Pairing
WINE AND FOOD

Pairing
WINE AND FOOD

LINDA JOHNSON-BELL

Burford Books

Printed in the United States of America.

10 9 8 7 6 5 4 3 2 1

Library of Congress Cataloging-in-Publication Data is on file with the Library of Congress.

To my boys!

CONTENTS

Preface to the New Edition

Welcome to the 2012 edition of *Pairing Wine and Food*. Since I first wrote this book in 1999, the international wine scene has known some real changes. There are two that I wish to briefly touch upon here, as they will influence the way in which food and wine is matched.

First is that the war waging between "Old World" and "New World" has shifted. Where there was once a clear demarcation between, say, a Sauvignon Blanc from Bordeaux and one from New Zealand, the Old World classic model was considered the more subtle, complex, and traditional. But what I am seeing, hearing, and tasting now is that the distinction is not so clear-cut anymore. There are New World winemakers striving and succeeding in making wines that closely resemble their classic models and there are even more Old World winemakers who are making international, homogeneous, non-*terroir*-driven wines. While the Californians were trying to copy the Bordelais, the Bordelais were trying to copy the Californians. It has become quite a confusing mess.

So now we speak of "traditional" versus "non-traditional" in the trade. Within every region I visit, whether I am in Pessac-Léognan, Chianti Classico, or Rioja, I am hearing the same debate: Are these wines being made in an international style (overly extracted fruit, dominant oak, high alcohol, and so forth)? Or are they traditional: Do they taste as though they come from Pessac-Léognan, Chianti Classico and Rioja? If I closed my eyes, could this be Cabernet Sauvignon/Merlot, Sangiovese, and Tempranillo from anywhere? I am loath to admit that when I close my eyes in Bordeaux lately, sipping a wine of 15.5 percent alcohol, I wonder if I am in the Barossa Valley.

The second change worth mentioning is partly responsible for the first one: climate change. Perversely, as European producers aimed to up the sugar/alcohol content in their wines, so to create the heavy, bold, alcoholic wines the New World consumers prefer (due to their hot climates), Mother Nature started doing it for them. So now the effect is two-fold. According to a study conducted by researchers at Stanford University in California, there could be "50% less land suitable for cultivating premium wine grapes in high-value areas of Northern California even as some cooler parts of Oregon and Washington state would become correspondingly better for growing grapes" (the study's author is Subhash Arora: visit www.climatechangeand-wine.com for more information). High alcoholic levels in a wine, whether a deliberate style-choice made by a winemaker or an unavoidable result of the changing climatic conditions, erase a grape's varietal character, its distinctive characteristics. Combined with high yields or other less than meticulous winemaking techniques and we are soon unable to distinguish a Primitivo from a Pinot Noir. Some varieties only do well in cooler climates. There are a few things a winemaker can do to mitigate the damage, but ultimately, we will be seeing more and more replanting around the world: A very expensive and time-consuming process. This is far too broad and controversial a topic to tackle here, but the relevance to food and wine pairing is that it has become increasingly difficult to consistently describe regional styles when attempting to explain a wine's taste.

I have still based my research here upon the classic models, but sadly, most of the wines I met more than twenty years ago, the wines that seduced me, educated me and thrilled me, are now unrecognizable to me. Happily, the best cure for my malaise is further exploration, and as I travel north and east, as I stealthily creep my way back towards the places from which wine first came, I am finding that there is still much to learn, to taste, and to thrill. I am again meeting wines that speak to me of their soil, of their birthplace. The world's vineyards have already begun their remapping, taking us into an exciting future that may very well allow a return to past viticultural glory.

—Linda@TheWineLady.com

Introduction

I very immodestly consider myself a wine expert, and a purist at that. At first, I never paid very much attention to food. It was simply what came with my wine. I cringed when waiters in restaurants brought the food menu first, treating the wine selection as an afterthought. Anyone who didn't consider wine as first and foremost, and who didn't insist that the food bow to the superior power of the grape, was a heathen, in my book. But no more. I no longer ridicule food writers or those attention-hungry chefs who become pop stars (well, not as much as I used to). For I have married the enemy: a foodie.

Do not get me wrong, I am not a stranger to good food. I come from one of those rare American households where fast food and cola drinks were verboten, where dinner was a formal ritual, and where every meal was fresh. In addition, for more than twelve years I wallowed in gastronomic excess while living in France, scouring the daily markets for the freshest produce, making hundreds of pots of homemade confiture, and attending almost every Michelin-star restaurant opening. I even prepared and ate things that still wriggled in the dish when served. I did the French thing—wholly and completely. But as the editor of a French wine magazine, I did it from a wine drinker's perspective. With hindsight, however, I realize that a love and knowledge of food was slowly infusing into my subconscious, without my knowledge or consent.

My foodie owns a wonderful restaurant on London's Portobello Road. I found myself surrounded. I had no choice but to convert. Now, all day long, magnificent odors waft about me. I find myself engrossed in conversation with the chefs over how long squid should be marinated for the ceviche, which spices would best liven up the vegetarian dishes, and which wines would best complement the new menus.

Suddenly I was speaking another language. I was dragged out to the English countryside and force-fed a diet of freshly picked wild raspberries, duck egg omelets, muntjac chops from the neighbors' land with juniper berries, homegrown salads filled with nasturtium leaves, flowers, rose petals, chives, arugula, three different varieties of mint, lavender, and rosemary from the garden. Not to mention fresh oysters with horseradish and lime, sashimi of salmon with wasabi and fresh ginger, sweet potato with peanut and coriander pesto, roast pork with crackling, and banoffee pie. My foodie had introduced me to the other side of the equation—my taste buds couldn't keep up. It worked. I was seduced. He didn't get me drunk, he just got me properly fed—something I was told could never happen in England!

It was fun. It was interesting. And suddenly it all made sense. We can only really know and understand wine and the taste of it if we know and understand the same about food. They are mated for life.

The tradition of enjoying food and wine together is nothing new . . . obviously. Man has been enjoying all the musts of all the vines ever yielding their fruit since Adam met Eve. In fact, I am sure that Adam and Eve had a lovely chilled carafe of their favorite tipple, most probably a Muscat from Alexandria, to enjoy with that apple, just as soon as they got rid of that pesky snake. Wine and fortified drinks were never a luxury, nor an indulgence. They were a necessity where fresh water was lacking.

We're pretty adept at this ancient ritual: We whip up a Filetto di Maiale Gratinato, deftly uncork a bottle of cool, crisp Chianti, throw on some Pavarotti, light some candles, *et voilà*! We've usually mastered this scenario (and what follows!) by the time we leave college. But why does this classic combination work so well? How did we know that the thyme, rosemary, and sage as well as the pecorino in this pork fillet dish would go so nicely with the Sangiovese grape in the wine? We are all familiar with the golden rules of wine service, passed to us through years of Sunday lunches with the family or gleaned from the jacket flaps of recipe books. Rules such as "white meat takes white wine, and red meat, red wine"; "white wine before red"; and so on. But did you ever stop to think why? Why do food and wine taste the way they do, and why are these tastes so varied?

With today's plethora of international foods and wines available, the choices can become overwhelming. If you are confused as to how to match wine with food, put away your vodka tonic and despair no more. It is easier than you think. For, despite the apparent complexity of matches, you have been deceived. Most information available to us takes a generic and simplistic approach: We are told that lamb goes well with red wine, for example. Or it goes to the other extreme and is overly specific: Icelandic lamb of a specific age with a curry and coconut milk sauce with a dash of coriander and parsley goes well with "so-and-so's wine of one or two particular vintages of the last decade, unattainable in the States, made of an obscure grape variety, served at 15° Celsius."

In fact, it is not the lamb you should be worrying about at all. Here is the secret: Marry the dominant flavor of the dish (usually found in the sauce) to the dominant grape variety of the wine. This is the crux of the situation. Basic ingredient meets basic ingredient (worry about texture and weight later).

The next secret to know is that nature has taken care of food and wine pairings for us: Wine grapes and foodstuffs that are soil bedfellows will marry well. Following the lead from the European regional food and wine pairings is the key to then extrapolating and experimenting with your own matches. What to do if you do not live in Puglia, Rioja, Provence, or the Mosel Valley?

Every country or region that is known for a particular specialty produces a wine or other alcoholic beverage intended to strike the perfect accord with its food. Usually it is also a homegrown product created from pretty much the same ingredients that are in the food. The Romans drink Frascati Superiore Secco with their spaghetti alla carbonara, the Swiss enjoy Chasselas with their cheese fondue, the North Africans choose fig alcohol and mint tea with their couscous, the Russians serve vodka with their borscht, and the Scandinavians appreciate aquavit with their gravlax.

These rich food and drink pairings are often regional. In France, one drinks Riesling with choucroute garnie à l'alsacième, Sancerre with Chavignol cheese, and Sauternes with foie gras. None of this has come about by accident, but by design—nature's design. Wine is simply made from grapes, and grapes are fruit, which are grown just like any other fruit or crop. Fruits born of the same soil, in the same climate, and of the same environment, very naturally make perfect bedfellows.

Living in the United States, or any New World country for that matter, makes food and wine pairings difficult. The US is a smorgasbord of international cuisine with exciting and creative twists continually infusing our culture, but it has no native wine grapes, and has imported a mishmash of every European noble grape variety instead. This is why we need to study the elements of food and wine more closely.

An Indian lamb curry dish may be better with a spicy, acidic white such as a Gewürztraminer, whereas a classic lamb roast in gravy with roast potatoes and mint sauce would prefer a rich Pauillac or New World Cabernet Sauvignon. (Note that Cabernet Sauvignon is the dominant grape variety used in the Cabernet Sauvignon, Cabernet Franc, and Merlot-Bordeaux blend in Pauillac.) But we can make things even easier. It is not just about Indian food going best with spicy whites and Chinese with tannic reds—but about the sweet, sour, salty, or spicy flavor of the food going with the sweetness, acidity, bitterness, or astringency of the wine. Nowhere does there exist a complete compilation of dishes with an explanation of why things taste the way they taste, and therefore match or don't match. This guide will provide that information.

In addition to listing specific dishes, you will also be given an explanation from the specific to the general. Illogical, you might say, but working first with specific flavors, then their groups, then the dishes, does make sense. You will discover the reasons why some pairings work and others don't, how the classic marriages developed, how to vary taste themes without disastrous results, and the industry secrets and remedies when dealing with wine's sworn enemies.

So with more food and wine choices available than ever before, where does one begin? If you understand the workings of flavor groups, then you will easily master the game of food and wine matches. This guide will put you in control of your palate and your imagination. Part 1 explains what gives wine its taste, and we go much farther than simply the grape variety—we go to its true origins and examine everything about its composition. In part 2, we do the same with food, thus making very clear the analogous relationship of food and wine. In part 3, the extensive cross-reference should cover every imaginable match you could conceive. If you find any oversights or omissions, please do not hesitate to let me know!

When you understand why food and wine taste as they do, you can understand why and how the classic rules have developed, which then gives you the freedom and confidence to break or adapt them in clever and personal ways.

Take sweet white wines, for example. The English call them "dessert" wines—how shortsighted! A good sweet white can be served alone as an aperitif, with a first course of foie gras or quiche, with a main course of roast pork stuffed with prunes or apricots, with a fruit salad or a green salad made with walnuts, and is sublime with blue cheese, Roquefort, mild and strong goat cheeses (but not the sweet, creamy kind), and Epoisses or Beaufort cheeses. And all of this before you even get to dessert! Another surprise is Champagne. We forget that there are enough variations in Champagne styles to take a meal from beginning to end—nothing beats ending a meal with a light and digestible Champagne.

So break all the rules. The essential element is that both personalities are respected and complemented, and that neither one is dominated. If a wine has brought forward an aspect of the food, and the food has reinforced an element of the wine, then a successful match had been made.

Let pleasure be your guide.

—Linda Johnson-Bell
Linda@TheWineLady.com

PART ONE

The Taste of Wine

When I first started learning about wine, I was twenty years old and studying in Paris. The French family with whom I was living was a noble old family that, like many others, had little more than their titles and the crumbled remains of a château as reminders of their glorious past. My baroness had a heart of gold. Her dear husband, although I adored him for it, was a clever, quite frugal conniver, who had turned cheating the system into his livelihood. One evening, early in the year, they organized a dinner party for all the family to view the new American arrival. For this auspicious occasion, they brought out a bottle of wine that, I was proudly told, had been produced by one of their family members in Bordeaux. As prior gustatory forays at my Californian girls' school had only introduced me to the delights of California coolers and strawberry daiquiris, I was very intimidated and was trying desperately to keep my virgin palate in the closet.

The wine was presented with what I thought then was great style and tradition. With hindsight, I can assure you that it was pure blundering pomp. I tasted it. They all looked at me. What was I supposed to say? That it tasted good? Did it? How was I supposed to know? I had nothing with which to compare it. Because I did appreciate that it had a little more "oomph" than my last gallon of Gallo Burgundy, I said so—but not in so many words, of course. The rest of the family was served the wine, and very soon we had duly drained the last drop from the bottle. Yet it sat there, empty, until one of the cousins pointed out that we were in need of more refreshment. Baron de Radin scowled at the cousin, picked up the bottle, and took it back to the kitchen. He reappeared a few minutes later with a fresh bottle, this time served without any of the previous hullabaloo. I noticed that he had uncorked it in the kitchen. Glasses were happily refilled, and we drank on.

But wait a minute. Something was definitely very strange. This glass of wine tasted distinctly unlike our first glass. I discreetly looked at the bottle that was still proudly on display in the middle of the table and confirmed that, yes indeed, it was the same wine as the first. Actually, it was even the same bottle as the first! It had the same little water stain on top of the *m* in *mis en bouteille*. Being an inexperienced young Yank, I said nothing and kept drinking, deciding that there must be more to this wine game than I thought. I looked around the room, and no one else seemed even to bat a taste bud. This went on all evening; the bottle kept disappearing and coming back to the table full.

The party became quite gay. Le Baron now only needed a cursory glance from the cousin before performing his hostly duties. After five more bottles of decidedly inferior red brew had been served, I decided to investigate. I followed le Baron into the kitchen on the pretext that I was going to help clean up. And what did I spy? Le Baron bending over the family's precious heritage, pouring the contents of a two-liter container of Felix Potin's twelve-franc-a-liter, generic red wine through the funnel I'd seen him use to fill up the Renault Cinq last week. He saw me and my aghast expression, and shot me a conspiratorial smile accompanied by a hissing *"Dites-rien, d'accord?"* I agreed, and morosely went back out to join the other guests.

Voilà. One of my very first interludes with French wine. Believe it or not, that very same bottle appeared on the table every time we had important guests for dinner—and I never said a word.

LEARNING ABOUT WINE

I continued my wine education on my own by soaking off and saving the bottle labels of every wine I tasted, even bothering wine waiters in restaurants. I would then glue the labels into my wine notebook and write down the date, the place, the meal, and my companions, then note my impressions. At the beginning, I could usually only muster an "I like this" or "I do not like this." Not a very encouraging start but it did actually work because, before too long, I could look at all the wines I did like and find their common denominator, thereby determining my first preferences. Eventually, I was able to detect differences among the wines and then was able to put names to these tastes.

You may be asking: Why go to all this bother? Today wine labels are increasingly informative, telling you what sort of foods the wine will match, often even including information on the region's climate or soils. But not having to rely on commercial copy scripted by the wineries' PR team, and learning the ground rules about what goes into the taste of wine—which you will learn from this section of the book—will help you to assess and taste wines, better understanding your preferences and better matching your food and wine. The first lesson we learn when tasting wines is what we like and do not like. This is half the battle. The other half is learning why you like them or do not like them. If you can then find the common denominators—grape variety, wine style, regional preference, and so on—you have come a long way, and the rewards will be many!

WHAT IS TASTE?

So what is taste? We tend to take our sense of taste for granted. Do you realize that—just as with our senses of hearing, sight, and touch—we constantly taste things even when we are not eating? For the senses of smell and taste are so closely linked that we always taste what we smell and vice versa. The two work in conjunction. Furthermore, our sense of sight also aids our sense of taste. Our whole sensorial repertoire tells us what a piece of burned toast is going to taste like even before we put it into our mouth.

In the same way that different people have different strengths of eyesight or hearing, so people are born with different abilities in the areas of taste and smell, which are further influenced by our cultural and sensorial past. So each individual has uniquely tuned physiological mechanisms that release or stimulate a reaction and therefore a personal minimum and maximum threshold of taste and smell perception. Like the other senses, smell and taste serve as a source of information for our brains. Our sensorial logic then discriminates and identifies those different sensations.

When we taste something, we experience a sensation in special parts of the mouth: the taste buds. These are dispersed throughout the mouth, and some have specific sensors: Sourness is recognized with the tip of the tongue; sweetness with the flat of the tongue; bitterness under the tongue; tartness on the inner surface of the cheeks.

We have tried endlessly to create a finite classification of flavors, but as each individual will interpret a substance differently, a standard of measurement can only be vague and subjective. However, we do know that we can objectively classify the larger taste groups of sweetness, acidity, saltiness, sourness, and bitterness. But even with these groups, the boundaries are far from precise. It is difficult to establish a clear demarcation between one type and another because the taste of individual foods or wines comes, in fact, from a combination of these basic flavors. Also, our ability to perceive the flavors themselves is influenced by other factors such as temperature and flavor combinations.

HOW A GOOD UPBRINGING ENSURES GOOD TASTE

What influences a wine's taste? First of all, what is wine? Wine is simply the result of the partial or entire alcoholic fermentation of fresh grapes or the juice of fresh grapes. It tastes like the things it contains; therefore the predominant flavors of wine come from the skin, or just beneath the skin, of the grapes used to make it.

In the simplest terms, wine is composed of: water (between 75 and 90 percent), alcohols, acids, polyphenols (or coloring agents), sugars (fructose and glucose), carbon dioxide, and aromatic components (chemical). In addition, there are all the components of wine that we cannot see, smell, or taste, such as vitamins, proteins, amino acids, and so on. Each of these plays an important role in the taste of a wine.

Like human beings, a wine's taste is going to depend a great deal on both its origins and its upbringing. In fact, the French use this very word *upbringing,* or *élevage,* when describing a wine's early life.

The taste of a wine is therefore the result of the combination of many factors, starting with the unique characteristics of grape variety, or varieties, used to make it. The next factors are how the vines were planted, grown, pruned, and treated; the soil and subsoil; the general climate of the vineyard's region; and sometimes even the climate of the surrounding areas. Were the vines grown on a fertile valley floor or clinging to a steep slope? Did they have to fight for food or were they overfertilized and -watered? Did they get too much sunshine or just what they needed? Were they allowed to produce all the fruit they wanted (the French call this *pissing* the vines) or were they pruned and obliged to produce fewer but better-quality grapes? The vintage year will also affect the taste of a wine, as the weather and growing conditions are never the same from one year to the next.

The vinification method, how the wine was treated before being bottled, and how long it has been left to mature in the bottle all add to its unique flavor combination. Will it be a flash-in-the-pan sort of wine or will it mature nicely and develop even more character as it grows old? All in all, has it been disciplined or spoiled rotten? A spoiled wine, like a spoiled child, will be lazy, brash, and superficial. A wine with character will behave more subtly and will reveal its strength and personality as you get to know it.

WHAT DOES WINE TASTE LIKE?

The taste elements of both wine and food are the same: sweetness, acidity, bitterness, and astringency.

The sweetness in the taste of wine comes from the fructose and glucose, types of sugar, in the grape and from the alcohol produced during the fermentation. The alcohol is not sweet in itself; it just underlines those components that are, and helps to counteract the acidity and tannins, making the wine seem sweeter.

The acidity comes from the tartaric and malic acids in the grapes. Malic acid is green-tasting and can make wine very bitter, which is why the fermentation processes chosen by the winemaker are so important in achieving a balance; they will affect the malic acid levels in the wine.

Bitterness and astringency come from the tannins in the grapes. There are very few tannins in white wines, so most discussion of tannins is reserved for the reds.

The Taste of Acidity

The sour-tasting substances in wine are the acids: tartaric, malic, and citric are in the grape; succinic, lactic, and acetic result from fermentation. The total acidity of a wine depends upon whether the growing season was too cold—in which case the grapes are too-acidic and underripe—or too hot, in which case the grapes become overripe and lack acids. White wines generally have more acidity than reds. It is the amount of acid that is important: Too little and the wine is bland and flabby, too much and it is vinegary. The right amount of acid, in balance with the wine's other components, makes the wine look and taste crisp, clean, and lively, as well as ensuring longevity.

Tartaric acid is unique to grapes and to wine and represents one-quarter to one-third of the total acid composition of wine. It is the strongest acid, and it strongly influences the pH of a wine. The pH measures the concentration of hydrogen ions, which for wine means its dryness. The lower the pH, the safer the wine is from diseases and from oxidation, and therefore the greater its aging potential. The tartaric acid content decreases as the grape ripens, then varies depending upon the harvest weather conditions.

Malic acid is found in every part of the grapevine. It is the most fragile of the acids, which allows for its easy transformation into lactic acids (called malolactic fermentation), which diminishes considerably the overall acidity of a wine. The hotter the year's weather, the faster the acid decreases during the ripening process, which is why there is more of it when the weather has been cooler. All red wines are allowed to go through a complete malolactic fermentation. White wines can either go without, go partially, or go entirely through this second fermentation. It depends upon the juice's initial acid and sugar levels and the style of wine desired. If a winemaker wants a crisp and "green" white wine, then the malolactic fermentation is halted or not even allowed to begin. For a "buttery," smooth white, the malolactic fermentation is permitted for longer or until its completion.

Acids give a wine its shine or brilliance—especially the tartaric acids, which renew the wine's color. It is the presence of malic acid that often gives a wine an apple smell, and in the mouth we can sense the amount of acids by the irritation of our gums and the inside of the mouth.

The Taste of Tannins: Bitterness and Astringency

The most important of the three types of polyphenols, or coloring agents, tannins give a wine texture rather than taste. Tannins that are "condensed" are present in the grape, and those that are "exogene" are procured from the wood during barrel aging. In the stalks, skins, and seeds there are tannins that are released during fermentation and pressing, giving the wine its specific character and contributing to its aging capacity. Storing, or aging, the wine in new oak introduces additional tannins, which are transferred from the wood's fibers. These are more common in red wine than in white. Tannins obtained from the oak barrels can improve a wine's aging potential, complement its texture, and fill it out, but only if the wine itself has a solid backbone of acids, fruit extracts, and condensed tannins. Oak aging cannot replace raw materials that are lacking in the first place.

The wine's red color fades as the anthocyanins, another tannin, diminish with age. The more mature a wine, the more yellow or brown the "disk," or surface, becomes. The combination of these coloring agents can give the wine a sour taste and a drying sensation in the mouth. This is called "astringency." Different tannins from different-aged wines and wines from various regions will have distinct sorts of astringency. For example, young Bordeaux will have tough, astringent tannins, while old Bordeaux will have velvet-soft tannins. The more tannin is present in a wine's youth, the more it makes the sides of your mouth pucker, and the longer the wine will take to mature. Don't buy a recent-vintage Bordeaux Premier Cru and expect it to go down like velvet; it is meant to age and mature in the bottle. This is why bottle-aging is so important, as we will see later.

The Taste of Sweetness

There are three major sweet-tasting substances in wine: the sugars and poly-alcohols, both originating in the grape, and alcohols from fermentation.

Each style of wine has a different level of sugar depending upon the grape's maturation when harvested. Sweet wines contain several dozen grams of sugar per liter, while a dry white wine normally contains less than two grams per liter. The sugars, along with the alcohols, give the wine body and are visible because of the "legs" formed on the side of the glass. The sugars don't really have any odor but could eventually contribute to the overall expression of the wine. And it is the sugar that gives the wine its sweet taste, its fatness, and its unctuousness.

Alcohol is an important element in wine—it gives it great-looking legs. It is produced during fermentation when enzymes created by the yeasts change the sugar of the grape juice into alcohol, carbon dioxide, and heat. It is the proportion of alcohol to glycerine that determines the limpidity, or the "body," of a wine, which we observe as legs or tears. More alcohol and the wine is thinner, thus the legs run down the side of the glass more quickly. The more glycerine is present, the thicker the wine will be, and thus the more slowly the legs will drip down the side of the glass. It is also primarily the amount of ethyl alcohol that will determine the sweetness of the wine.

The Taste of Bubbles

Carbon dioxide is the principal product, along with ethyl alcohol, of the alcoholic fermentation. It is present in both still wines and effervescent wines. If the wine is effervescent, carbon dioxide manifests itself as bubbles. Like tannin, bubbles do not have an odor or taste as such, but the bubbles help to release the wine's perfumes and definitely alter its texture. If anything, you can detect an acidic taste edge while it pricks and tickles the tongue.

For a Fragrant Smell

Aromatic components (chemical substances) exist in minuscule quantities in wine and are issued from various chemical groups: alcohols, acid, ethers, and so on. For example, the presence of ethyl acetate might smell like vinegar, phenylethyl acetate like rose, ethyl caproate like soap, menthol like mint, and vanillin like vanilla.

What is important to note is that these are all visual, olfactive, and gustative results born of the wine itself, its contents. In addition to these, there are other man-made manipulations, such as adding fabricated yeasts to the grape juice to jump-start fermentation, and other measures taken to rectify nature's flaws of low sugars and high acidity, which also alter the smell and taste of wine. We'll discuss these later.

THE SMELLS OF WINE

The following is an exhaustive list of the various smells a wine can have. A wine's smell can tell us a lot about how it was made, where it is from, how old it is, and whether or not it is of good quality. Identifying a wine's smell also develops your taste memory, which is indispensable when trying to establish what kind of wine you prefer as well as when matching food and wine. Do not forget that smell and taste remain subjective senses; not everybody will taste the same odor or identify it as the same thing. Also remember that despite the general rules and guidelines of winemaking, there are always exceptions.

Family of Smells	Examples	Comments
Floral	Acacia Carnation Hawthorn/May blossom Honeysuckle Narcissus Vine Wildflowers	These are considered to be good odors and are found in young, dry white wines and sparkling wines.
	Broom Jasmine Lime blossom Rose Violet	These are more present and heavy and are found in serious white wines that will age, as well as in some red wines. Look for rose in a Gewürztraminer or Muscat.
	Geranium	A very strong presence of this flower usually indicates a misuse of ascorbic acid.
Fruit		You may have noticed that in a good wine, especially in a sweet one, the fruit aromas evolve as the wine matures. In reds, they become almost jammy and take on the smells of compote, dried fruit, and stewed fruit; in whites, they become deliciously tropical.
	Lemon	An elegant perfume that lightens the bouquet and gives the wine freshness.
	Apricot Peach	You are likely to find these odors in top white wines of considerable strength meant for aging, and in sweet wines.
	Blackcurrant Raspberry Small red fruit	The typical and easily recognizable principal smells found in red wines meant for early drinking and in those red wines meant for aging that are drunk when young.
	Blackberry Mulberry	The original odor associated with quality in reds.
	Quince Strawberry	Depending on the grape variety and the soil type, these perfumes can be evident in a wine maturing or on the decline.

Family of Smells	Examples	Comments
	Bergamot Lemon Orange Tangerine	These are powerful and elegant smells and are very characteristic of Muscatel-like fortified wines. Also found in Australian Rieslings and in the Sémillon grape.
	Cherry Redcurrants	A subtle perfume that is considered a good odor. Think Cabernet Sauvignon or Pinot Noir.
	Apple	Can be either good or bad thing. If it smells like an overripe apple or beet, it is a sign of oxidation or problematic malolactic fermentation. If it smells like a golden or green apple in a young, dry white wine, then it is good.
	Banana Pear	When there is too much of this smell, it almost resembles nail polish. It is a very simple odor usually found in white wines of little originality, whose fermentations were jump-started with industrial flavored yeasts, in Primeur red wines, and in "technological" rosés.
	Plum Raisin	These are pretty rare in wines; you might detect them in some young, simple reds.
	Guava Kiwi Lychee Papaya Passion fruit	Considered to be original and agreeable smells, if not too strong, in certain white wines (Gewürztraminer, for example).
Nuts and dried fruit	Hazelnut Grilled almond	These are considered to be aromas of great class, especially when present in the tertiary bouquet of the top well-built and solid white wines such as a mature white Burgundy.
	Dried fig Walnut	Very classic aromas found in aged, fortified wines as well as in top wines at their peak of maturity.

Family of Smells	Examples	Comments
	Prunes	A bad sign. This usually means that a red wine that has faded or died, or is an indication that there was a problem with oxidation, probably due to bad storage/conservation conditions.
Vegetable	Cut grass Herbaceousness Stalk or stems	Considered a bad thing, these smells are usually the result of bad harvesting practices; grapes that are too crushed or not de-stalked well. You also find these odors in "technological" wines that are past their prime.
	Fern	A very distinguished odor that is found in white and red wines meant for long-term aging.
	Cut hay	A nice odor present in certain red wines.
	Juniper Incense Pine Resin Turpentine	These are powerful perfumes that are found in red wines from regions of southern or meridian climates, of pine forests.
	Humus Lichen Marsh Mushroom Undergrowth Wet straw	Considered to be desirable odors, they are linked to the phenomenon of reduction in the bottle and so are found in top red wines that have undergone a number of years of bottle aging.
	Dry leaves Herbal infusion Tea Tisane or herbal tea Tobacco	Smells that usually indicate a certain amount of aging and evolution. Found in both red and white wines meant for aging.
	Mint Eucalyptus	Characteristic smells of Cabernet Sauvignon grown in Australia, South Africa, or California.
	Dust Earth	Not considered desirable, these odors usually disappear with a little airing.
	Green pepper	The dominant odor usually associated with a young Cabernet Sauvignon or Cabernet Franc wine. If too strong, it means that the grapes were harvested while underripe.

Family of Smells	Examples	Comments
Spices and herbs	Basil Bay Cinnamon Lavender Nutmeg Thyme	Power odors found in red wines and certain mature white wines issued from vintages of substantial warmth and sunshine.
	Licorice Pepper	Considered very elegant and noble, these aromas are often present in the best reds from the best *terroirs*.
	Aniseed Cloves Fennel	In small amounts, these are acceptable smells.
	Garlic Onions	Not so good. Usually means that the wine suffered reduction in the bottle.
	Vanilla	A very pleasant perfume that can bring balance and harmony to the wine if not overpowering. Usually found in wines that have been aged in new oak barrels.
	Truffle	A very strong odor that can sometimes resemble aspects of the vegetable family (underwood and humus), or even the animal family (sweat, urine). If present in old wines, it is an expression of quality but definitely needs aeration if we are to fully appreciate it.
Animal	Amber Civet (cat) Musk	Powerful and surprising odors that are usually appreciated if they are found in well-developed, aged, and evolved red wines.
	Game	A very powerful aroma usually found in very old red wines—Pommards can definitely smell a bit gamey.
	Cat urine	Found in Sauvignon Blanc grapes that were picked while underripe, or when yields were too high.

Family of Smells	Examples	Comments
	Fur Game Leather Sweat Wet dog	A very particular odor appreciated by those who go in for this sort of thing. Found in great red wines after a long and perfect maturation.
	Chicken gut Fox	Bad smells associated with wines that have been poorly vinified or are from hybrid grape varieties.
Roasted	Burnt Grilled Smoke Toast	Can be lovely when found in some white wines of distinction. Aged white Burgundies often have these notes.
	Cacao Chocolate Coffee	Very desirable aromas found in the top red wines when at their apogee.
	Burnt wood Creosote Rubber Smoke Tar	Smells characteristic of certain red wines while in the process of maturation. They often disappear once the wine is fully mature.
	Caramel	A heady, heavy perfume, like the quince, usually indicates that the wine is maturing too quickly or that it was vinified at too high a temperature.
	Flint Gunpowder	Typical of dry white wines of the Loire Valley. A very pleasing smell and taste that is reportedly due to the flinty soil.
	Honey Wax	Lovely perfumes that develop in mature white wines of great class.
	Acetate Nail polish	Disagreeable smells found in poorly made young red wines or "technological" rosés.
	Beer Cheese Cider Dirty dishcloth Milk Sauerkraut Yeast Yogurt	A whole pack of not-so-lovely odors caused by poorly managed fermentations.

Family of Smells	Examples	Comments
	Cattle shed Mold Pigsty Soap Stagnation	Again, odors considered to be not so good and that are linked to poor quality.
Alcohol	Eau de vie Kirsch Old marc	Perfumes present in very heady wines rich in alcohol.
	Graphite Iodine	Sometimes found in wine and not considered to be good signs.

Translated and adapted from *La Dégustation,* pp. 48–53, G. Gribourg/C. Sarfati, Edisud, France, 1989.

THE GRAPES

All the factors we have looked at are important in telling you about the taste of a wine, but the single most important factor is the grape variety or varieties from which the wine is made. In winemaking, just as in cooking, if you use inferior raw materials and do not adjust the proportions of the ingredients correctly, your final dish will fall short of the mark.

Do not forget that the grape is a fruit or a crop like any other, and crops come from different regions for a reason. Bananas come from the tropics, figs from the Mediterranean, apples from temperate areas like Britain or the American Northwest. It would be foolhardy to try to grow these fruits in places other than their indigenous habitat, or where the growing conditions are totally different. They might survive, but they would probably not be as good. So why do we do it with the noble European grape varieties? The Chardonnay grape is at its optimum in Burgundy, as is the Cabernet Sauvignon in Médoc and Graves, the Merlot in St-Emilion or Pomerol, the Kékfrankanos in Sopron, Hungary, the Nebbiolo in Piedmont, and the Tempranillo in Rioja.

The *Vitis vinifera* vines that produce wine grapes are indigenous to the Mediterranean, Central Europe, and Southwest Asia. Any wine grapevines in the New World were brought there: They are not native. When noble European grape varieties are grown in new, adopted soils, they produce different tastes and styles, usually as a result of the warmer climate. Once I would have argued that these new models were not only different, but also inferior. I'm mellowing with age and am now resigned to stating that "different" interpretations on the classic models should be allowed!

These international interpretations on the classic European models make food and wine pairings more difficult, but certainly more fun: Chardonnay could have an unoaked Chablis (Burgundy) taste, an oaked Meursault (Burgundy) taste, an Alto Adige (Italy) taste, a Carneros (California) taste, or a Maipo (Chile) taste. And a Sauvignon Blanc from Graves (Bordeaux) is a *completely* different animal from its New Zealand counterpart. Know that for the purposes of this book, I am using the European models as guides unless otherwise specified.

Not All Grapes Can Go It Alone

Some grape varieties—despite occasional flirtations—do very well on their own: Pinot Noir, Sauvignon Blanc, Riesling, Chardonnay. Others are best when blended with other grape varieties: Merlot, Cabernet Sauvignon, Cabernet Franc.

Why? Take Bordeaux wines as an example, where Cabernet Sauvignon is the main ingredient of the recipe, the "flour." Merlot, because it is a sweeter and softer grape than the Cabernet Sauvignon, has traditionally been used to soften the tannins of the Cabernet Sauvignon, and so is the "sugar" of the recipe. Cabernet Franc is added as the "spice," giving its own special character, and there are minute doses of Petit Verdot and/or Malbec. Combining the taste elements of all the varieties gives each Bordeaux appellation its unique flavor.

Each Bordeaux appellation has a designated "recipe" according to which grape varieties do better in that area because of the soil and microclimate. And within this recipe, each winemaker makes individual variations according to which grapes did better than another in any particular year, and according to the personal tastes of the château owner and winemaker. In the same way, when cooking, we follow a basic recipe yet will vary the proportion of ingredients (meat, vegetables, spices, and flavorings) according to our personal taste, the seasonal availability of ingredients, and perhaps our financial resources.

The Style Parameters of the Grape Varieties

Every grape variety produces grapes that have a specific chemical constitution and therefore possess a particular aromatic potential, in varying degrees of intensity and quality. Some varieties are considered to have no interest at all; these are usually hybrids. The varieties considered rich in primary aromas, such as Muscat, Gewürztraminer, or Riesling, produce wines that taste as though you've just bitten into a grape. These are the varieties that are vinified in such a way as to preserve or amplify these aromas.

Then there are the varieties susceptible to an aromatic potential of interesting secondary aromas: Gamay, Pinot Noir, Marsanne, Cabernet Sauvignon, Grenache, Chardonnay, Syrah, and Chenin. Only vinification can reveal the hidden aromatic potential of these grapes.

Finally we have those varieties that develop through vinification and continue to evolve with aging: Pinot Noir, Cabernet Sauvignon, Syrah, Nebbiolo, and Sangiovese, for example. Take a Gamay from Beaujolais and a Pinot Noir from Burgundy, and it will be the Pinot Noir that will still taste amazing after sitting in your cellar for five or ten years, not the Gamay, no matter what a winemaker does to it. Each grape variety has a finite aromatic and taste potential.

A grape variety, from the start, either is meant for aging or is not. There are varieties that produce wines with a balance of sugar, acid, and tannin that gives them the structure needed to sustain aging. Then there are varieties that produce wines meant to be drunk while young, as they reveal themselves best while still youthful, and whose sugar, acid, and tannin balance is relatively light.

Winemakers can try to squeeze as much as they like out of grapes by letting them overproduce and by extracting as much flavor during the vinification as possible. For example, to get the most out of a variety that does not have much aroma, such as the Ugni Blanc, a winemaker can vinify the must, or grape juice, with little or no oxidation and at very low temperatures, thus eking out a little more flavor. But this will only be a superficial result. Nature has provided built-in limits.

To make a grape happy, all you need to do is to provide a perfect environment. In its optimum site of acclimation—the place where the soil, climate, and growing conditions are all perfect—each variety will find its optimum individual and specific sugar, acid, and tannin balance. For example, in Alsace, the Gewürztraminer will always be sweeter than the Riesling. In the Côtes du Rhône, Carignan will always be more acidic than Grenache, and in Burgundy, Pinot Noir will always be more tannic than Gamay. In the right region and conditions, each grape variety is reaching its own taste potential.

The White Grapes

To help you identify grape varieties, here is a list of the major white grapes. White wine grape varieties generally smell and taste like citrus and other tree fruit, such as lemon, orange, grapefruit, or apple. In mature white wines, or in sweet white wines, we often taste more exotic or tropical fruit, like pineapple, mango, apricot, pear, melon, and lychee.

Both red and white wines can have odors and tastes such as mineral, spice, herbs, tobacco, hay, yeast, honey, caramel, and nuts. The tastes come from the grape variety, the soil, the yeasts (if indigenous yeasts are not used to start fermentation), the fermentation period, or the oak used for aging.

Chardonnay

An easygoing kind of grape, the Chardonnay seems to want to please everyone. It does its best to adapt to every soil, every climate of every country, and every winemaking style. Who would believe that the same grape could give us a wine that is steely, mineral, and salty as well as one that is fat, buttery, oaky, and lightly sweet? But the Chardonnay does just that. And nowhere are its many personalities better illustrated than in the *marno-calcaires* soils of Burgundy. Indeed, Burgundy is the perfect region in which to observe varietal variations and provides a strong defense for the unique variable of soil type. From the cool climate and *calcaire* soil of Chablis to the warmer Mâcon, the Chardonnay adapts perfectly, becoming more aromatic and supple as it moves farther south. Take it out of its native Burgundy altogether and it quickly becomes attuned to its adopted land's climate and environment.

Chardonnays from northern Italy are well structured, acidic, and mineral, and those from southern France are light and fruity; those from Chile are vibrant with fruit and light oak; from New Zealand's cooler regions, the wines become intense with balanced fruit; and from California, they are often tropical, oaky wines.

Chenin Blanc

Good Chenin Blanc is one of the world's most underrated grape varieties. It is true that Chenin Blanc from a very cold year can produce a sour wine, but with a little sunshine, its true colors are revealed. This happens best in its home, the Loire Valley. The Chenin Blanc has several very distinct sides to it. When harvested at optimum maturity, it produces a dry, firm, elegantly floral wine, such as a Savennières. It also produces sparkling wines of good quality in Saumur and Vouvray. When harvested late so that noble rot (*selection de grains nobles*) is successfully achieved—when the grapes are deliberately allowed to shrivel and intensify on the vine before harvesting—then the most succulent and famous sweet wines are the result: Coteaux du Layon, Bonnezeaux, and Quarts de Chaume, all apples and apricots with nutty, honey tones and underlined by a high acidity that helps to carry it all along. These are long-lived, but not as fat or ageless as Sauternes.

Outside the Loire Valley and into warmer climates, Chenin Blanc unfortunately becomes a fairly innocuous thing. New World versions are at best fruity, but lacking any of its crucial steeliness or complexity. Nor does this grape lend itself to high yields: Overproduction is truly merciless. Having realized this, the South Africans and others are starting to nurture older vines in an attempt to get more concentrated and complex fruit (older plants give fewer, more concentrated grapes, while younger plants produce higher yields of lighter fruit).

Gewürztraminer

There is no more distinctive or aromatic grape than the Gewürztraminer. Alsace is its home and there it produces, if yields are kept reasonably low, a rich tapestry of fruity, floral, and spicy tastes. Its texture in the mouth is round, rich, and smooth. Like the Riesling, it can be harvested late (*vendanges tardives*) to produce a very classy wine—and in certain years, when the weather is perfect and noble rot is attained, the results are amazing. Although often described as "spicy," the first impression is frequently of roses and lychees. When made in the dry style, it is still opulent but it does not fare well in warm years or warm climates, where the heat lets its acid levels plummet, leaving it overly sweet, oily, and flabby.

Germany's Pfalz and Baden regions run a close second to Alsace, and lighter versions come from Austria and Italy's Sudtirol. Outside Europe, the wines are usually off-dry, easy, and without much character. But growers who take it seriously in cooler climates such as Washington State and Oregon are producing some great results.

Marsanne

Native to the mid–Rhône Valley, this variety is one of the Rhône Valley Hermitage staples, and when coupled with Roussanne produces Hermitage, Crozes-Hermitage at St-Joseph. It has also been planted farther south in France and in Australia. When young, it is a discreet wine that becomes more floral as it ages, moving toward notes of wax, honey, and nuts. On the palate, the wines are supple, fat, and round.

Müller-Thurgau

A cross between Riesling and Silvaner, this variety's creator, German Dr. Hermann Müller, was trying to combine the quality of the Riesling grape with the reliability of the Silvaner. Since Silvaner is an early-maturing grape, it is very popular in cold vine-growing regions, as it matures before the worst weather arrives. But Müller-Thurgau turned out to make a rather flabby, mediocre wine, especially when a product of Germany's high yields. It does much better in New Zealand, Washington State, and some parts of Italy, and it is the most common variety grown in England. At its best, it charms us with its floral scents of privet and flowering currant leaves.

Muscat

You may have noticed that most grapes taste of everything but grapes, as we have always thought of them. Muscat is a "grape"-tasting grape and is also one of the oldest grape varieties in the world. Alsatian Muscats are elegant, dry, rose-scented wines, usually drunk as an aperitif. The very sweet, fortified Muscats of the south of France and the Rhône (Frontignan, Lunel,

Rivesaltes, and Beaumes-de-Venise) are drunk with desserts. Australia produces darker, heavier liqueur Muscats of high quality. Italy's fizzy, low-alcohol, sweet Moscatos, such as Asti Spumante, are refreshing and versatile, and who can ignore the delectable Moscatel de Setúbal from Portugal?

Pinot Blanc

You may think that the Pinot Blanc is an innocuous little grape, but it has quite a lot to say for itself, which is difficult for a grape that is a mutation of a mutation. The Pinot Blanc, originally from Burgundy, is a white mutation of the Pinot Gris, which is a mutation of the Pinot Noir! The Germans, French, and Italians have long appreciated its startling resemblance to light, unoaked Chardonnay. Indeed, this resemblance is physical as well as gustative, as it is very difficult to tell the plant vines apart. A well-made Pinot Blanc will remind you of apples, butter, and warm, sweet sap. The Alsatian version contributes something to almost every meal, its delicacy present yet discreet.

Pinot Gris

Pinot Gris, as just mentioned, is a mutation of the Pinot Noir grape, and comes in many packages and under several names, but it finds its full expression in Alsace, where it is known as Tokay Pinot Gris, although the Hungarians are insisting that Tokay be dropped from the name so there is no confusion with their famous Tokaji. It skirts seductively between the steeliness of the Riesling and the spicy voluptuousness of the Gewürztraminer, never making up its mind. It is smoky, spicy, nougaty. At the other extreme, it produces a light, crisp, dry wine, the Pinot Grigio, in Italy.

Riesling

The true Riesling of German origin is one of the world's great grape varieties. Like Sauvignon Blanc, it has both a strong personality—one that is better off without the influence of oak—and high acidity, but it is far more adaptable. It thrives in the cool climates of Europe, especially in Germany and Alsace and, to some extent, the warmer climates of Australia, although high yields in such a climate can render it "soapy." It is very susceptible to noble rot, which means that it can produce wines in many styles, from the dry to the intensely sweet. Because of the high acidity and sugar levels, Rieslings can age for many years. Wherever it is grown, whether it is old or young, and no matter which wine style it has produced, you should always be able to detect a vivid fruitiness and a lively acidity. If too sweet, it loses its personality and becomes heavy and cloying. It should sing to you of honeysuckle, crunchy green apples, spiced baked apples, quince, and orange, and of that famous 'tarry' aroma.

Sauvignon Blanc

This grape is responsible for many of France's great white wines: from the gorgeously noble Sauternes and its many satellites (Barsac, Cadillac, Loupiac) to the crisp, elegant, and delicate Sancerre with its steely, stony, white-flower aromas typical of the Loire Valley's flint soils. Transported to other soils, it is quite transformed; perhaps that is why it is rarely recognized. New Zealand's refreshing version is an explosion of gooseberries, freshly cut grass, and tropical fruit. Be careful if you detect the lingering odor of tinned asparagus, green beans, or an exaggerated herbaceousness—almost a stemminess—as these are considered, not surprisingly, to be undesirable and are certainly due to too-high yields. My favorite expressions of this grape are the white Bordeaux and the northern Italians. I have also recently tasted stunning Sauvignons from Croatia and Slovakia, while visiting Italy. They possess none of this cartoon-character pastiche-ness of the New World Sauvignons: They are subtle, discreet, and mineral, with mature fruit and fresh acidity.

Sémillon

One member of the trio of the famous white Bordeaux blend (Sauvignon Blanc, Muscadelle, and Sémillon), Sémillon makes an unforgettable sweet white wine—Sauternes, Barsac, Cadillac, and so on—and, of course, the dry white Bordeaux, the Graves and Pessac-Léognan. There is a good reason that it is usually part of a blend, as on its own it creates a dry white wine that is at best lightly citrus-fruity, slightly herbaceous like the Sauvignon Blanc, but usually lacking originality. Heavily oaked, as in the Barossa Valley, it produces a fat, vanilla, lemony wine. It has won great acclaim for its results in an unusual dry white from Australia's Hunter Valley. Other New World countries have married it to Chardonnay to pad out the yield shortages of the extremely popular Chardonnay grape.

Ugni Blanc

A grape possessing many names and roles—surprisingly, considering its lack of distinction and originality. Or perhaps, this is just what makes it the perfect candidate for ubiquity. Known as Ugni Blanc, Clairette Ronde, and Muscadet in Aigre in France, and as Trebbiano in Italy, whence it originates. Legend has it that Ugni Blanc was brought to southern France during the fourteenth century, probably via Avignon, the seat of the papal court. It is the most planted variety in both France and Italy (where it was even blended with Sangiovese in Chianti), stealing its way into all of our favorite Provençal, Rhône, and Bordeaux blends—not to mention its importance in brandy. This is because it will grow vigorously, providing high yields, in almost any warm-climate conditions, withstanding disease and rot. At best, as a varietal, it makes a light, white, and crisp wine, low in alcohol and high in acidity. At worst, it is boring and tasteless.

Viognier

Native to the Condrieu region of the Rhône Valley, this grape is the stuff of heady, perfumed, yet dry, full-bodied opulence. It is all lime blossoms, musk, apricots, and peaches. On the palate, it is well rounded and mellow, despite its high acidity and alcohol content, making it a wine of great class. However, it is considered unreliable and needs to reach a perfect maturity in order to express itself fully. This is best assured when it is planted on the south-facing slopes of the Rhône Valley. Still, if the weather is not right, there is no crop at all—and even when all goes according to plan, the yields are low, which means high prices. Also grown in Languedoc-Roussillon and California with excellent results, it has been designated a trendy new grape.

The Red Grapes

Now let's look at the major red grape varieties. Red wine grape varieties generally taste like the red fruit family: black and red cherry, redcurrant and blackcurrant, raspberry, strawberry, and plum. As we have seen, both red and white wines can have odors and tastes such as mineral, spices, herbs, tobacco, hay, yeast, honey, caramel, and nuts. The tastes come from the grape variety, the soil, the yeasts (if indigenous yeasts are not used to start fermentation), the fermentation period, or the oak used for aging.

Barbera

Usually part of a blend, the most valuable contribution of the Barbera grape is its naturally high acidity. Hailing originally from Piedmont, it is best matched with grapes of higher tannin content and body (such as its nemesis Nebbiolo), as it produces red wines lighter in style and earlier maturing than Barolo, with pronounced astringency. Because of its high acidity, it does well in warm and hot climates. It has been very successfully grown in Argentina, where it produces a warm, juicy, and intense wine with strong undertones of its typical sour-cherry notes. It is also very popular in California's hot Central Valley because of this high acidity.

Cabernet Franc

Another blending grape, this variety adds a touch of spice and reliability (it matures easily in all weathers) to the formidable Bordeaux blend (usually no more than 20 to 25 percent), along with Cabernet Sauvignon and Merlot (and traces of Petit Verdot and Malbec). It would not stand a chance as a single variety in Bordeaux (although we should not forget the Château

Cheval Blanc, which is usually 66 percent Cabernet Franc, 33 percent Merlot, 1 percent Malbec), yet it totally holds its own in the Loire Valley, where it offers us the aromatic, tannic, red-fruity Saumur-Champigny, Bourgueil, and Chinon. It does well in cool, inland climates, and produces fabulous results in Argentina, Long Island New York, and New Zealand. One place it is not really suited for is the overly warm Napa Valley, where it was planted in order to obtain the Californian "Bordeaux" blend Meritage. I also must add that I have enjoyed several spicy, personable, and intense bottles from Hungary.

Cabernet Sauvignon

The Cabernet Sauvignon grape, like the Chardonnay, has become one of those overtransported, overplanted, abused grape varieties victimized by the trendsetters of the New World. The result is that there are so many versions of this grape, we forget what it does best: a trio act, in Bordeaux. Yes, it is adaptable, but it shouldn't be made to perform every trick under the sun. Under ideal climatic conditions, it produces an aromatic, tannic wine that ages and evolves elegantly yet powerfully. If harvested when underripe or with enormous yields, the results can be truly mediocre: the wine too tannic and light-bodied with very violent green pepper and herbaceous odors. If the climate is too warm and the grapes are overripe, the resulting wines can have very jammy, baked, fortified flavors and will lack structure. This grape needs blending. There is nothing more fatiguing and boring than these hugely alcoholic, tannic single-varietal beasts that are being produced and sold at eye-watering prices—so pretentious. A perfectly balanced Bordeaux is what we are after, and if achieved it will have notes of blackcurrants, cedar, cigars, lead pencils, green pepper, mint, and dark chocolate.

Gamay

Gamay is a native of the granite soils of Beaujolais, and if you truly know how this grape variety works, you will understand why Beaujolais Nouveau is best drunk immediately—and I mean within a few days! It was the grape variety deemed too "common" by the medieval king Philip the Bold, who demanded that all the Gamay on the Côte d'Or be uprooted in favor of the "nobler" Pinot Noir of Burgundy. But the vineyard workers (peasants, back then) insisted on keeping a few plantings, as that was what they relied upon to give them sustenance. Because it was considered inferior and because it was not treated seriously, it was drunk before it could even be bottled. It is true that when Gamay is given a very short *cuvaison* (the time spent in the vat) and is of a high yield, it produces Primeur wines that are light but fresh and very aromatic with notes of red fruit and bananas. However, I am always reminded of an aftertaste of a copper coin. When allowed to macerate longer, as with the Crus of Beaujolais—wines from ten specially designated villages—the wine can be very well rounded, elegant, and enjoyable.

Grenache

Although originally from Spain, where it is fruity powerhouse, this grape is best known for its great works in France's Rhône Valley: Châteauneuf-du-Pape, Côtes du Rhône, Gigondas, and so on. Again, here is a grape variety that is best used as a blend (with Syrah, Cinsault, and Mourvèdre), but is often used as a single variety in southern France and in the New World. When not of high yields, the wine has a dark robe and is rather aromatic, with notes of pepper, raspberries, and herbs, with supple acids, a round, fat texture, generous alcohols, and a rustic edge. When yields are too high, the wine is light-colored and tastes a bit oxidized, or like cheap cherry bonbons. It is very popular in South Africa, Australia, and California because it is very susceptible to rot and mildew and thus is better suited to dry climates.

Malbec

Again, a grape variety that is used in the red Bordeaux blend, where the Cabernet Sauvignon, Cabernet Franc, and Merlot dominate its personality. However, this dark, tannic grape (also called Auxerrois) comes into its own in southwestern France, where it can be a major component in the lushly rustic, dark, and brooding Cahors, Buzet, Bergerac, Côtes de Duras, Côtes du Frontonnais, Côtes du Marmandais, and Pécharmant. In Argentina, it produces the best reds: velvety, vigorous, aromatic, and worthy of cellar aging. In Chile, it tends to be blended with the softer Merlot and is gorgeous. Almost anywhere it is grown, Malbec seems to retain its lovely tastes of blackberries, blackcurrants, lavender, and spices.

Merlot

In the red Bordeaux blend, I like to think of the Merlot as the sugar in the recipe, the Cabernet Sauvignon as the flour, and the Cabernet Franc as the spices. Merlot gives softer, plumper, and juicy, early-maturing wines that are sweeter—a perfect complement to the tannic Cabernet Sauvignon and the spicy Cabernet Franc. The Merlot tastes of plums, roses, blackcurrants, and rich fruitcake. There are Bordeaux appellations where the bulk of the blend is Merlot-based, such as Pomerol and St-Emilion. As an unblended varietal wine it does well in California; the warmer climate accentuates its natural sweet suppleness and thus gives it a commercial appeal. However, I find most of the Merlots grown in warm climates and served up as single varieties lack structure, acid, and character. It needs the company of other grapes to show off its potential, as hotter climates do bring out its spicier, plummier side, but the allure is a superficial one. It produces light, grassy wines in northern

Italy, and if blended does well in New Zealand and South Africa. Chile also seems to get it to stand rather well on its own.

Mourvèdre

Originally a Spanish grape, known there as Monastrelli, its robust aromas are better known in Provence's Bandol region and in the Rhône Valley, where it is often blended with Syrah and Grenache. The south of France has embraced it as one of its trendy varietals. It does best in hot climates, where its tastes of blackberries, game, and leather can be appreciated. Because it is a rather tannic, highly colored, and robust grape, its wines need aging, which will further enhance its wild, gamey character. South Australia and California (as a "Rhône Ranger") are both doing good things with it.

Nebbiolo

The small, thick-skinned Nebbiolo grape produces some of the driest, biggest, and toughest of intense red wines, capable of long bottle aging. When well made and matured, it is a magical confusion of prunes, tar, licorice, violets, roses, chocolate, and spicy fruitcake. Its stronghold is Piedmont and thereabouts in northwest Italy, where its two most famous wines are Barolo and Barbaresco. It is rare outside Italy and this is probably a very good thing, as other versions tend to be uninteresting and harsh. But keep an eye out for examples from Sonoma, Paso Robles, Santa Maria or Santa Barbara. There is even a German winemaker experimenting with it . . . interesting!

Periquita

This is a very versatile grape variety native to southern Portugal also known as Castelão and João de Santarém. It also has five or six other names, all of them unpronounceable and impossible to spell. It was named Periquita (small parrot) by José Maria da Fonseca after the small farm where he started his winemaking operation. I guess he too found the other names too difficult to spell! It is often dismissed as very ordinary, but when aged in wood, I think it makes a most original wine. It has a silky texture and full-bodied sweetness, yet is powerful with a pleasant bite. If you want a taste of Portugal, try the indigenous grape varieties, not the ubiquitous Chardonnays and Cabernet Sauvignons. There are hundreds more grape varieties in Portugal, all capable of creating the most characterful brews.

Pinot Noir

When asked if I prefer Bordeaux or Burgundy, I quickly jump at the chance to enthuse passionately about the seductive superiority of the Pinot Noir. When grown correctly (cool climate, small yields), a Burgundy reaches the pinnacle of sophistication and elegance so often associated with the Bordeaux, but then surpasses it, flaunting its sexy, animal-like charm. The Burgundy seems to overflow exuberantly, oozing sensually out of its glass, while the Bordeaux, however moving, sits upright, always a bit restrained in comparison. It is the mature Pinot Noir's complex flavors of raspberries, strawberries, cranberries, violets, game, compost, allspice, tobacco, and hay, coupled with its silky, velvety texture, that are so captivating. Pinot Noir is the most precocious of the fine-wine grapes to grow and vinify. Relatively low in tannin and acidity, it needs a cool climate. Too little sun leads to pallid, thin-tasting wine. With too much warmth, Pinot Noir can develop jammy, baked flavors, losing its elegance and silkiness. Even the best New World Pinot Noirs lack the magical complexity of the greatest Burgundies, where it is perfectly at home in the *argilo-calcaire* soils and cool climate. My favorite secret is that the Pinot Nero in Italy's Alto Adige region can rival Burgundy's Volnays, at a fraction of the price.

Pinotage

Mistakenly considered an indigenous grape variety of South Africa, technically this is actually a cross between Pinot Noir and Cinsault (since 1926). It produces everything from light, fruity wines to robust, distinctive, and hearty reds with strong tannic backbones, and flavors of plums, brambles, flambéed bananas, and smoky oak. One of the best offerings from South Africa, it is a lovely, original-tasting grape variety.

Sangiovese

Taste a Sangiovese (blood of Jove) and you will immediately conjure images of Italy. As the major component of the famous Chianti wine, it is actually grown all over Italy. In Chianti Classico, the producers are moving away from the incredibly boring Super-Tuscan Cabernet Sauvignon beasts and toward producing more classic Sangiovese-only wines—experimenting with rootstocks in order to bring Sangiovese back to its original potential. Sangiovese is also responsible for Brunello di Montalcino, Vino Nobile di Montepulciano, Carmignano, Rosso di Montalcino, and Rosso di Montepulciano. As with the other late-maturing grape varieties we have seen (Grenache and Mourvèdre), it needs a hot climate in order to produce the richness and alcohol content required for bottle aging. In cooler climates, it tends to have sharp acids and bitter tannins. It is a very rich, robust wine that will do well with long bottle aging. Styles vary from light, astringent, and ordinary to a full-bodied, firm, slightly spicy red (with bitter cherry, tobacco, and herb flavors).

Syrah

Called Shiraz in Australia and South Africa, Syrah is the magic varietal behind the Rhône Valley's famous Hermitage, Côte-Rôtie, Cornas, St-Joseph, and Crozes-Hermitage. At home in the valley's granite soils, it produces wines that are deep in color and aroma. When young, they display floral and fruity (raspberry) notes. Once matured, this evolves into notes of black pepper, leather, spices, and game. Syrah is a very versatile grape and can be grown in almost any climate, although yields need to be kept down and overripeness must be avoided or the wine can become heavy, flabby, and too tannic. Some winemakers then fall into the trap of harvesting when the grapes are not at all mature, which gives equally mediocre results. Outside France, in Australia and California, Syrah is used both as a single variety and in blends with good results.

Tempranillo

Often labeled as Spain's Cabernet Sauvignon, Tempranillo is the mainstay of most of its reds. It does well in its native Rioja because it is not too high in alcohol or acidity, despite the hot climate. These are rich, dark grapes that make wine capable of bottle aging. We know it best as an oaky (often over-oaked!), mellow, sultry, vanilla-rich red. Without oak, its fruity notes are more evident.

Zinfandel

It has been established that Zinfandel is a variant of the Primitivo of southern Italy (Puglia) and a Croatian grape I cannot spell. The Californians like to consider it a native grape, but remember, the United States has no native *Vitis vinifera* grapes, so this is factually impossible. In California, it became best known back in the 1970s and 1980s as a White Zinfandel. So much so that most consumers assumed that it was a white grape and not red! After the "blush" trend faded, winemakers started producing more red Zinfandel. A good Zinfandel is robust, spicy, blackberry-ish, interesting, and, in my opinion, by far the most individual variety coming out of California. If yields are respected and the grapes are grown in cooler hillside regions, the results are worth cellaring for many years.

WHY ARE NEW WORLD WINES SINGLE-VARIETAL WINES?

Have you noticed that most of the New World regions produce and market mostly single-grape-variety wines, while European wines are identified by geographic region? This is usually what puts us off the Old World wines. Other than memorizing which region or appellation is allowed to grow which grapes, how are we supposed to know that Sancerre is made from Sauvignon Blanc? That red Rioja is made from Tempranillo, Barolo from Nebbiolo, or Vouvray from Chenin Blanc?

Most credit for the fact that New World wines are identified by the grape variety, and not the region, goes to Robert Mondavi. In California in

1966, he started the single-variety craze, using the dominant grape in the wine as its name as opposed to its geographic origins. Because California had no specific geographic areas legislated for growing specific grapes, winemakers had no choice but to name the wine after the grape that was in the bottle. This also suited their winemaking: presenting single varietals rather than blends. And there is a reason for that.

The United States is a "New World" wine country: It has no indigenous wine grapes, only table grapes. The species of *Vitis* in the US is *labrusca,* not *vinifera,* as in Europe, or the "Old World." So it was the European immigrants who brought their rootstocks with them from Germany, France, Portugal, Hungary, and so on. Pre-Prohibition, Americans were drinking their wines as Europeans do, because they were European. Families grew their own grapes in their gardens and made their own wines, and families sat down to drink wine for dinner. When the suffragettes went on the warpath against spirit-drinking rabble-rousers and wastrels, domestic wine drinking inadvertently got caught up in the fray. And when it came to drafting the Eighteenth Amendment, wine became included in the definition of the prohibited liquors. In the decade or so of Prohibition, an entire generation of wine consumerism and winemaking techniques was crippled. Domestic wine cultivation did not really get under way again until the 1960s, when it became vogue to retire to a winery in Napa!

By this time, winemakers had to start reeducating their public from scratch. And the collective national palate had become accustomed to sweet drinks such as homemade wine, powdered-wine kits, Coca-Cola, beer, and fruit juices. Complex, blended wines from Bordeaux, for example, were simply too difficult to be understood. Further, the fledgling winemaking industry found it easier to market a single "famous" grape name than to try to teach the complicated European appellation system. For example, in the Bordeaux blend of Cabernet Sauvignon, Cabernet Franc, Malbec, Petit Verdot, and Merlot, Merlot is the sweetest grape in the recipe. And a sweet, fluid, non-tannic Merlot is easier to sell than an intense Bordeaux blend.

More important, winemakers needed the freedom to plant whatever grape they wanted to, wherever they wanted to, to see what did best where. They did not want to be tied down to formulaic blends; they wanted to experiment and create. They eschewed the European appellation system and did not want regulated geographic areas . . . until they figured out two things: Yes, as they experimented, certain grapes were truly doing better in certain areas and making a name for themselves; also, by capitalizing on this geographic distinction they could market these as quality wines and make more money.

So, by going back to the idea of *terroir,* or soil—a concept they were scathing about only a decade earlier—winemakers began clamoring to have their specific piece of soil designated as a special vine-growing area, or an AVA (American Viticultural Area). Napa Valley was the first appellation designated by the Bureau of Alcohol, Tobacco and Firearms (BATF) in 1981. This means that wines labeled with one county or vineyard as the appellation need consist of 75 percent grapes from that county or vineyard, whereas wines from AVAs are required to have 85 percent. To establish an AVA, the grower or winery must petition to the BATF and provide evidence that their area possesses a unique character for grape-growing. It is difficult to dispute that there exists a difference between a Chardonnay from Carneros and one from the Russian River Valley. But for now, whether this difference is due to "unique character" or not is debatable (in this author's opinion). Many question the rigor with which these areas were created. Tim Mondavi once explained to me that "the AVAs are only meant to be a statement of origin and not a guarantee of quality." This is a valid point. But the opposition—people who happen to own land outside the AVAs—contend that to market specific vineyards, such as Stag's Leap (made famous by such wineries as Clos du Val, Pine Ridge, and Silverado), detracts from the reputation of the larger appellation of Napa Valley, upon which they rely so heavily. So how large a role do geographic features play as opposed to local politics? The bickering continues. Also questioned is why there should be such a system. Is it truly a move toward quality or is it surrendering to the irresistible lure of the higher prices that could be gained for AVA-controlled wines? At least everyone is clear on the importance of one point: finding a system that is standardized yet not stifling.

During a trip to South Africa a few years ago, I was amazed by the number of estates that were growing anywhere from six to seven white varieties as well as the same number of red grapes. I'd drive out and see Sauvignon Blanc parcels next to Riesling parcels and Syrah next to Pinot Noir (complete climatic opposites!) How could one estate accommodate such a fruit salad? I asked. The standard answer was that "my land has the topographic and soil variations needed to fully support the physiological needs of each variety." I found that quite difficult to believe. Occasionally I got an honest answer: They wished to have enough varieties on hand to respond whatever way market trends went. Alternatively, they threw their hands up and explained that they were simply experimenting. They were starting with ten white and ten red varieties, scattered in all different expositions, and were aiming to slowly narrow down the parcels until they found the one perfect grape/soil combination. That, I can understand and admire.

The New World wine countries are just that, new. Yes, many have had viticulture brought to them as far back as the 1500–1600s by the European settlers, but that is still relatively new. Further, a few hundred years does not render a visiting grape variety "native." When you know that the roots of cultivated vineyards have been found in Georgia as early as 9000–7000 BC and that in a properly historical context, *France* is New World, then you can begin to understand that these countries need much more time to find their way.

AMERICAN AVAs

Remember that US AVAs do not require a specific grape to be grown in that area. Winemakers are free to grow whatever they want. This is unlike Europe, where a wine producer, for example in Rioja, will be required to grow and use Tempranillo as a primary red grape. These named areas are not telling us what grapes are grown there, nor are they guaranteeing quality. But some of names will be very familiar to you, as affinities are being created between certain grapes and regions, such as Cabernet Sauvignon in Napa Valley, Chardonnay in Russian River, and so on.

CALIFORNIA
Central Coast and Santa Cruz Mountains

Arroyo Grande Valley
Arroyo Seco
Ben Lomond Mountain
Carmel Valley
Central Coast
Chalone
Cienega Valley
Edna Valley
Hames Valley
Happy Canyon of Santa Barbara
Lime Kiln Valley
Livermore Valley
Monterey
Mount Harlan
Pacheco Pass
Paicines
Paso Robles
San Antonio Valley
San Benito
San Bernabe
San Francisco Bay
San Lucas
San Ysidro District
Santa Clara Valley
Santa Cruz Mountains

Santa Lucia Highlands
Santa Maria Valley
Santa Rita Hills
Santa Ynez Valley
York Mountain

Central Valley

Alta Mesa
Borden Ranch
Capay Valley
Clarksburg
Clements Hills
Cosumnes River
Diablo Grande
Dunnigan Hills
Jahant
Lodi
Madera
Merritt Island
Mokelumne River
River Junction
Salado Creek
Sloughhouse
Tracy Hills

Klamath Mountains

Seiad Valley
Trinity Lakes
Willow Creek

North Coast

Alexander Valley
Anderson Valley
Atlas Peak
Benmore Valley
Bennett Valley
Calistoga
Chalk Hill
Chiles Valley
Clear Lake

Cole Ranch
Covelo
Diamond Mountain District
Dos Rios
Dry Creek Valley
Green Valley of Russian River Valley
Guenoc Valley
High Valley
Howell Mountain
Knights Valley
Los Carneros
McDowell Valley
Mendocino
Mendocino Ridge
Mount Veeder
Napa Valley
North Coast
Northern Sonoma
Oak Knoll District of Napa Valley
Oakville
Potter Valley
Red Hills Lake County
Redwood Valley
Rockpile
Russian River Valley
Rutherford
Solano County Green Valley
Sonoma Coast
Sonoma Mountain
Sonoma Valley
Spring Mountain District
St. Helena
Stags Leap District
Suisun Valley
Wild Horse Valley
Yorkville Highlands
Yountville

California Shenandoah Valley

El Dorado
Fair Play

Fiddletown
North Yuba
Sierra Foothills

South Coast

Antelope Valley
Cucamonga Valley
Leona Valley
Malibu-Newton Canyon
Ramona Valley
Saddle Rock–Malibu
San Pasqual Valley
Sierra Pelona Valley
South Coast
Temecula Valley

OREGON

Applegate Valley
Chehalem Mountains
Dundee Hills
Eola-Amity Hills
McMinnville
Red Hill Douglas County
Ribbon Ridge
Rogue Valley
Southern Oregon
Umpqua Valley
Willamette Valley
Yamhill-Carlton District

WASHINGTON

Horse Heaven Hills
Lake Chelan
Puget Sound
Rattlesnake Hills
Red Mountain
Snipes Mountain
Wahluke Slope
Yakima Valley

MULTISTATE
Columbia Gorge, Oregon and Washington
Columbia Valley, Washington and Oregon
Snake River Valley, Idaho and Oregon
Walla Walla Valley, Oregon and Washington

NEW YORK
Cayuga Lake
Finger Lakes
Hudson River Region
Long Island
Niagara Escarpment
North Fork of Long Island
Seneca Lake
The Hamptons, Long Island

VIRGINIA
Monticello
North Fork of Roanoke
Northern Neck George Washington Birthplace
Rocky Knob
Virginia's Eastern Shore

TEXAS
Bell Mountain
Escondido Valley
Fredericksburg in the Texas Hill Country
Mesilla Valley
Texas Davis Mountains
Texas High Plains
Texas Hill Country
Texoma

MICHIGAN
Fennville
Lake Michigan Shore

Leelanau Peninsula
Old Mission Peninsula

OTHER

Alexandria Lakes, Minnesota
Altus, Arkansas
Arkansas Mountain, Arkansas
Augusta, Missouri
Catoctin, Maryland
Central Delaware Valley, New Jersey and Pennsylvania
Cumberland Valley, Maryland and Pennsylvania
Grand River Valley, Ohio
Grand Valley, Colorado
Haw River Valley, North Carolina
Hermann, Missouri
Isle St. George, Ohio
Kanawha River Valley, West Virginia
Lake Erie, New York, Ohio, and Pennsylvania
Lake Wisconsin, Wisconsin
Lancaster Valley, Pennsylvania
Lehigh Valley, Pennsylvania
Linganore, Maryland
Loramie Creek, Ohio
Martha's Vineyard, Massachusetts
Middle Rio Grande Valley, New Mexico
Mimbres Valley, New Mexico
Mississippi Delta, Louisiana, Mississippi, and Tennessee
Ohio River Valley, Indiana, Kentucky, Ohio, and West Virginia
Outer Coastal Plain, New Jersey
Ozark Highlands, Missouri
Ozark Mountain, Arkansas, Missouri, and Oklahoma
Shawnee Hills, Illinois
Shenandoah Valley, Virginia and West Virginia
Shenandoah Valley, Virginia and West Virginia
Sonoita, Arizona
Southeastern New England, Connecticut, Massachusetts, and Rhode Island
Swan Creek, North Carolina
Warren Hills, New Jersey
Western Connecticut Highlands, Connecticut
Yadkin Valley, North Carolina

WHICH GRAPES MAKE WHICH WINES

Name	Region/Country	Color/Type	Grape Varieties
Ajaccio	Corsica, France	Red	Sciacarello, Grenache, Cinsault, Carignan
		White	Ugni Blanc, Vermentino Blanc
		Rosé	Barbarossa, Nielluccio, Sciacarello, Vermentino Blanc, Carignan, Cinsault, Grenache
Albariño	Galicia, Spain	White	Albariño
Alenquer	Alenquer, Portugal	Red	Camarate, Mortagua, Periquita, Preto Martinho, Tinta Miuda
		White	Vital, Jampal, Arinto, Fernao Pires
Alentejo	Alentejo, Portugal	Red	Alfrocheiro, Aragonez, Periquita, Tinta Caiada, Trincadeira, Alicante Bouschet, Moreto
		White	Antão Vaz, Arinto, Fernão Pires, Rabo de Ovelha, Roupeiro
Almeirim	Almeirim, Portugal	Red	Castelao Nacional, Poeirinha, Periquita, Trincadeira Preta
		White	Fernao Pires, Arinto, Rabo de Ovelha, Talia, Trincadeira das Pratas, Vital
Aloxe Corton	Burgundy, France	Red	Pinot Noir
Amarone della Valpolicella	Veneto, Italy	Red	Corvina, Rondinella, Molinara
Anjou-Saumur	Loire, France	Red	Cabernet Franc, Cabernet Sauvignon, Pineau d'Aunis (Chenin Noir)
		White	Chenin, Chardonnay, Sauvignon Blanc
		Rosé	Cabernet Franc, Cabernet Sauvignon, Gamay, Côt, Groslot
Apremont	Savoie, France	White	Jacquère, Chardonnay, Aligoté
Arbois	Jura, France	Red	Poulsard Noir, Trousseau, Pinot Noir
		White	Savignin, Chardonnay, Pinot Blanc
Asti Spumante	Piedmont	White sparkling	Moscato
Auxey Duresses	Burgundy, France	Red	Pinot Noir
		White	Chardonnay
Bairrada	Portugal	Red	Baga, Alfrocheiro, Camarate, Castelão, Jaen, Touriga Nacional, Aragonez
		White	Maria Gomes, Arinto, Bical, Cercial, Rabo de Ovelha, Verdelho

Name	Region/Country	Color/Type	Grape Varieties
Bandol	Provence, France	Red/rosé	Mourvèdre, Grenache, Cinsault, Syrah, Tibouren, Xalitor
		White	Bourboulence, Clairette, Ugni Blanc, Sauvignon Blanc
Barbaresco	Piedmont, Italy	Red	Nebbiolo Michet, Nebbiolo Lampia, Nebbiolo rosé
Barbera d'Alba	Piedmont, Italy	Red	Barbera
Barbera d'Asti	Piedmont, Italy	Red	Barbera, Freisa, Grignolino, Dolcetto
Bardolino	Veneto, Italy	Red	Corvina, Rondinella, Molinara, Negrara, Rossignola, Barbera, Sangiovese
Barolo	Piedmont, Italy	Red	Nebbiolo Michet, Nebbiolo Lampia, Nebbiolo rosé
Barolo Bianco	Piedmont, Italy	White	Arneis
Barsac	Bordeaux, France	Sweet white	Sémillon, Sauvignon Blanc, Muscadelle
Bâtard-Montrachet	Burgundy, France	White	Chardonnay
Beaujolais	Burgundy, France	Red / White	Gamay / Chardonnay, Aligoté
Beaumes-de-Venise	Rhône Valley, France	Vin doux naturel	Muscat
Beaune	Burgundy, France	Red / White	Pinot Noir / Chardonnay
Bellet	Provence, France	Red / Rosé	Braquet, Folle Noir, Cinsault, Grenache, Rolle, Roussanne++
		White	Rolle Roussanne, Spagnol, Clairette, Bourboulence ++
Bergerac	Southwest France	Red	Cabernet Sauvignon, Cabernet Franc, Merlot
		White	Sémillon, Sauvignon Blanc, Muscadelle
Bianco di Custoza	Veneto, Italy	White	Trebbiano, Garganega, Tocai Friulano
Blanc de Blancs	Champagne, France	Sparkling white	Chardonnay
Blanc de Noirs	Champagne, France	Sparkling white	Pinot Noir, Pinot Meunier
Blanquette de Limoux	Languedoc, France	Sparkling white	Mauzac, Chardonnay, Chenin Blanc
Bonnes Mares	Burgundy, France	Red	Pinot Noir

Name	Region/Country	Color/Type	Grape Varieties
Bonnezeaux	Loire Valley, France	Sweet white	Chenin Blanc
Bordeaux	Bordeaux, France	Red White	Cabernet Sauvignon, Cabernet Franc, Merlot, Malbec, Petit Verdot + Sauvignon Blanc, Sémillon, Muscadelle
Botticino	Lombardy, Italy	Red	Barbera, Schiava Gentile, Marzemino, Sangiovese
Bourgueil	Loire Valley, France	Red	Cabernet Franc
Brouilly	Beaujolais, France	Red	Gamay
Brunello di Montalcino	Tuscany, Italy	Red	Sangiovese
Bull's Blood	Eger, Hungary	Red	Kékfrankos, Cabernet Sauvignon, Merlot
Burgundy	Burgundy, France	Red White	Pinot Noir Chardonnay
Buzet	Southwest France	Red White	Merlot, Cabernet Sauvignon, Cabernet Franc, Merlot Sémillon, Sauvignon Blanc, Muscadelle
Cadillac	Bordeaux, France	Sweet white	Sémillon, Sauvignon Blanc, Muscadelle
Cahors	Southwest, France	Red	Malbec, Merlot, Tannat, Jurançon Noir
Canon-Fronsac	Bordeaux, France	Red	Merlot, Cabernet Franc
Capri	Campania, Italy	Red White	Piedirosso Falanghina, Greco
Carmignano	Tuscany, Italy	Red	Sangiovese, Canaiolo Nero, Cabernet Sauvignon
Cassis	Provence, France	Red/rosé White	Grenache, Carignan, Mourvèdre, Cinsault Ugni Blanc, Sauvignon Blanc, Grenache Blanc, Marsanne ++
Castel del Monte	Puglia, Italy	Red	Uva di Troia
Cava	Catalonia, Spain	Sparkling white	Xarel-lo, Parellada, Macabeo, Chardonnay
Chablis	Burgundy, France	White	Chardonnay
Chacoli de Guetaria	Northwest (Basque), Spain	Red White	Hondarribi Beltz Hondarribi Zuri

Name	Region/Country	Color/Type	Grape Varieties
Chambertin	Burgundy, France	Red	Pinot Noir
Chambolle-Musigny	Burgundy, France	Red	Pinot Noir
Champagne	Champagne, France	Sparkling	Pinot Noir, Pinot Meunier, Chardonnay
Chassagne-Montrachet	Burgundy, France	White	Chardonnay
Châteauneuf-du-Pape	Rhône Valley, France	Red	Grenache Noir, Cinsault, Syrah, Mourvèdre
		White	Grenache Blanc, Bourboulenc, Roussanne
Chianti	Tuscany, Italy	Red	Sangiovese, Canaiolo ++
Chinon	Loire Valley	Red or white	Chenin Blanc, Cabernet Sauvignon
Clos de Vougeot	Bugundy, France	Red	Pinot Noir
Colli Orientali del Friuli	Veneto, Italy	Red	Merlot, Cabernet Sauvignon, Pinot Nero
Condrieu	Rhône Valley, France	White	Viognier
Corbières	Languedoc Roussillon, France	Red	Carignan, Grenache, Cinsault ++
		White	Roussanne, Clairette, Cinsault, Grenache, Bourboulenc, Ugni Blanc, Maccabeau, Marsanne
Cornas	Rhône Valley, France	Red	Syrah
Corton	Burgundy, France	Red	Pinot Noir
Corton-Charlemagne	Burgundy, France	White	Chardonnay
Côte Chalonnaise	Burgundy, France	Red / White	Pinot Noir / Chardonnay
Côte de Beaune	Burgundy, France	Red	Pinot Noir
Côte de Nuits	Burgundy, France	Red / White	Pinot Noir / Chardonnay
Côte Rôtie	Rhône, France	Red / White	Syrah / Viognier
Coteaux d'Aix-en-Provence	Provence, France	Red /Rosé	Cabernet Sauvignon, Carignan, Cinsault, Cournoise, Grenache, Mourvèdre, Syrah
		White	Bourboulenc, Clairette, Grenache Blanc, Sauvignon Blanc, Sémillon, Ugni Blanc

Name	Region/Country	Color/Type	Grape Varieties
Coteaux du Layon	Loire	Sweet white	Chenin Blanc
Côtes de Bourg	Bordeaux, France	Red	Cabernet Sauvignon, Cabernet Franc, Merlot, Malbec, Gros Verdot, Prolongeau
		White	Sauvignon Blanc, Sémillon, Muscadelle, Merlot Blanc, Colombard
Côtes de Duras	Southwest France	Red	Cabernet Sauvignon, Cabernet Franc, Merlot, Malbec
		White	Sauvignon Blanc, Sémillon, Muscadelle, Chenin, Mauzac
Côtes de Montravel	Southwest France	White	Sémillon, Sauvignon Blanc, Muscadelle
Côtes de Provence	Provence, France	Red/rosé	Carignan, Cinsault, Grenache, Mourvèdre, Tibouren ++
		White	Clairette, Sémillon, Ugni Blanc, Vermentino Blanc/Rolle
Côtes du Jura	Jura, France	Red	Poulsard Noir, Trousseau, Pinot Noir
		White	Sauvignon Blanc, Chardonnay, Pinot Blanc
Côtes du Rhône	Rhône Valley, France	Red/rosé	Grenache Noir, Cinsault, Syrah, Mourvèdre, Pinot Noir, Gamay ++
		White	Clairette, Roussanne, Bourboulenc, Viognier, Picpoul, Marsanne ++
Côtes du Roussillon	Roussillon, France	Red/rosé	Carignan, Cinsault, Grenache, Syrah, Mourvedre, Maccabeau Blanc
		White	Maccabeau Blanc, Grenache Blanc, Tourbat Blanc, Marsanne, Roussanne
Crémant d'Alsace	Alsace, France	Sparkling red/rosé	Pinot Noir
		Sparking white	Riesling, Pinot Blanc, Chardonnay
Crémant de Bourgogne	Burgundy, France	Sparkling rosé	Pinot Noir
		Sparkling white	Pinot Noir, Chardonnay, Pinot Gris, Pinot Blanc, Gamay, Aligoté
Crémant de Loire	Loire, France	Sparkling	Chenin Blanc, Cabernet Franc, Cabernet Sauvignon, Pineau d'Aunis, Pinot Noir, Chardonnay

Name	Region/Country	Color/Type	Grape Varieties
Crépy	Savoie, France	White	Chasselas
Crozes-Hermitage	Rhône Valley, France	Red White	Syrah Marsanne, Roussanne
Dão	Portugal	Red White	Alfrocheiro Preto, Bastardo, Jaen, Tinta Pinheira, Tinta Barroca, Tourigo Nacional Bical, Cercial, Malvasia Fina, Verdelho, Encruzado, Assario Branco, Barcelo, Borrado das Moscas
Dolcetto d'Alba	Piedmont, Italy	Red	Dolcetto
Echezeaux	Burgundy, France	Red	Pinot Noir
Entre-Deux-Mers	Bordeaux, France	White	Sémillon, Sauvignon Blanc, Muscadelle
Falerno del Massico	Campania, Italy	Red White	Aglianico, Piedirosso Falanghina
Fiano d'Avellino	Campania, Italy	White	Fiano
Fitou	Languedoc, France	Red	Carignan, Lladoner, Pelut, Grenache ++
Fleurie	Beaujolais, France	Red	Gamay
Fougères	Côteaux du Languedoc	Red White	Carignan, Cinsault, Grenache, Mourvèdre, Syrah Roussanne, white Grenache, Marsanne, Vermentino
Frascati	Latium, Italy	White	Malvasia, Trebbiano
Fronsac	Bordeaux, France	Red	Merlot, Cabernet franc, Cabernet Sauvignon, Malbec
Gaillac	Southwest France	Red/rosé White	Duras, Cabernet Sauvignon, Fer Sevadou, Gamay, Syrah, Merlot ++ Len de L'El, Amuzac, Sémillon, Sauvignon Blanc
Gattinara	Piedmont, Italy	Red	Nebbiolo
Gavi Cortese di Gavi	Piedmont, Italy	White	Cortese
Gevry-Chambertin	Burgundy, France	Red	Pinot Noir
Gigondas	Rhône Valley, France	Red	Grenache Noir, Syrah, Mourvèdre
Grave del Friuli	Friuli-Venezia Giulia, Italy	Red White	Cabernet Franc, Cabernet Sauvignon Chardonnay, Pinot Bianco

Name	Region/Country	Color/Type	Grape Varieties
Graves	Bordeaux, France	Red	Cabernet Sauvignon, Cabernet Franc, Merlot
		White	Sémillon, Sauvignon Blanc, Muscadelle
Greco di Tufo	Campania, Italy	White	Greco, Falanghina, Biancolella
Hermitage	Rhône Valley, France	Red	Syrah
		White	Marsanne, Roussanne
Irouléguy	Southwest France	Red/rosé	Cabernet Sauvignon, Cabernet Franc, Tannat
		White	Courbu, Manseng
La Clape	Côteaux du Languedoc, France	Red	Grenache Noir, Carignan, Syrah, Mourvedre
		White	Bourboulenc, Grenache Blanc, Malvoisie, Clairette
Lacryma Christi del Vesuvio	Campania, Italy	White	Coda di Volpe del Vesuvio
Lalande de Pomerol	Bordeaux, France	Red	Merlot, Cabernet Franc, Cabernet Sauvignon
Lambrusco di Sorbara	Emilia-Romagna, Italy	Sparkling red, semi-sweet	Lambrusco di Sorbara, Lambrusco Salamino
Limnos	Greece	White	Muscat of Alexandria
Lirac	Rhône Valley, France	Red/rosé	Grenache Noir, Cinsault, Mourvedre, Syrah, Carignan
		White	Roussanne, Viognier, Clairette Blanc, Grenache Blanc, Bourboulenc, Ugni Blanc, Picpoul, Marsanne
Lugana	Lombardy, Italy	White	Trebbiano di Lugana
Lussac	Bordeaux (St-Emilion), France	Red	Merlot, Malbec, Cabernet Franc, Cabernet Sauvignon
Mâcon	Burgundy, France	White	Chardonnay
Madiran	Southwest France	Red	Tannat, Cabernet Sauvignon, Cabernet Franc
Margaux	Bordeaux, France	Red	Cabernet Sauvignon, Cabernet Franc, Merlot, Carmenère, Malbec, Petit Verdot
Marino	Latium, Italy	White	Malvasia, Trebbiano
Marsala	Sicily, Italy	Red	Nerello Mascalese, Inzolia, Nero d'Avola
		White	Grillo, Catarratto, Pignatello, Calabrese

Name	Region/Country	Color/Type	Grape Varieties
Mercurey	Burgundy, France	Red White	Pinot Noir Chardonnay
Meursault	Burgundy, France	White	Chardonnay
Minervois	Languedoc Roussillon, France	Red/rosé White	Grenache, Syrah, Mourvèdre, Carignan Grenache Blanc, Bouboulenc Blanc, Maccabeau Blanc, Marsanne Blanche ++
Monbazillac	Southwest France	White	Sémillon, Sauvignon Blanc, Muscadelle
Montagny	Burgundy, France	White	Chardonnay
Montepulciano d'Abruzzo	Abruzzo, Italy	Red	Montepulciano
Montlouis	Loire, France	White	Pineau Blanc
Morellino di Scansano	Tuscany, Italy	Red	Sangiovese
Morey-St. Denis	Burgundy, France	Red	Pinot Noir
Morgon	Beaujolais, France	Red	Gamay
Mosel	Mosel, Germany	White	Riesling (or as named on label)
Moulin-à-Vent	Beaujolais, France	Red	Gamay
Muscadet	Loire Valley, France	White	Melon
Naoussa	Greece	Red	Xynomavro
Navarra	Navarra, Spain	Red White	Tempranillo, Garnacha, Cabernet Sauvignon Chardonnay
Nuits-St-Georges	Burgundy, France	Red	Pinot Noir
Orvieto	Umbria, Italy	White	Trebbiano Toscano, Verdello, Grechetto, Canailo Bianco, Malvasia Toscana
Pacherenc du Vic-Bilh	Southwest France	White	Arrufiac, Courbu, Gros and Petit Manseng
Palette	Provence, France	Red/rosé White	Mourvèdre, Grenache, Cinsault ++ Clairette, Ugni Blanc ++
Patrimonio	Corsica, France	Red/rosé White	Nielluccio, Grenache, Sciacarello, Vermentino Blanc Vermentino Blanc, Ugni Blanc
Penedès	Barcelona, Spain	Red White sparkling	Tempranillo, Garnacha, Carinena Cava

Name	Region/Country	Color/ Type	Grape Varieties
Pic St-Loup	Côteaux du Languedoc, France	Red	Syrah, Mourvèdre, Carignan, Cinsault
Picpoul	Rhône Valley, France	Red, white	Picpoul
Pomerol	Bordeaux, France	Red	Cabernet Franc, Merlot, Cabernet Sauvignon
Pommard	Burgundy, France	Red	Pinot Noir
Port	Duoro, Portugal	Fortified red Fortified white	Touriga Francesa, Touriga Nacianal, Bastardo, Mourisco, Tinto Cao ++ Malvasia Fina, Arinto, Cercial, Donzelinho Branco, Folgazão, Gouveio, Malvasia Fina, Moscatel Galego Branco, Rabigato, Roupeiro, Samarrinho, Semillon, Sercial, Verdelho, Viosinho, Vital
Pouilly-Fuissé	Burgundy, France	White	Chardonnay
Pouilly-Fumé	Loire Valley, France	White	Sauvignon Blanc
Pouilly-sur-Loire	Loire Valley, France	White	Chasselas, Sauvignon
Priorat	Tarragona, Spain	Red	Tempranillo
Prosecco di Conegliano-Valdobbiadene	Veneto, Italy	White	Prosecco
Puissegrain-St-Emilion	Bordeaux, France	Red	Merlot, Cabernet Franc, Cabernet Sauvignon
Puligny-Montrachet	Burgundy, France	White	Chardonnay
Quarts de Chaume	Loire Valley, France	White	Chenin Blanc
Quincy	Loire Valley, France	White	Sauvignon Blanc
Recas	Banat, Romania	Red White	Merlot, Syrah, Cabernet Sauvignon, Feteasca Neagra, Pinot Noir Pinot Grigio, Feteasca Regala, Chardonnay, Sauvignon Blanc
Reguengos	Portugal	Red White	Aragonez, Moreto, Periquita, Trincadeira Manteudo, Perrum, Rabo de Ovelha, Ropeiro
Reuilly	Loire Valley, France	White	Sauvignon Blanc
Rhine	Rhine, Germany	White	Riesling (or as named on label)
Rias Baixas	Galicia, Spain	Red White *	Caino Tinto, Souson Albarino, Treixadura, Caino Blanco

Name	Region/Country	Color/Type	Grape Varieties
Ribeiro	Spain	Red White	Caino, Garnacha, Ferron, Souson, Mencia, Tempranillo + Treixadura, Loureira, Albarino, Jerez +++
Ribera del Duero	Castilla y Leon, Spain	Red	Tempranillo
Richebourg	Burgundy, France	Red	Pinot Noir
Rioja	Rioja, Spain	Red White	Tempranillo, Garnacho Viura, Malvasia Riojana
Roera	Piedmont, Italy	White	Arneis
Rosso di Montalcino	Tuscany, Italy	Red	Sangiovese
Rosso di Montepulciano	Tuscany, Italy	Red	Sangiovese, Canaiolo Nero
Rueda	Rueda, Spain	White	Verdejo, Viura, Sauvignon Blanc, Palomino Fino
Rully	Burgundy, France	Red White	Pinot Noir Chardonnay
Sagrantino di Montefalco	Umbria, Italy	Red	Sagrantino
St-Joseph	Rhône Valley, France	Red White	Syrah Marsanne, Roussane
Salice Salento	Puglia, Italy	Red	Negroamaro, Nero d'Avola, Primitivo
Samos	Greece	White	Muscat Blanc à Petits Grains
Sancerre	Loire Valley, France	Red/rosé White	Sauvignon Blanc Pinot Noir
Saumur	Loire Valley, France	Red	Cabernet Franc, Cabernet Sauvignon
Sauternes	Bordeaux, France	Sweet white	Sémillon, Sauvignon Blanc, Muscadelle
Savennières	Loire, France	White	Chenin Blanc
Savigny-les-Beaune	Burgundy, France	Red White	Pinot Noir Chardonnay
Setúbal	Portugal	Sweet white	Moscatel de Setúbal, Muscat of Alexandria, Moscatel Roxo, Arinto
Sherry	Spain	Fortified	Palomino
Soave	Veneto, Italy	White	Garganega, Pinot Bianco, Chardonnay, Trebbiano
St. Péray	Rhône Valley, France	White	Roussanne, Marsanne
St-Amour	Beaujolais, France	Red	Gamay

Name	Region/Country	Color/Type	Grape Varieties
Ste-Croix-du-Mont	Bordeaux, France	Sweet white	Sémillon, Sauvignon Blanc, Muscadelle
St-Emilion	Bordeaux, France	Red	Merlot, Cabernet Sauvignon, Cabernet Franc
St-Estèphe	Bordeaux, France	Red	Cabernet Sauvignon, Merlot, Cabernet Franc, Malbec, Petit Verdot
St-Julien	Bordeaux, France	Red	Cabernet Sauvignon, Merlot, Cabernet Franc, Malbec, Petit Verdot
St-Véran	Burgundy, France	White	Chardonnay
Taurasi	Campania, Italy	Red	Aglianico, Piedirosso, Sangiovese, Barbera
Tavel	Rhône Valley, France	Rosé	Grenache, Cinsault, Clairette, Mourvèdre, Picpoul, Syrah, Carignan
Tokaji	Hungary	White	Furmint, Harslevelu
Torgiano	Umbria, Italy	Red White	Sangiovese, Canaiolo Trebbiano Tuscano, Grechetto, Malvasia, Verdello
Touraine	Loire, France	Red White	Cabernet Franc, Cabernet Sauvignon, Côt, Pinot Noir, Pinot Meunier, Pinot Gris, Pineau d'Aunis, Gamay Chenin, Sauvignon, Arbois
Vacqueyras	Rhône, France	Red	Grenache, Cinsault, Syrah ++
Valpolicella/Amarone	Veneto, Italy	Red	Corvina Veronese, Rondinella, Molinara
Vernaccia di San Gimignano	Tuscany, Italy	White	Vernaccia di San Gimignano
Vesuvio	Campania, Italy	Red White	Piedirosso, Sciascinoso Coda di Volpe, Verdeca
Vinho Verde	Portugal	White Red	Alvarinho, Arinto (Pedernã), Avesso, Azal, Batoca, Loureiro, Trajadura Amaral, Borraçal, Alvarelhão, Espadeiro, Padeiro, Pedral, Rabo de Anho, Vinhão
Vino Nobile di Montepulciano	Tuscany, Italy	Red	Sangiovese
Volnay	Burgundy, France	Red	Pinot Noir
Vosne-Romanée	Burgundy, France	Red	Pinot Noir
Vougeot	Burgundy, France	Red	Pinot Noir
Vouvray	Loire Valley, France	Dry or sweet white	Gros Pinot (Chenin Blanc)

MAJOR INFLUENCES ON THE TASTE OF WINE

We have already seen that there are a number of influences on the taste of a particular wine and have talked about the taste of wine in the context of its grape variety. In the descriptions of the grape varieties, I have referred to climate, soil, yields, and winemaking techniques. These all have direct influences on the grape's taste. Let's find out exactly how.

How Does Soil Type Affect a Wine's Taste?

Soil is defined by its richness in fertilizing elements (which affects the plant's vigor); its structure (whether it is compact, rocky, or muddy); its mineral composition (granite, chalk, or limestone); its color (red soils warm up faster in springtime than lighter-colored soils); and its topographic situation (on a hill, in a valley, or on a plain).

Soil—in combination with its exposure to the sun and other climatic elements—creates *terroir,* essentially the French word for dirt! *Terroir* is not a place but a happening, a combination of circumstances. *Terroir* defies description and cannot be reproduced or fabricated. Either it happens or it doesn't, and either a place has it or it doesn't. And a *terroir* can be wasted if the right grape variety is not married to it. Furthermore, designating a particular parcel of soil as an appellation does not automatically bestow upon it the title of *terroir.* Clearly *terroir* affects the taste of the wine to a considerable degree; it is, in fact, probably the major difference between a good wine and a great one.

Different grape varieties prefer certain soil types to others, and there is a good reason why some grapes match some soils better. Vines need soils that will store moisture reserves for droughts, drain excess water during heavy rains, and force the vine to grow deep roots to search for its nourishment, thereby developing character and strength. Vines on hillsides are going to need different soils from vines planted in valleys, which are vulnerable to stagnation and poor-draining pockets, thereby producing diluted, diseased fruit. As James Wilson, author of the book *Terroir,* so eloquently explains: "Vine roots are predatory in their search for lenses of fine-grained material and pounce on them ravenously. Roots are almost human in their perseverance to penetrate the barren layers and hardpan, passing through them without branching, in search of nourishing lenses." The characteristics of the vine must therefore complement the characteristics of the soil on which it is cultivated, and the balance among the variables is a delicate one.

For example, Syrah wines from the Rhône Valley's top *terroir* Les Bessards (which has an entirely granite soil) in the same year, in the same vineyard, of the same estate, will have a leather and spicy smell on the nose and the mouth will be very tannic. These wines will age very well. On the other hand, the same grapes from Meal (a *terroir* of stony soils on hills and terraces) have very fruity and delicate aromas, an elegant mouth with nice round tannins.

Take Bordeaux. In an oversimplification, the various proportions of grape varieties used in the blends are based on how suited each of the varieties are to the *terroir* in question. The Right Bank appellations of St-Emilion and Pomerol are a majority of Merlot, then Cabernet Franc, with Cabernet Sauvignon and Malbec in smaller doses because their soils welcome the Merlot more than the Left Bank appellations—say, the soils of Pauillac, which is Cabernet-Sauvignon-dominated plantings.

Another example is the Gamay grape. Philip the Bold was right. In the granite terrain of Beaujolais with its thin, sandy soils, it produces a fine and agreeable wine. Though when planted on the rich limestone soils found just a few miles toward the north on the Côte d'Or, the variety produces a wine that is light, thin, and not very pleasant. Closer to home, we need only taste the differences between a Zinfandel from San Luis Obispo, below Monterey or the Sierra foothills, and one from Amador County to understand. This observation can be made with other varieties and other *terroirs*. The only conclusion is clear: that each variety has a soil that best expresses its originality.

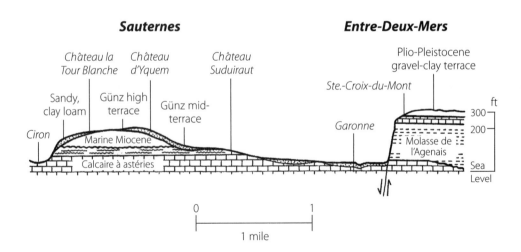

The story of soil: A geological slice of Bordeaux's soil composition. (Adapted from *Terroir* by James E. Wilson, Mitchell-Beazley, 1998.)

How Does Climate Affect a Wine's Taste?

A grape needs to mature on a vine before it is picked. If the weather is too cold, the grapes will not mature and will thus taste "green" and acidic. If it is too hot, they will reach maturity too quickly—but it will be a superficial maturity and not complete. White wines from a hot climate will lack acidity and therefore taste flabby and too sweet, while red wines will have too much alcohol and will have a very forward "first attack" before seeming to evaporate on the tongue and completely disappear before the wine gets down your throat. The correct climate is needed to ensure that the growing period, or the ripening period, is long and slow.

Furthermore, the warmer and sunnier the climate, the less distinction there will be among grape varieties and the less the varietal character will develop. This is because in cool-climate areas, higher levels of odor-active compounds are produced because the lesser amounts of sunshine and the cooler weather permit a longer, slower fruit maturation. We can smell these compounds (aromatic esters and aldehydes) as the familiar primary aromas of a grape variety. This is why climates that are too warm are really not conducive to quality grape-growing. There will also be less variation from year to year, and vintage will therefore be less of an issue.

Believe it or not, with a trained palate you can detect the climatic origin of a wine. You can taste whether it came from a hot climate or a cool climate—they taste quite different. You have probably tasted the difference yourself before but may or may not have realized what was making this difference. To put it simply, wines from a hotter climate will taste almost cooked or boiled, whereas wines from a cooler climate will taste fresher and cooler. Why?

For each grape variety, there is a specific climatic area where it best expresses its quality potential. For example, Riesling is perfectly adapted to the continental climate of Alsace, and the Pinot Noir to the continental climate of Burgundy. The Syrah is used to a temperate climate like that of the Rhône Valley, the Mourvèdre to a southern climate, and the Cabernet Sauvignon to the oceanic climate of the Bordeaux region. This is why there is such a difference between the way grape varieties taste in different countries. Chardonnay in Chablis is crisp and acidic, whereas in the Napa Valley it tastes oaky and tropical.

If a variety meant for a warm climate is grown in a cooler climate, its character is refined. For example, if the Grenache, of Spanish origin, is planted in the Côtes du Rhône, it produces finer, more delicate wines. And the inverse is true. If a variety is planted in a more southerly climate than its original home, then it will make a heavier wine, with heavier aromas and a higher alcohol content. Californians and other New World winemakers sometimes add acidity to a flabby wine grown in a too-warm location rather than take the risk of planting a variety in a place where it may not ripen every year, just as northern European winemakers add sugar sometimes (chaptalisation) in order to reduce acidity in under-ripe grapes in a cold year.

Sunlight permits and encourages the accumulation of sugars, but not sunlight alone. It cannot get the job done unless it is accompanied by the right temperatures—and most important is the sum of temperatures throughout the growing period of the vine. This is what people are referring to when they talk about "growing days" or "heat summation." The general rule is that the warmer it is during the period directly preceding the harvesting of the grapes, the higher the sugar levels will be and the lower the acidity. Inversely, the cooler the temperatures at this time, the lower the grape's sugar content will be, and the richer its acidity levels.

The synthesis of the polyphenols (coloring agents) also occurs in direct relation to the temperature. The warmer it is during the period just before harvesttime, the more color and tannins the red grapes will have when harvested.

The relationship among the sugar, acid, and polyphenols is a crucial one and is additionally influenced by the precipitation the vines receive during the maturation period. The best balance among them is achieved when the vines have a humid vegetative cycle (but not too wet) until the *veraison* (when the grape ripens from green to white or red-black) to permit an optimum growth then, finally, a rather dry period just before harvesting, so the sugars have reached their optimum levels.

To each type of climate, there is a corresponding type of wine, the character of which is defined by the balance of alcohol/acid and tannin.

Grapes grown in a warm and dry climate, such as the Mediterranean, will produce a wine that is rich in sugars and has relatively few acids, but is rich in polyphenols. An oceanic climate has fairly even temperatures with average sunshine, and produces grapes with average sugar and acid levels that are rather rich in polyphenols. A continental climate is one that produces grapes average in sugars, relatively acidic, and lacking a bit in polyphenols.

The majority of the world's vineyards are in areas that enjoy a Mediterranean climate, such as Italy, Greece, Spain, Portugal, North Africa, Asia, South Africa, Australia, California, and Chile. In this type of climate, the white wines won't have very much aroma and will lack acidity. To fix this, winemakers use technological advances such as fermenting at low temperatures and blocking the malolactic fermentation to obtain a fresh and aromatic white wine. This is fine, but one must be conscious of the fact that white wines of great quality should reflect and be typical of not only their vinification method, but also their climate, soil, and grape variety. In other words, yes, we can fix things, but in doing so we've changed them and inevitably altered their quality.

Now, just to throw a wrench in all of what I have just written, things are changing. With climate change, the world's vineyards are transforming. There is an entire international symposium and think tank dedicated to dealing with this issue, which is very real. Even in the span of my career I am noticing the changes. When I am in Bordeaux for the harvests, I can see it. And if I close my eyes, these wines coming out at 15.5 percent alcohol trick me into thinking I am in Napa. I know of winemakers in the Mosel who have uprooted their Riesling and are experimenting with Syrah and Pinot Noir. And we are all aware of the devastation to the Australian wineries, closing at an eerie pace. If you have to irrigate and fertilize and use every winemaking trick in the book to make at best a drinkable wine, then those grapes should not be growing there. I have always thought that Southern California should be growing Portuguese grape varieties . . . now we see it happening. This topic is too broad to treat in this work, but be aware that warmer and shorter growing periods are producing more grapes that are low in acidity and high in sugar—and thus alcohol—and that this erases the varietal character of a grape. The subtle variations and personalities of these grapes are becoming masked by high alcohol and too much oak. I find that more and more, these wines are all tasting the same!

How Does Yield Affect Wine's Taste?

One of the first issues that will greatly affect a wine's quality and taste can be influenced even before the grapes get into the winery. This is the vineyard's yields, or the volume of grapes the vineyard is allowed to grow. Every year, the minimum and maximum yields are fixed in the various appellations of Europe, depending upon weather and crop conditions.

Very much like rosebushes or other plants in our gardens, grapevines need to be treated in such a way that they do not go wild. A plant that is overnourished will actually produce more foliage than fruit. Too many leaves and too much fruit are both bad. For every grape variety, an augmentation of yields will dilute all its characteristics: color, sugar, acids, and tannins. Inversely, small yields will best show off the grape's character. The variation of yields depends upon several things: whether or not a prolific rootstock was chosen, the planting density of the vines, their fertilization and watering program, and the pruning techniques employed.

Planting Density

As we have seen, too many clusters on a branch and too many branches on a vine both allow a plant to produce too much fruit. However, another factor to consider is the number of plants, or vines, allowed to grow in any one area, such as a hectare of vines. The French call this the *pieds de vignes,* or the "feet of vines," planted. Vines that are planted very close together will have to fight for survival. They will have to struggle and compete with each other for the nutrients and water in the soil. Thus their roots will be forced to run deeper into the ground, unlike plants that are planted far apart, the roots of which tend to spread out horizontally and superficially and thus become lazy—everything they need is easily accessible to them. So, like a spoiled child, they will lack character. Stressing vines, whether by planting them closer together on hillsides or by heavy pruning, builds character and therefore allows a higher level of quality.

Why are plants sometimes planted farther apart? For monetary reasons usually. Fewer plants planted means less cost in terms of buying the plants and tending the parcel. When plants are close together, machine harvesters cannot fit between the rows to pick the fruit—it has to be done by hand, which means hand laborers, which is slower and more expensive.

It is also interesting to note that planting density is, or should be, tied to climate. In cooler climates, the density is traditionally about eight to ten thousand plants per hectare, while in warmer climates four to five thousand is more the norm. Any less than this and the quality can be compromised. So to obtain richer grapes, it is best to permit as few clusters as possible on the plant, which is achieved by planting the plants very close together. Before the phylloxera crisis—when the fungal infection spread like wildfire through the vineyards and decimated many wine-producing areas—there were some plantings in Champagne and Burgundy that were as dense as twenty thousand plants per hectare!

Pruning

If a vine were not pruned, it would develop terrifically during the first few years, exhausting its growth and shortening its life. It would bear less fruit, and the quality of the grapes would not be as good. It is necessary to control the growth of a young vine in proportion to its strength and the depth of its root system; therefore, pruning is individual to every vine. Pruning can be performed at two stages during the year: in the December or January after the harvest when the vines are in hibernation, and in July or August, called "green pruning" because the vines are in their vegetative cycle.

The Age of the Plants

Another factor affecting yields is the age of the vines. Older vines that have been well pruned and not squeezed to maximum production will slowly yield fewer, more concentrated grapes as they get older. Vines are just getting interesting when they hit thirty years or more. So it is best if they arrive at that ripe age in a sober fashion. Vines that *pissent*—a very elegant French term for being overworked—are drained and worn out by the time they are twenty.

Even the age at which a winemaker allows a plant to start producing fruit is an important factor in a wine's overall taste and quality. On average, a new plant is pruned very severely and not allowed to produce any fruit until it is three or four years old. At either end of the spectrum, there are extremes. Those winemakers who are very commercially driven will sometimes let two-year-old plants produce fruit, and lots of it, while I know of a young winemaker who runs a family business in Germany who won't let the plants produce one grape until they are seven years old! Which would make the better wine in your opinion?

Determining Yield

So when determining yield, it is not enough to ask how many hectoliters per hectare have been produced. Other questions are equally important. How much pruning was done and how often? Are heavy fertilizers used? Is irrigation allowed? Which rootstock was chosen? How many plants per hectare are there? How old are the plants? When were they first allowed to produce fruit? And so forth. These are all variables in the final equation of quantity and therefore quality.

How Does the Winemaking Technique Affect the Wine's Taste?

Having looked at the magic trilogy of soil, climate, and grape variety, there are those who would say there is a fourth element that is even more important (I wouldn't). Is that person a magician who makes it all possible, whose gentle hand leads the juice on the path of a greater beverage—or are the winemakers the ultimate intruders, manipulators who permanently imprint their personal style and interpretation of the grape onto each bottle? The answer is: all of the above. It depends on the winemaker's politics and methodology. Some winemakers claim that they are simply standing back and letting the fruit express itself, although meanwhile they maximize the extraction of color and flavor when fermenting. Others might say they prefer to allow the soil to speak for itself and opt for winemaking methods that are more hands-off.

These two different philosophies can be illustrated rather well in Burgundy. It is interesting to take a particular domain and try to determine whether its wines from different villages or vineyards reflect their variety and where they are grown, or if the common denominator of each wine is the style in which it has been made. I have tested this. I studied in great detail a particular winemaking family with parcels in four or five of the well-known appellations in Burgundy. Up and down Burgundy, in all the blind tastings, you could actually pick out their wines—the style of the wine was definitely stamped with their technique rather than with the different wine parcels. You could barely tell the difference between the Pommard, the Volnay, and the Mercurey! All their wines were delicious, mind you, and the wine style was very elegant, but it became boring and completely counteracted the beauty and the point of Burgundy.

Another aspect of winemaking, and a rather modern one, is the advent of the flying winemaker. These are freelance winemakers who make wine for any number of clients anywhere in the world. Again, there are bad and good things in this. The original idea was supposed to have had something to do with spreading and communicating badly needed viticultural information to certain wine regions. Frenchmen were flying to Australia and California, Australians to Portugal, all of them to Hungary and Bulgaria. Top flying winemakers have become celebrities in the wine world. They have up to a couple of dozen clients around the world. But at what point do information and knowledge stop being shared and personal style preferences take hold, creating homogeneity?

CHOICES FOR THE WINEMAKER

There are many choices a winemaker has to make—and they will *all* affect the final taste of the wine.

From which rootstock/clone of which grape . . . how many plants to plant in a hectare, at which distances and where . . . on a slope or in a valley . . . to irrigate? To fertilize? How much to prune and when . . . and on it goes . . .

Hand or Machine Harvesting?

Handpicked grapes will arrive at the winery in better condition. Those that are ripest, least bruised, and healthy will be distinguished from those that are unripe, bruised, and rotten. Also, any unwanted debris can be avoided. This means a cleaner wine, less vulnerable later to unwanted flavors. However, handpicking is labor-intensive and therefore very expensive. Most of the traditional vineyards continue this practice, while modern ones plant their vines farther apart on purpose so that harvesting machines can fit between the rows and do the picking. Despite any hand sorting later in the winery, this means more bruised grapes and debris.

To Partially or Fully Separate Stems and Stalks?

Before maceration and fermentation, the winemaker has to decide how much, if any, of the stalks to separate from the grapes. If they are allowed to remain in contact with the must (the unfermented grape juice) and the must is rather delicate or light (due to either the grape variety, the style of wine, or dilution caused by rain), then they can turn the wine sour and astringent. The wine could even taste of sticks and branches. If the must has the strength to take it (an intense red variety in a good year), then leaving some stalks and stems in with the rest of the grape can give it more structure, as these parts of the grape contain tannins, acids, and some minerals.

How Long to Macerate the Wine

The length of time the skins remain in contact with must is only relevant when making red or rosé wines. This is what gives the must its color, flavor, and structure. A long maceration is used for the noble grape varieties such as Cabernet Sauvignon, Pinot Noir, Nebbiolo, and Syrah because they have better-quality skins. Other red grape varieties will need less time in the vat. If they are macerated for too long, the skin extracts will make the wine taste bitter, green, and hard.

How to Start and at What Temperature to Ferment the Must

The first fermentation that grape juice undergoes is the alcoholic fermentation. This is simply allowing the yeasts to convert the juice's sugars to alcohol. The only problem is that sometimes the yeasts do not get going on their own and need a jump start. Ideally, a winemaker can use indigenous yeasts from that vineyard, but if for some reason this is not possible, a winemaker can purchase commercial yeasts and use them to initiate fermentation. Yeasts of this sort can be bought in different flavors, such as apricot, banana, or peach, in order to give an otherwise light raw material more appeal. It also ensures that the fermentation will be successful and reduces, if not eradicates, the risk of using native yeasts. I dread this practice and think that when commercial yeasts are overused, the wine never tastes integrated or cohesive. However, I am not a winemaker, so I will never have to make the decision; sometimes I think I have to keep my opinion to myself.

Assuming things get off naturally, red wines are allowed to ferment at a higher temperature than whites to extract more color and flavor. But beware: If allowed to ferment at too high a temperature, the yeasts will become inactive and the fermentation will come to a halt, or the wine will taste cooked or boiled.

Whether to Allow a Partial or Full Malolactic Fermentation

This is the second fermentation, and is when the malic acids (which taste like green apples) are transformed into lactic acids (which taste like yogurt), making the wine more supple. It is usually only applied to white wines, as they can be more acidic. A winemaker can allow a partial or full malolactic fermentation, and this greatly alters a wine's taste. As a matter of fact, one can usually tell if the wine has undergone such a fermentation or not. Typically, a wine from a cool climate, like Champagne or Alsace, might need a partial or full fermentation to soften some of the acids without losing their crisp, apple-like tastes and smells. In wines made from grapes in a warmer climate, on the other hand, the winemaker might not let it occur or the wine would be too flabby and sweet.

The Length of Barrel Aging and the Sort of Wood Program

After fermentation, the wine is usually put into containers of various sizes for aging. The container chosen is most often an oak barrel. This choice merits an entire book alone. Red wines, depending on their quality and structure, will usually be aged for anywhere between six months and two years. White wines are usually aged for less than six months, or not at all.

Of all the decisions a winemaker has to make about oak—whether to use it during fermentation, aging, or both; to use new oak, used oak, or both; how long to use it; light, medium, or heavy toast—one of the most important (toasting is also crucial) will be the selection of its origins, but not for the reasons that most of us would assume. The question is not Alliers, Nevers, or Limousin (all French oak forests), and the argument should not be French versus American or even Slovenian, Hungarian, or Russian, for there are variations in quality and confusion of hybrids in all these places. The primary factor in the selection of oak quality is tight grain versus wide grain, and only secondarily how much is used; too much of even the best oak is too much.

Even oak trees have their problems of soil, site, and climate, and forests in cooler climates produce trees that have tight grains. This permits a more subtle transfer of vanillin and less extraction of the aggressive oak flavors.

Over-oaking is a big problem in modern winemaking. It started with the late-1970s California trend of showing off your new and expensive, imported French oak barrels. But today there is still the even worse offense of hoping that the oak barrels will provide the tannins, flavor, and complexity that the fruit is lacking. The problem is often not that there is too much oak, but that there is not enough good fruit. When used as the key ingredient, oak can mask many faults and deficiencies. Oak should be the spice of the recipe, not the flour!

Competent winemakers will evaluate the structure of the wine and decide how much oak it can take. They may put only one-third of the wine in new oak, one-third in two-year-old oak, and the last third in stainless steel.

This is what one refers to as a "wood program," and again, it is all about balance and getting the best recipe to fit the raw material. Red wine that has spent too long in new oak will taste dry and harsh, while white wine that has spent too long in new oak often ends up tasting bitter and resiny.

What Effect Does Aging Have on Wine?

It is a known fact that a wine is a living entity that improves with age and changes with its evolution—that is, if it is made from a grape variety that is physiologically intended to improve with age, if this grape variety is grown in the most suitable climate, and if the appropriate winemaking techniques have been applied. If that is the case, there will be a definite difference between what we call the primary aromas of a wine, or its grape variety while young, and the more developed smells that come from oak and bottle aging, what is called the wine's bouquet.

What Is Maturation?

Assuming that everything goes well until bottling, wine will continue to mature. In very simple terms, the maturation of a wine is the function of its composition, its origin (terroir), and its vintage. No two bottles from the same Bordeaux château, of two different years, will develop and mature in the same number of years.

When we say we are letting a wine mature, we are waiting for all its components to fall into balance with one another. A good wine is one that is balanced and harmonious. The acids, alcohols, tannins, and fruits have all blended into one, creating a personality, a character. A less good wine will never fall into place because the components were never there to start with: The fruits will die; the tannins will fade away into nothing instead of softening and holding the wine together; the acids, the backbone and life of the wine, may become flabby or disappear. When tasting a young wine, we look for all of these elements and try to determine how well the wine is made and how it will mature. We can be rather certain of a wine's character, but we never really know whether that character will endure until we test it years later.

During bottle aging, red wines deposit little plaques and grains of coloring agents and other molecules, which bond and fall to the bottom of the bottle. The heavier clusters settle faster than the smaller ones, which need years to settle. As these coloring agents settle in the bottles, the intensity of the wine's color diminishes, becoming more and more reddish brick, and finally yellowish, as the anthocyanins, or coloring agents, in the tannins soften and diminish while the tannins do. When we say that the tannins "soften," we mean that the wine has reached a point of balance in its development curve. The harsh edge is taken off, and the wine's texture is smoother and less drying.

Polymerization progresses continually as the wine ages so that tannic wines for long aging become gradually harder and more tannic before reaching a peak when they are more tannic than they were in the barrel. Then the slope starts a gradual decline. The extra-large molecules lose their ability to combine with other proteins, and their astringency diminishes. At the same time they are combining with other components in the wine, becoming insoluble and precipitating to form the characteristic deposit. At this point the wine is in its mature, mellow phase and is softer, richer, and rounder: This is maturity.

If kept too long, the increasingly large polymers gather strength once more, a sort of final wind, and become dry and astringent once again. This is compounded by the fact that the wine is also losing its fruit and gaining volatile acidity. It is drying out, or dying. Knowing at which moment to open a wine is a skill acquired, happily, through much practice!

Certain wines will reach maturity sooner than others, and not every wine will have the same length of maturity. In general, the duration of a wine's ideal maturation period is the length it needed to reach it. If a 2010 Latour will reach its apogee in 2030, then we can hope to be able to enjoy our bottles for twenty years.

WHAT DOES A MATURE WINE TASTE LIKE?

To best describe how a mature wine tastes, imagine the following analogies:

Young	Mature
Fresh cherries	Black cherry jam
Citrus fruit	Tropical fruit
Fresh red fruit	Cooked warm red fruit
Fresh fig	Dried fig
Green pepper	Black pepper
Honeysuckle	Honey or caramel
Green apples	Apple crumble
Orange juice	Orange liqueur
Peanuts	Grilled almonds
Freshly cut grass	Wet straw or hay
Cinnamon gum	Mulled wine

Does this give you an idea? Proper aging adds depth and complexity to an odor. Plus there are some odors that are not even apparent in a wine until some oak aging or bottle aging has taken place, such as cigar and tobacco smells, and the smell of mushrooms and undergrowth. There is no "young" smell analogy for these.

HOW TO TASTE WINE

There are many techniques developed by wine professionals that help you to maximize the taste experience.

When we taste a wine, we are looking out for many things. We are tasting for balance among the acids, tannins, alcohol, and fruit sugar—acids for the backbone, tannins for preservation and longevity, alcohol for its structure, and fruit for its taste. The better a wine is made, the more balanced it will be and the longer it will last.

Tasting a wine is merely breaking down the different components of taste and analyzing them. Anyone can do it, but it does take concentration and practice. The more you taste, the more "memory" you will have and the more information you will collect with which to create your own standards. As your skill increases, you will be able to blind-taste the difference between a red and white wine, recognize a Cabernet Sauvignon grape or a Pinot Noir, know whether the wine is from France, the United States, or Australia, determine if a wine was made in a hot or cool climate, and be able to tell a young wine from an older one. Further, when I am working as a wine judge, it is important that I taste objectively. My personal opinion has no place in the exercise. I may not get on with Portugal's Vinho Verde wines, but when faced with a flight to judge and score, it is my job to know that wine's correct profile and judge it accordingly: I may not like it, but I have to be able to determine whether it is well made or not.

The process of tasting a wine is basically broken into three categories: sight, smell, and taste. Fill the glass no more than one-third full when tasting and never more than half full when at the table.

Sight

With the glass held vertically, look down on it from directly above. This will allow you to view the wine's surface, clearness and depth of color, and any carbon dioxide (bubbles) that may be present.

With the glass tilted almost in a horizontal position against a white tablecloth, look at the wine (red) at its center as well as its rim. The center, or the "eye" of the wine, will determine its hue and help you to know its age. The lighter, or rubier, red a red wine is, the younger it is. Once it is in the red-brick, orange tones, you know it is older. By looking at its rim, you can also determine its age. The younger the wine, the thinner the watery rim will be; the older the wine, the thicker.

Now look at the wine horizontally with your eyes directly at its "disc" level. This enables you to observe the wine's "robe" or color, which, as described above, will help to determine the wine's age. With white wines, the color will tell you a lot about its weight and taste intensity. A very light, watery color will almost mean a light, watery wine. You will also be looking for deposits. In an older red, this would be normal; even if decanted well there may be bits that escaped. And with whites, deposits used to mean that it was a wine with good extracts and was considered perfectly natural and desirable. However, in today's world, most people prefer wines to be as stable and (in my opinion) as sterile as possible so as to better survive the conditions imposed by international transport and storage. But don't get squeamish if there are bits of pulp or fining material in your Pouilly-Fuissé: Wine is fruit juice, *non*?

Next, tilt the glass so a little wine covers the sides. Examine it again horizontally at eye level, but look for the little tears or legs running down the side of the glass. Are they slow and languorous or thin and rapid? The slower the legs run the more glucose (sugar) is present in the wine, and the more watery the legs are or faster they run, the more alcohol is present in the wine. This will already give you a first idea of how the wine may taste.

Smell

Before swirling, smell the wine. This will permit you to smell any varietal qualities or characteristics.

Then swirl the glass and smell again. Either use one or both nostrils. It sounds odd, but experiment with each nostril; you might be surprised at the differences. You should be looking for major faults and noting the differences from when the wine was still. Here you'll find more intense aromas for young wines and a bouquet for mature wines.

If you think you've detected a fault, or if you can't seem to "wake up" the nose, continue swirling, or cover the glass and shake it violently once or twice.

CAN YOU TASTE WINE FAULTS?

Improper harvesting and production techniques, handling, and storage can all cause wine faults. Here are a few you might discover when tasting wine.

What It Tastes Like	What Happened	When It Happened
Rot and a bitter herbaceousness like crushed green leaves	The grapes were damaged by hail or were rotten, or there were leaves and other foreign objects with the grapes.	During harvest
Herbaceous (in excess)	The grapes were roughly treated and poorly de-stemmed, de-stalked, and crushed, or the grapes were immature at harvest.	Arrival at winery
Bitter; stalks, stems, and branches	The grapes were pressed too violently, which bruised the skin.	Pressing of white grapes
Dry, sour, and astringent tannins	The *cuvaison* (vatting time) was too long.	Fermentation
Thin and light	The *cuvaison* was too short.	Fermentation
Taste of cooked caramel	The temperature was too high.	Fermentation
Lacks color and structure	The temperature was too low.	Fermentation
Earthy, manure-type smells	*Brettanomyces* (*Brett*), a strain of yeast, is liked by some but disliked by many Californians. In small amounts it adds character; in large amounts it is considered offensive.	Fermentation
Flavor of fresh dirt or cement	Dekkera is another wild yeast of the genus *Brett*. Liked by some in France, it can also come from contaminated equipment and barrels.	Fermentation
Taste of the lees	There was no racking or not enough.	Racking
Taste of oxidation (flat and aldehydic)	There was too much racking.	Racking
Tastes oxidized, musty, stale, and dirty	The container was opened and reclosed.	*Elevage* (winemaking process)
Tastes of a moldy *cuve* or tank	The container is dirty or moldy.	Elevage

What It Tastes Like	What Happened	When It Happened
Smell of rotten eggs	Too much hydrogen sulfide from bacterial contamination. Can sometimes be cured by airing.	*Elevage*
Smell of burned matches	Too much sulfur dioxide was used. Can sometimes be cured by airing.	Preparation and cleaning of oak barrels
Taste of sulfur	Too much sulfur is used.	Preparation for bottling and bottling
Heavy deposits	Poor filtering.	Preparation for bottling and bottling
Taste of rotten cork	Bad cork.	Preparation for bottling and bottling
Smells like musty cardboard or a damp basement	The wine is corked. This is caused by trichloranisol (TCA), a compound released by molds that can infest the bark from which corks are made. One theory is that you cannot get TCA without chlorine, which is used to bleach corks, so if corks aren't properly rinsed and dried after bleaching, this problem can occur.	Preparation for bottling and bottling
No fruit flavor left, off-color	Wine is madeirized, or subjected to oxygen or heat through poor storage. It ends up tasting like Madeira or sherry.	Storage
Sharp, tart, green, thin, like an unripe grape	Excessive acidity, excessive fixed or volatile aciditor, a high proportion of tannins, or too much ethyl acetate.	Fermentation
Smell of rotten eggs, garlic, onion, or even skunk	Reduction of a wine results in a smell of mercaptans, which are formed by yeast reacting with sulfur in the lees.	During primary alcoholic fermentation
Vinegar smell	Volatile acidity. This indicates the presence of acetic acid caused by bacteria. Airing can help.	Fermentation

Taste

Some people advise taking a small sip, but I tend to take large mouthfuls as it helps me to feel or "chew" the wine's texture more easily. Or I take a small first sip, go through my analysis, and then take a second, much larger, sip and rinse it through the mouth like mouthwash to either confirm or discount my first impressions. It's up to you to decide what works best. This first taste is meant to judge the *première bouche* or "first attack." Is it soft or firm, smooth or sharp? How soon afterward do you feel the tannins, the acids, the texture?

Swish the wine around in your mouth. Go ahead and make that gurgling, airy noise between your teeth to aerate the wine. Swallow a tiny bit. Concentrate on what is happening on your tongue and on the sides of your mouth. Are you experiencing a puckering, drying sensation? Young, tannic wines will do this. Is it velvety smooth, with softened tannins indicating an older wine, correctly aged? Is it like butter, all creamy and almost thick? This is where the "mouth" is determined. Is it ample or thin? Here also you can fully analyze the wine's flavors, its intensity, and its texture.

Spit the wine, breathe out through the nose and palate, and concentrate on the back of your mouth. Here we analyze the "finale," or finish, of the wine. The better the wine, the longer it will linger in the back of the palate. Here also the balance of the tastes and aromas is important. A wine that has a delicious up-front and fruity attack, and an ample, warm mouth, may often disappoint us once it gets to the finish. An overly alcoholic wine with lots of heavy fruit, spice, and oak flavors up front will fool us until the finish, where it is short or even nonexistent, a certitude that the wine is unbalanced. Even an immature wine will show some signs of the shape of its future; and a complete lack of finish, at any stage, is a bad one.

How Does the Wine's Temperature Affect Its Taste?

If ever you are served a wine, either red, rosé, or white, that is really chilled, be wary. When a wine is super-cold, you can no longer taste it, and therefore any attributes or faults it may have are masked. Often inexpensive rosés or Primeur reds are served like this for that very reason! Drinking wines that are too warm has the opposite effect. Every aspect of the wine is laid bare before us and to its worst advantage. And beware: Contrary to popular belief, room temperature can often be too hot.

Last summer, I ordered a bottle of red Burgundy in a restaurant, and as I had noticed that the wine rack was directly over the hot, vibrating stereo system next to the kitchen door, I asked for an ice bucket. The waitress looked a bit confused, went away, and then came back to the table, smugly announcing that the Burgundy I ordered was indeed "a red wine, madam,

and is served at room temperature." I replied, even more smugly, that room
temperature in that particular room, at that particular moment, was near, or
over, 25°C and that the Burgundy I had ordered was meant to be enjoyed at
16–17°C, so could she please bring an ice bucket? She didn't look convinced,
but grudgingly complied. This happens to me all the time. And I am not
particularly fond of boiled Pinot Noir.

Remember that the word *chambré* in French is the adjective form of the
word *chambre,* or "room." When château walls were feet thick and there was
no central heating, room temperature was between 16° and 18°C at most (if
they were lucky!). Serving a red at 20–25°C often alters the taste of the wine.
When serving a red wine that has not come from the cellar and is warm,
you should not refer to this as chilling the wine because you are not, you
are simply bringing it back to the temperature at which it should be served.
A red wine served too warm is too heavy, alcoholic, and flat tasting. At the
correct temperature it will be lively and more flavorful—too cold and it will
have no taste at all.

SERVING TEMPERATURES	
Sparkling wines	
Simple sparkling (Cava, Crémant, Saumur, non-vintage Champagne)	5–7°C/41–45°F
Sweet sparkling	4–7°C/39–45°F
Finest sparkling and vintage Champagne	6–9°C/43–48°F
White wines	
Simple, sweet whites (Anjou Blanc, Muscat, German QbA)	4–8°C/39–46°F
Simple, crisp, dry whites (Muscadet, Sancerre, Sauvignon Blanc, Pinot Blanc)	6–8°C/43–46°F
Complex dry whites (Burgundy, Graves, Rioja)	9–11°C/48–52°F
Medium sweet whites (German Spätlese, Auslese, New World Riesling)	10–12°C/50–54°F
Finest sweet whites (Classed-growth Sauternes, top German wine, late-harvest wine)	5–9°C/41–48°F
Finest dry whites (Mature white Burgundy, Graves, top New World Chardonnay)	10–12°C/50–54°F

Rosé wines	
Simplest should be most chilled	6–8°C/43–46°F
Red wines	
Early-drinking reds (Loire, simple Beaujolais, Côtes du Rhône, vins de pays)	10–12°C/50–54°F
Simple reds (Young Bordeaux and Burgundies, New World reds)	14–15°C/57–59°F
Complex, mature reds, notably Pinot Noirs (Burgundy, New World Pinot Noir, Italian and Spanish reds)	16–17°C/61–63°F
Mature fine reds, notably Cabernet Sauvignons (Classed-growth Bordeaux, serious New World Cabernet, Côtes du Rhône)	17–18°C/63–64°F
Fortified wines	
Dry (Fino sherry)	9–11°C/48–52°F
Medium (Amontillado sherry, Madeira, white port)	10–12°C/50–54°F
Sweet (Cream sherry, tawny port, vintage port)	15–16°C/59–61°F

Getting It All Together

These are just some of the decisions that affect the final product—the wine you drink—but they give you a pretty good idea of why wines taste as they do. And as all this information on wine has probably made you hungry, let's move on to the tastes of food.

PART TWO

The Taste of Food

The first sign that I was to have a special relationship with food was at birth. My mother delights in recounting the fact that I was the first baby in the history of the hospital to finish my first bottle and ask for more. The affair continued well throughout my childhood and is marked by another memorable anecdote—my personal favorite. At the gustatorily naive age of twelve, our Girl Scout troop embarked on a backpacking adventure near the Grand Canyon. This was to be a foray into the true wild. We were all out-fitted with special backpacks, space blankets, and lightweight cooking gear. To top it off, we made a noble attempt to keep the trip authentically austere by spending a fortune on powdered food of the type used by astronauts. We very halfheartedly planned our daily menus entirely from a selection of aluminum foil packets.

But I would not have it. Carry a thirty-pound pack—yes; piddle in the middle of the woods with no toilet paper—yes; run the risk of meeting a coyote—yes; but eat powdered scrambled eggs—*no!* So as the rest of the troop was outside loading the Suburban, I quickly raided the kitchen, taking four eggs, a pack of bacon, a frozen sirloin steak and a large potato with fresh butter and chives, some Parma ham, and some cantaloupe. Tucking these safely into my pack, I smugly set off with the rest of the girls.

I waited, sadistically, until we had suffered a day and a half of powdered meals. Then early one morning, as everyone was tucking into their cornflakes in powdered milk, I buttered my miniature frying pan and broke open the eggs. I threw on the bacon and sat back, sipping my hot tea, imagining the feast to come. The odor soon wafted over to the others' tent and very soon furry caps emerged. "Eggs, *real* eggs!" The next instant the entire troop was sitting round my fire trying to figure out how to divide four eggs into fifteen portions. I left them to it, as they didn't know what I had up my sleeve for dinner that night! Needless to say, I didn't earn any badges on that trip.

FROM WINE TO FOOD

We are now moving, in a sense, from one food group to another, because most of the principles we established in part 1 can be applied to food. We know a lot more about wine than we think we do, just by being food lovers. In fact, some may argue that learning about wine is probably easier than learning about food as there are an even greater number of variables affecting a food's taste than there are for wine.

The things that are important to a grape's quality—and therefore the quality of the wine—are the same things that we look for when choosing our food. We all prefer fresh food to stale, colorful to pale, tasty to bland, and purity to ambiguity.

The only problem with today's food industry is that we cannot count on any of the homegrown ingredients that were taken for granted by all country dwellers until the 1940s. Unlike wine, we have very little idea of where our food comes from. There are no appellation restrictions for tomatoes or potatoes, for example; we know only that our eggs are free range or that our meat is Texan and organic; and other than the rare markets of local fresh produce, we have to rely on large supermarkets that can ship their goods from anywhere in the world. So where good farming used to be directly responsible for good cooking and good eating, it seems that good shopping is the modern equivalent.

Nature has a reason for everything. Interestingly, the more I learn about food and wine, the more I find myself referring to gardening encyclopedias! I think that is the beauty of the industry. It marries so many disciplines: history, geography, chemistry, climatology, geology, ecology, and agriculture.

FOOD'S NATURAL INFLUENCES

The analogies between food and wine are endless. Food, like wine, needs to be grown in good soil with enough sunlight and rain; it must be produced in small yields and with careful harvesting and preparation techniques. Just as there are different grape varieties, so there are different varieties of tomato, of mushroom, of potato, of apple. Then, just like wine, each variety is further differentiated by its origins. The same things that provide a country or region with its variances in wine (the landscape, vegetation, soil, and climate) lend a food its diversity. And just as there is a grape variety suited to a set of geographic conditions, so is there a geographic set of conditions ideal for a food item: Figs grow at their best in the Mediterranean, apples in the northeastern United States, salmon in Norway, butter in Normandy, beef in Scotland, truffles in the Perigord, goat cheese in the Loire Valley, Parma ham and Parmesan cheese in Tuscany, and so on.

Even in blending, there are similarities between food and wine. Just as a fine Bordeaux is blended from the very best of a winemaker's *cuvées,* so is the fine, sweet, corn cereal, polenta. There are four types of polenta grain and an authentic way to make polenta. The finest producers strive for smaller yields to maintain quality. Then they mix the four grains each year according to their flavor and quality and to the secret recipe or blend of the individual producer. Doesn't that sound familiar?

THE MANIPULATION OF FOOD AND WINE

Cooking methods, like winemaking techniques, can change the original flavors and therefore greatly vary the choice of a suitable wine pairing. We know that winemaking techniques (apart from the other factors of climate, soil, and so on) can change the taste of the grape. Take Chardonnay, for example. If you ferment and age it in oak barrels rather than stainless steel, it will taste oakier. If full malolactic fermentation is allowed, then it will taste more buttery. This means that we can't say that Chardonnay always goes with such-and-such a dish; we need to identify a particular style of Chardonnay, such as a steely, mineral-complex Chablis, or a buttery, oaky, sweet Napa Valley.

The same scenario is true for food. Take the most basic: hamburger. What kind of ground beef are you going to use for the patty? Do you buy organic, lean, fatty, or grain-fed? The origin of the meat will already be a factor in the resulting texture and taste. Then, how are you going to cook it? Are you going to opt for an outdoor barbecue, sauté it in a frying pan, grill it, or roast it in the oven? Four different cooking methods produce four distinctly different tastes.

Now add the condiments. Will you use onions, garlic, Tabasco sauce, olive oil, or ketchup? Will you top it with Cheddar, Swiss, or blue cheese? Perhaps you'll add some bacon and avocado? Finally, are you going to put it on a sesame seed bun, a grilled ciabatta, or a toasted and buttered roll? The final taste results are infinite. And each one of these choices could vary the final choice of wine. If your hamburger was barbecued, you might try a spicy Zinfandel, especially if the coals were mesquite. With a pan-fried hamburger, perhaps a Merlot; with blue cheese, a heavy, oaky Chardonnay.

COOKING AND PREPARATION METHODS

The way in which a food is cooked has an enormous impact on the way it will taste. Just imagine the difference between a hard-boiled egg and a fried one; a raw carrot and a boiled one; or a grilled steak and a beef stew. Two things define all cooking methods: the variations of heat; and the variations of the amount of liquid used. The more liquid is used and the less heat applied, the more the food's texture is softened and the more the flavor is intensified. The less liquid and more heat applied, the more the food's flavor is intensified, while its color and flavor are preserved or increased and its texture becomes crispy. To put it simply, fast, hot, and dry preserves taste, while slow, moderate, and moist intensifies flavors. And when it comes to matching wines, a general guideline is that those foods prepared with a light method of cooking (poaching or steaming, for example) would usually require a fruity, lightly acidic wine rather than a heavy tannic one, even if the poached food has a spicy or heavy sauce to accompany it.

Steaming

A delicate cooking method that helps foods retain all their freshness, flavor, and texture by using no liquid at all, just tenderizing the food in steam. Steamed foods, such as vegetables or Oriental dishes, usually need slightly acidic, fruity white wines.

Poaching

Poaching is a very gentle simmer in liquid (try fresh oysters poached in Champagne with julienne carrots and leeks as a potage). The amount of water, stock, or wine in which the food is poached depends on the food itself. Once the food is cooked, the cooking liquid can be boiled until it has reduced, then used as the basis for a sauce. Poaching is usually used for foods with delicate textures and tastes, because this method tends to preserve both. As with steaming, it will result in a very delicate dish, regardless of flavorings, and would do well with a fruity, light- to medium-bodied wine— probably a white, as you don't see much "poached steak" on menus!

Boiling

Because boiling doesn't add flavor to foods, this method has more to do with texture than taste. It is used for tenderizing tough pieces of meat, which are submerged in water or stock at a high temperature. The flavors of the food also tend to be toned down, especially if the food is salty (think of that Christmas ham). The texture of boiled meat needs a medium to heavy red.

Shallow-Frying/Stir-Frying

This method is most successful if performed quickly and at a very high temperature. There are many variables in this method, including the kind of fat used and the depth of the pan (from a deep pan to a wok). Frying is primarily meant to preserve a food's color and flavor, although it does intensify the taste a little. It will produce a dish with a relatively light texture and simple flavor, compared with the heaviness and flavor complexity of a stew, for example. As the sauce is often created in the frying process, its taste will also influence the choice of wine. Usually, a light, fruity, acidic red or white is best—nothing too oaky, too tannic, or too sweet.

Deep-Frying

Despite what we might think, when we immerse foods in a large, deep pan of boiling fat, it is better to use more fat, not less. According to my *Larousse Gastronomique,* food fried in plenty of hot oil is sealed immediately and therefore does not absorb the fat but becomes crisp, firm, and cooked through. When too little fat is used, on the other hand, this sealing process cannot take place; the fat is absorbed into the food and the pieces stick to one another and become soggy. I learned this while perfecting my *frites* technique in Paris. I also learned a trick from the lady who owns my local bar in Venice: When she is deep-frying her array of mouthwatering *cicheti* (bar snacks), especially her *mozzarella in carrozza,* which she let me watch her make one morning, she adds beer, Prosecco, or sparkling water to her batter . . . light as a feather. If cooked correctly, deep-fried foods are surprisingly light and delicate and are best complemented by light, fruity, acidic wines.

Braising, Casseroling, and Stewing

Generally used for red meats, such as beef and lamb, these methods can also be applied to veal, pork, and venison. The idea is to exchange flavors, so lots of vegetables, spices, and herbs are used. Large cuts of meat can be marinated before braising because, as with boiling, this method softens the food's texture. If done slowly, the flavors of the foods are intensified. The results are complex and heavily textured, which means we can match these dishes with full, oaky whites or tannic, rustic reds.

Grilling

A method requiring very intense heat, grilling works by sealing all the nourishing juices into the meat by the crust formed on the surface. Because it is fast and does not allow time for the meat to tenderize, it is usually reserved for the best cuts of meat. Grilling, like roasting, uses dry heat, but it is faster than roasting. It tends to produce more intense and smoky flavors. Grilled meats need mature, full reds with tannins and heavy, dark fruit.

Roasting

Roasting is the complete opposite of steaming, poaching, and boiling because it uses dry heat to intensify the taste and add a unique flavor. The flavors are concentrated on the outside, browned layers of the meat where juices have evaporated, which gives a slightly caramelized flavor to the crusty surface—like crackling, for example. This is how the English like their meats, hence the proverbial Sunday roast. Smooth, elegant, and mature reds will best match the juicy, flavorful cuts of meat that are reserved for this most noble of methods.

THE WEIGHT OF FOOD

The cooking method employed combines with the food's weight and texture to produce the variables of taste. Faced with a tender fillet of sole, we may decide to preserve its texture and weight by steaming it, or to change its texture and weight by frying it in butter, which will make it heavier and denser. Like wine, we analyze a food's texture, weight, and consistency, as well as its basic taste. We use all of these clues to form an opinion and a match.

What we mean by *weight* is very simply the substance or heaviness of the food or of the dish. Compare a salad to a lamb stew that has been in your Crock-Pot overnight. The salad is the lighter dish in weight, in substance, and also in its concentration of flavors. The lamb stew is the more substantial, heavy dish. You may have put the same spices in both dishes—say, basil and parsley—but that doesn't mean that the two dishes are going to take the same wine, as their respective weights will require different wines.

When matching wines to a dish's taste and weight, it is easier to match light wines to light dishes. You can also use a light wine for a heavier dish to cut through it and freshen it, although the more traditional match is a heavier, rustic wine to complement it. Imagine foie gras with a rich and sweet Sauternes, or Indian food with a spicy Gewürztraminer; these two pairings are matching food and wine of similar weights.

THE TEXTURE OF FOOD

Texture is quite a different thing from weight. Think about how a wine feels in your mouth. Is it dry and slow to go down, or heavy or smooth? Is it "puckery" because of its young tannins? Or light and crisp, due to its acidity? Perhaps it tastes round and smooth as a result of the glycerine? Imagine a light, acidic Sancerre (the Sauvignon Blanc grape) with briny, fresh oysters. Imagine a velvety Pauillac or St-Julien (Cabernet-Sauvignon-dominated) with a tender spring lamb roast. Imagine an unctuous, fat, sweet Sauternes with an equally unctuous fat, sweet foie gras (Sauternes has more acidity than sugar, hence the match). In these pairings, the texture of the food and wine match.

However, you can also use contrasting textures. Take our foie gras again but this time, marry it with a bubbly, crisp Pinot-Noir-based Champagne. Now you have the spicy robustness of this grape contrasting with the sweet smoothness of the foie gras, and the crisp, effervescent texture of the Champagne contrasting with the rich creaminess of the foie gras. A contrasting marriage in this case is just as effective.

Matching the Categories of Taste, Weight, and Texture

Food	Wine
Acidic foods	Acidic wines, fruity and aromatic, off-dry
Fatty/oily foods	Acidic wines with a rich, full flavor; rosés, not tannic reds
Fishy foods	Fruity, aromatic, full-bodied, off-dry whites and rosés
Salty food	Sweet whites; low-tannin reds
Smoked foods	Oaked, rich, and fruity whites; spicy reds
Spicy food	Fruity, young, low-tannin, moderate-alcohol reds; whites with some residual sugar and light acidity
Sweet food	Sweet wines of equal or more sweetness
Vinegary foods	Fruity, light, and dry or slightly sweet whites, of equal acidity

THE IMPORTANCE OF SAUCES: THE NITTY-GRITTY OF THE ISSUE

So far we have looked at the cooking method, the weight, and the texture of the food. All of these before we even get to the variable of the sauce! Imagine you have before you a poached chicken breast—a fairly innocuous beast that needs a bit of livening up. Are you going to smother it with a lemon and cream sauce? A mushroom and Marsala sauce? A tomato and onion sauce? And in that lemon and cream sauce, will you use tarragon or parsley? In the mushroom and Marsala sauce, garlic or cloves? And in the tomato and onion, basil or curry? The equation is becoming more complex, isn't it?

Sauces change not only the flavor of the dish but also its texture and weight. A sauce made with butter, olive oil, cream, or egg yolks will give the dish more body. Sauces with these bases will also be very rich and will need an acidic wine to cut through the heaviness and provide some balance. Again, there is a wide spectrum even here, with an herb butter sauce being very much lighter than a béarnaise or hollandaise sauce. The former needs fruity, crisp, aromatic wines, like a minerally Chablis or a Sancerre, while the latter needs acidity also, but with more substance, like an oaky Chardonnay or an Alsace Pinot Gris.

The whole thing could easily become overwhelming—but the beauty is that you are in control and can do as you like. Despite all the influences that precede it, the sauce will contain the magic clues essential for making a good wine match. Think of the sauce as the liquid seasoning for the food. Sauces usually have a base: cream, tomato, red wine, white wine, vegetable stock, or meat stock. And to these bases, we can add more layers of flavors, or we can stick to the basic ingredients.

Oil-based sauces are actually rather light and in general work well with dry red wines. An olive oil and herb sauce on pasta or roast vegetables will go nicely, not surprisingly, with a medium-weight Italian red such as Barbera. The sesame seed oil you might use in a Chinese stir-fry works with a spicy, sweet white, not only because the oil is light, but because the spices used in the stir-fry are best with a richer, honeyed, fruity wine. Spicy, sweetish whites, such as a Gewürztraminer, will also complement the soy sauce used in Chinese cooking; a wine that had a lot of tannin or is very oaky would become even drier and coarser on the palate with a salty sauce such as soy. Fruity whites and rosés with a touch of sweetness will temper the saltiness and keep the textures balanced. Hazelnut and walnut oils used in salads need oaky, fruity whites like a New World Chardonnay.

Barbecued sauces need a sweet, warm-climate red such as a Zinfandel or Shiraz because the warm fruit is sweetish and the tannins can hold up to such a sauce, where a sweetish white would be crushed. Oak-dominated reds would not do so well, however, so stick to the fruit.

Tomato sauces and vegetable purées used as sauces are usually on the acidic side and so need an acidic yet fruitier counterbalance, such as a Sauvignon Blanc, or a fruity red Italian, or a Merlot if there is meat in the sauce.

You will find specific sauce and wine matches in the sauces listing in part 3.

After establishing the base of the sauce, the next step is usually adding the herb or spice dimensions. Although they are carefully chosen to match the sauce's base, they often end up with a starring role. Try putting curry with coconut milk. The milk will sweeten it a bit, but there will be no mistaking that the curry is the dominant flavor of the sauce, and of the dish.

SPICES, HERBS, AND CONDIMENTS

Who can deny the historical, cultural, and economic impact the spice trade has had on the world? Spices have always been more than a simple seasoning. Spices were associated with wealth, exotic travel, the discovery of new continents, sovereignty, and power. From the East came sailing ships laden with spices, textiles, and perfumes to the great empires of Greece, Rome, Mesopotamia, Arabia, and Egypt.

Long before the Christian era, the Greek merchants thronged the markets of southern India. Epicurean Rome spent a fortune on Indian spices, silks, and brocades. Rome fought the Parthian Wars largely to keep open the trade route to India; there may have been no Crusades and no expeditions to the East without the lure of Indian spices. And Venice's trading heyday ended once the New World was discovered and the Portuguese found a land trail to India, bypassing Venice. Spices were such royal luxuries that men were willing to risk their lives for them. This is hard to believe when spices cost so little today.

And what did they use the spices for? To enhance and vary the taste of their foods, certainly, and also to mask the taste of food that was slightly off and would otherwise be thrown away. Some spices were also used for preserving meat and other food without refrigeration. Cloves, for example, were a popular preservative in the sixteenth century. They contain a chemical called eugenol that inhibits the growth of bacteria and are still used to preserve some modern foods like Virginia ham. (When you run out of mints, try sucking on a clove for a few minutes to freshen your breath quickly and make your mouth feel great.) If spices were not available, then food could not be preserved during the winter months and there would be nothing to eat—simple.

Spices also can be used as anti-oxidants as they possess antibiotic properties. Spices intensify saliva flow and the secretion of amylase, neuraminic acid, and hexosamines. They clean food and bacteria from the mouth and may even help to prevent infection and cavities. They also protect the mucus in the mouth against thermic, mechanical, and chemical irritation. Spices increase the secretion of saliva rich in ptyalin, which facilitates starch digestion in the stomach, making carbohydrate-rich meals more digestible. Spices may also activate the adrenocortical function and fortify resistance and physical capacity. Stroke and blood pressure can be markedly diminished or augmented by means of spices. Indeed, the medicinal uses of herbs and spices would fill another book.

What Are Spices?

Spices shape a people's culinary personality. Both are products of a particular place and its environment. The climate will dictate which spices and plants will thrive in the area. A hot climate will produce some pretty fiery-tasting spices and thus infuse the cuisine and entire culture with a similar personality. Subconsciously we associate countries with their family of spices—it suits them. Mention chili peppers and we immediately imagine ourselves lying on a beach in Mexico with a glass of chilled tequila. And before you can say "allspice" or "cinnamon," I am on that French ski slope sipping my mulled wine and brushing up my après–ski skills. (Let's forget for the moment the fact that these spices, like most others, are indigenous to tropical climates. We are permitted such daydreams because they have been in Europe since the ninth and tenth centuries—long enough to allow a bit of poetic license.)

Technically a spice, or condiment, is an aromatic plant with no permanent woody stem above the ground. Spices and condiments are natural plants, vegetable products, or mixtures of the two, in whole or ground form, which are used for imparting flavor, aroma, and piquancy to foods. Since spices may comprise different plant components or parts, we can assume that herbs are then part of spices and condiments, and we will group them all together here for the sake of clarity . . . and brevity.

There are about seventy known spices grown in different parts of the world. This variety lies in the fact that a spice not only can vary by the plant from which it originates, but also the different parts of the plant—each one having its unique taste. Where with wine we were concerned with the aromas located in and under the skin, then, here we faced with even more infinitesimal choices!

Why such importance given to spices in our discussion? Because they form the basis of our argument. They are the primary ingredients used to flavor food and are often the dominant base of a dish to which we are trying to match a wine. They are indispensable to the culinary art. Spices are to food what grape varieties are to wine. Basic ingredient meets basic ingredient.

The Components of Spices and Herbs

Even in something as apparently invariable as a spice or herb, there are qualitative requirements, and climate, soil, and yields are of great importance. Herbs and spices, like vine plants, do not do very well with too many fertilizers or manures. Like the vine, they just need the appropriate soil, moisture, and light, and each one has a natural habitat or climatic origin. If you really want to get carried away, you could use fresh spices imported from their native lands, but most of us are happy enough to grow them on our windowsills or to stick with the cultivated variety found in jars in the local supermarket.

The Botany of Spices and Herbs

Here are the principal parts of a plant and some well-known examples of spices and herbs produced from them.

Part of Plant	Spices and Herbs
Aril	Mace
Bark	Cinnamon and cassia
Berries	Allspice, black pepper, and juniper
Bulbs	Garlic and onion
Flowers	Cloves and saffron
Fruit	Cardamom and chilies
Leaves	Bay leaves, mint, and marjoram
Kernels	Nutmeg
Rhizomes	Ginger and turmeric
Roots	Angelica, horseradish, and lovage
Seeds	Aniseed, caraway, celery, and coriander

Classifying Spices and Herbs

According to the *Larousse Gastronomique,* all condiments (which are of vegetable origin) are classified by their dominant flavor. This is the classification they apply.

Flavor	Spices and herbs
Salty	Sea salt
Acidic	Vinegar, verjuice, lemon juice, capers, sea-fennel, nasturtiums
Bitter	Garlic, shallots, onions, mustard, horseradish
Bitter aromatic	Paprika, dill, anise, basil, coffee, cinnamon, chervil, coriander, cumin, turmeric, tarragon, fennel, juniper, clove, bay, mace, mint, nutmeg, parsley, saffron, sage, thyme, vanilla
Sweet	Sugar, honey
Fat	Oils, butters, fats

We know that spices and herbs, while very healthy for you, are not considered to have any nutritional value. For example, a dry bay leaf has the following composition: moisture; protein; fat; fiber; carbohydrates; total ash; calcium; phosphorus; sodium; potassium; iron. It also contains the following vitamins (listed in milligrams per 100 grams): 0.10 vitamin B_1 (thiamine); 0.42 vitamin B_2 (riboflavin); 2.0 vitamin B_6 (niacin); 46.6 vitamin C (ascorbic acid); 545 International Units vitamin A. It contains 410 calories per 100 grams.

THE SPICES AND HERBS

If you grow herbs at home and wish to use them for cooking, the best time to cut them is when they are in bloom. Some herbs should be cut at the beginning of their blossoming, others toward the end: thyme in May and June, mint in July, sage at the beginning of June, fennel during the end of August and most of September, and marjoram at the beginning of July. Each herb, like each grape variety, has it optimum harvesting or maturity period. When drying your herbs, tie them loosely in bunches and hang them in a shady and aerated place. To preserve them throughout the year, keep them in a dark, dry container. Or cut them fresh and freeze them.

Allspice

Pimenta officinalis
Allspice or pimenta is made from the dried, unripe berries of the allspice tree and derives its name from the fact that the spice possesses the combined flavor and aroma of cloves, nutmeg, cinnamon, and black pepper.

Uses: Ketchup, soups, sauces, pickles, canned meat, gravies, relishes, pies, puddings, mulled wines, curry powders, mincemeat pies, poultry dressing, spicy breads and cakes.

Basil or Sweet Basil

Ocimum basilicum
Native of northwest India and Persia, basil is an annual of the mint family. The flavor is warm, sweet and somewhat pungent. The odor is aromatic, fragrant, and sweet. According to *Larousse Gastronomique,* basil was considered a royal plant that could only be picked by the sovereign (*basileus*) with a golden sickle.

Uses: Pesto sauce, soups, meat pies, eggplant, zucchini, some cheeses, cooked peas and string beans, used with or instead of oregano in tomato-based dishes.

Bay Leaves

Laurus nobilis
Bay leaves grow from an evergreen, hardy tree or bush cultivated since antiquity in Mediterranean countries. The aroma of the crushed leaves is delicate and fragrant. The taste is aromatic and bitter. It is not to be confused with the leaves of the bay rum tree family from Puerto Rico or with the California bay laurel. The taste is warm, slightly spicy, and sweetish.

Uses: Spanish, Creole, and French soups, sauces, stews, marinades, game, shellfish, tomato sauce, and vinegar.

Capers

Capparis spinosa

Capers are the unripe buds of *Capparis spinosa,* a low-trailing or prostrate, bushy shrub with dense foliage growing in the south of Europe, North Africa, and India. The tiny buds open when the sun rises and close again when it sets. Once cut, they remain closed. The capers are then graded on copper sieves. The smaller the bud, the higher its quality grade. Usually they are cured and prepared in salt. The bitter, vinegary taste is rather pronounced, so very few capers are needed when cooking.

Uses: Fish and meat sauces, garnish for cold roasts and salads, seasoning for pickles and relishes.

Chilies

Capsicum annum

Chilies, also called red peppers, are the dried, ripe fruit of the capsicum plant, and can be used as a vegetable as well as a condiment. Originating in the American tropics, the plant bears single flowers; its fruit is usually pendant and provides all the forms of red pepper, cayenne, paprika, and chilies. The varieties of chili are broadly divided into two groups: the long, pungent type, including the pickling type used as a spice; and the bell-shaped, non-pungent or mild, thick-fleshed type.

Uses: In all types of curried dishes, roasted and ground with other condiments such as coriander, cumin, turmeric, and farinaceous matter to make curry powder. It is also used for seasoning eggs, fish, meat, sauces, chutneys, pickles, frankfurter sausages, and Tabasco sauce.

Chervil

Anthriscus cerefolium

Chervil is an annual herb native to Europe, although it does not do well in very hot weather. It can be used both for seasoning salad and as a garnish. It tastes similar to mild parsley and aniseed.

Uses: For garnishing and seasoning, chopped finely and sprinkled over fish, soups, salads, sauces, egg dishes, French dressing, and as part of the *fines herbes* combination.

Chives

Allium schoenoparasum

The chive is a perennial herb belonging to the onion family and is a native of Europe. Chives are completely immune to cold and can also withstand drought. Although the mildest member of the onion family with a light, delicate onion flavor, they can also be a bit tangy or even hot.

Uses: Potato salads, green salads, omelets, cheese bread, soups, stews, with or in cheeses.

Cinnamon

Cinnamomum zeylanicum

A cousin of cassia, cinnamon is a tree spice that consists of layers of dried pieces of the inner bark of branches and young shoots from the evergreen tree. The quality of cinnamon depends, among other factors, upon the region where it is grown. Cinnamons from Sri Lanka and the Seychelle Islands are considered the best. Every part of the tree—the bark (whole or powdered), wood, leaves, buds, flowers, fruit, and roots—can be used in one way or another. The taste is warm and spicy with a delicate, musky perfume.

Uses: Candies, liqueurs, soaps, dental products, chewing gum, sweets, cakes, and breads.

Clove

Eugenia caryphyllus

The clove is the air-dried, unripe fruit bud obtained from a medium-sized, evergreen, straight-trunked, tropical tree. Clove is the second most popular spice, being next only to black pepper. The term *clove* is derived from the French word *clov* and the English *clout*, both meaning "nail," due to its likeness to a broad-headed nail. It has been mentioned as far back as the first century BC, usually for its antiseptic properties as it contains eugenol. The Chinese imported it to Europe in 1265. Initially the taste reassembles that of allspice, but actually it has an almost fruity aspect.

Uses: Sweet and savory dishes, baked goods, cakes, chocolate puddings, desserts, sweets, syrups, stews, gravies, ketchup, and sauces, especially tomato.

Coriander, Cilantro

Coriandrum sativum

Native of the Mediterranean region, the seed of the umbelliferous coriander plant is one of the richest sources of vitamins C and A. It has a parsley-like aroma with a bold, sage flavor and a tangy, citrus taste.

Uses: With lamb, stuffing, sausages, pasta dishes, in curries, in cheeses, for garnishing, in Mexican salsa, chutneys, salad dressing, Oriental stir-fries, and spicy dishes.

Cumin

Cuminum cynimum

Cumin seeds are long and spindle-shaped, dried yellowish to grayish brown in color, and are either five-sided, smooth, or covered in hairs. Believed to be native of Egypt, Syria, and the eastern Mediterranean region, the aromatic seed-like fruit has a peculiar odor that is strong and heavily pleasant to some, but rather disagreeable to others. Its flavor is warm and spicy but slightly bitter. Cumin is one of the oldest spices known since biblical times, mostly appreciated for its medicinal effects on stomach upset and wind!

Uses: Mixed spices, curry powders for soups, pickles, seasoning breads, cakes, and cheeses.

Dill

Anethum graveolens

Anethum graveolens, rather than Indian dill, is the dill indigenous to Europe and cultivated in England, Germany, Rumania, Turkey, and the United States. Used whole and ground, the ripe, light brown seeds emit an intense, herbal aroma resembling that of caraway or mild aniseed. The delicate fronds are also used.

Uses: Fish, especially salmon, light sauces, butter, carrot soup, breads, deviled eggs, pickles, cucumbers, sauerkraut, dill pickles. Can be used as a substitute for caraway.

Fennel

Foeniculum vulgare

Fennel seed is the dried, ripe seed of this flowering umbelliferous plant, an Italian native cultivated in Mediterranean countries, Romania, and India, as it does best in mild climates. It has a sweet aroma resembling aniseed. Fennel seeds are classified for trade purposes according to their place of origin, those from Lucknow in India being considered the best. The thickened leaf stalks are blanched and used as vegetable. The leaves, which are reported to have diuretic properties, are also used for flavoring, and the roots are regarded as purgative.

Uses: Leaves are used in fish sauce and for garnishing. The dried seeds are used as seasoning in soups, meat dishes, sauces (coquilles St-Jacques), liquors, bread rolls.

Garlic

Allium sativum

A member of the onion family, garlic has a stronger flavor than any of the other members of its family. It grows under much the same conditions as the onion except that it prefers a richer soil in a higher elevation. A well-drained, moderately clayey loam is best suited for its cultivation. Garlic has long since been recognized all over the world as a valuable condiment for foods and a popular remedy for various ailments and physiological disorders—such as vampirism! It is used all over the world for seasoning dishes. In America about 50 percent of the output of fresh garlic is dehydrated and sold to food processors for use in mayonnaise products, salad dressings, tomato products, and meat preparations.

Uses: Raw garlic can be used in the manufacturing of garlic powder, garlic salt, garlic vinegar, and flavored croutons. Fresh garlic is used chopped in sauces and salad dressings, in most cooking, and on its own, roasted whole.

Ginger

Zingiber officinale

Ginger is the dried underground stem or rhizome of the plant. Ginger, like cinnamon, clove, and pepper, is one of the most important and oldest spices and grew originally in Bengal and Malabar. It consists of the prepared and sun-dried rhizomes that either have the brownish outer cortical layers intact or have the outer peel or coating partially or completely removed. To improve their appearance, some grades of ginger are bleached by liming. According to available historical records, ginger was certainly known to and highly esteemed by the ancient Greeks and Romans, who obtained this spice from Arabian traders via the Red Sea. It was introduced into Germany and France in the ninth century and to England in the tenth. Since the ginger rhizome can be easily transported in a living state for considerable distances, the plant has been introduced to many tropical and subtropical countries. It is now cultivated everywhere. The crop thrives well in sandy or clayey loam soils. The aroma of ginger is pleasant and spicy and the flavor penetrating and slightly biting, due to antiseptic or pungent compounds it contains.

Uses: Gingerbread, candies, ginger ale, curry powders, certain curried meats, cordials, soft drinks, bitters.

Horseradish

Cochlearia armoracia / Armoracia rusticana

Horseradish is a near relative of turnip, cabbage, and mustard. It is one of the oldest condiments and is a well-known, large-leafed hardy perennial. It is the thick, white, fleshy root of horseradish that is highly prized as an appetizing condiment. A native of the marshy districts of Eastern Europe, it is grown in the United States, where about fifteen million pounds are processed annually for consumption with food. In England it has become an institution as it balances with the richness of the traditional roast beef. The common type has broad, crinkled leaves and produces roots of high quality. The root contains a pungent, acrid, and vesicating volatile oil. The pungency is due to the presence of sinigrin, a sulfur containing glucoside. It is also very rich in vitamin C.

Uses: Cream, sauce, or relish.

Juniper

Juniperous communis
Juniper is an evergreen shrub sometimes attaining the height of a small tree. The fleshy berry-like fruits do not ripen until the second year. The plant flowers in March or April and the fruits ripen in August or September of the second year. It is the dried berries that we use. Juniper fruits have a gin-like aroma and a sweet taste with a somewhat bitter aftertaste.

Uses: Seasoning gin (commercial), sauces, stuffings, with venison, hare, guinea fowl, and game.

Mint

Mentha spicata
Mint is a popular, old household remedy for relieving colds and coughs. It belongs to the genus *Mentha,* which consists of about forty species, *spicata, arvensis,* and *piperita* being the three most crucial for producing the world's demand for peppermint oil and menthol. Sunny weather with moderate rainfall is conducive to its luxuriant growth and high menthol content. It has a refreshing, sharp, and cleansing taste.

Uses: Chutneys, meat (lamb), fish, sauces, soups, stews, vinegar, teas, tobacco, and cordials. The fresh leaf tops of all the mints are used in beverages, fruit cups, applesauce, ice cream, jellies, salads, Middle Eastern salads, and rice dishes.

Mustard

Brassica nigra (true mustard), *B. alba* (white mustard), *B. juncea* (brown mustard)
Table mustard seems to always be a mixture of two or more of these three mustard varieties. Mustard seeds can be brown, black, or white. Black and brown seeds are considered more aromatic, while the white or yellow seeds have more flavor. Once the oil is procured from the mustard seed, it is dried into powder, which is mixed with water to create the mustard we serve as a condiment.

Uses: Soups, stews, gravies and sauces with white meats, as a condiment for red meat, in curries, on sandwiches.

Nutmeg

Myristica fragrans

Nutmeg is the dried seed (kernel) of the peach-like ripe fruit of the evergreen tree, *Myristica fragrans*. Nutmeg is used as a condiment and although I promised not to explore the other uses of all of these spices, it is fascinating to know that nutmeg is also a stimulant, carminative, astringent, and aphrodisiac. But we most commonly think of it as a main ingredient in our goulash and mulled wine!

Uses: Potato and cheese dishes, breads, cakes, cauliflower, milk puddings, and sauces.

Onion

Allium cepa

Onions, we know about. They are well known to every country and culture because they can grow practically anywhere and be used in almost anything in various forms. For these reasons the onion has also always been considered a very inexpensive flavoring and has been used for both cooking and as a seasoning. Mild onions are used for cooking or as a salad, while pungent varieties are used as seasoning. Onions are even used as a vegetable dish in onion rings or salad. Onions can be eaten cooked, raw, in powdered form, caramelized, grilled, or deep-fried.

Uses: Bases of soups and sauces, in salads, seasoning for most meats, fish, poultry, vegetable dishes, and in pickles, dressings, chutneys, and relishes.

Oregano

Origanum vulgare

Origanum, oregano, and wild marjoram are the dried leaves of an aromatic, branched perennial herb. The color of the dried herb is light green. The camphor-like aroma is strong and aromatic. Oregano has a pungent aroma, a hot, peppery flavor, and a warm, fragrant, and hot peppery taste that is slightly bitter. The plant owes its usefulness as a culinary herb to its volatile oil. Botanists and herb growers classify it as the "pizza herb." It is also the essential ingredient of chili sauce and is used in chili con carne and other Mexican dishes.

Uses: Any tomato-based dish, from spaghetti to stewed tomatoes, soups, meat dishes, pork, fish, egg dishes, salads, vegetable soups, zucchini and eggplant dishes, marinade for beef or lamb, and breads.

Parsley

Petroselinum crispum

Parsley—a native of Sardinia and widely and extensively cultivated in the Mediterranean and the United States—is a hardy, aromatic, biennial herb, although it can sometimes last up to four years. The color of the dried herb is green. Its aroma is pleasant, fragrant, spicy, and very fresh. In the US, parsley is always used as a garnish and adorns the side of a plate. Oddly enough, no one dares eat it, probably because it looks limp and lifeless and we are certain that it has made its rounds on several other people's plates that day. But actually it is the best way to cleanse your palate between courses or after a meal. The fresh leaves mask even the heaviest culinary odor. Parsley is a cool-weather crop, growing best in a rich, moist soil, amenable to deep cultivation.

Uses: Eaten fresh, as seasoning for grilled, sautéed meats, tomato-based pastas, soups, stews, salads, tabbouleh, butters for seafood, omelets, relishes, and vinaigrette.

Black, Green, and White Pepper

Piper nigrum

Black pepper is one of the most popular everyday spices. It is the dried, mature, but unripe berries (fruit) of *Piper nigrum,* a branching vine or climbing perennial shrub mostly found in hot and moist parts of southern India. Black, white, and green pepper all come from the same plant, and all can be used either ground or whole. The spikes and fruits are ready for harvest when they are fully mature and start yellowing. At this stage, whole spikes are removed from the tall vines. Either the spikes are kept for a day or so, then the berries are removed by rubbing or scrubbing and dried in the sun; or the spikes are dried in the sun for a few days on mats or on clean concrete floors, then turned over and over. Later, the berries are removed by rubbing, threshing, or trampling. When completely dry, the outer skin of the berries becomes shriveled and dark brown to black. Generally 100 kilograms/220 pounds of fresh berries yields about 26–39 kg/57–86 lbs. of black pepper. Of course, the yield of pepper varies widely in different areas depending upon factors such as elevation, temperature, distribution of rainfall, soil fertility, cultural practices, variety of pepper, and the age of the pepper vine (sound familiar?). In India the yield varies from 110 to 335 kilograms per hectare/100 to 305 pounds per acre.

Uses: Used as a preservative for meats and other perishable foods, and as a seasoning for everything.

Rosemary

Rosemarinus offinalis

Rosemary is an exotic, leafy, evergreen shrub. This is probably why it has a pungent, piney, mint-like taste with a slight ginger undertone. The fresh leaves can be used as a garnish, and when dried and powdered they are used as a seasoning. It is a very hardy herb that does well on kitchen windowsills as well as in gardens.

Uses: Marinade for beef, pork, lamb, hearty soups, tomato and garlic sauces, roast chicken, breads, dressings, and stews.

Saffron

Crocus sativus

Saffron is the most expensive spice in the world. It consists of the dried stigmas of *Crocus sativus,* a bulbous perennial native of Southern Europe and cultivated in Mediterranean countries. True saffron must not be confused with either meadow saffron or safflower, which are occasionally used as adulterants of true saffron. It takes over two hundred thousand dried stigmas from seventy-five thousand handpicked flowers, to make 450 grams/1 pound of real saffron. The color is bright yellow-red, the aroma powerful, somewhat bitter, and exotic. The principal coloring agent of saffron is the glycoside crocin; the bitter substance is the glucoside picrocrocin.

Uses: In Spanish rice specialties, paella, fish soups, and Scandinavian breads. It's also divine in black chocolate.

Sage

Salvia officinalis

Sage is the dried leaf of *Salvia officinalis,* one of the two sage species indigenous to England. It is also a member of the mint family. Native to Southern Europe, it is a hardy sub-shrub that grows almost anywhere. Yugoslavian sage is considered by the trade to be the best quality. It has a very distinctive, sophisticated odor, with notes of lemon that, although warm, can be a little bitter.

Uses: In pork sausage, meat loaf, seasoning in meat dishes and in making poultry stuffing, game dishes, liver, sauces, cheese soufflés, vegetables, breads, and teas.

Tarragon

Artemisia dracunculus

Called tarragon, French tarragon, or estragon, the dried leaves and flowering tops of this plant are well known for their intriguing flavor. The aroma is warm, aromatic, and reminiscent of anise, with a little tang, and it goes very well with cream- and cheese-based sauces.

Uses: Cream soups, béarnaise sauce, egg and cream dishes, mayonnaise, mustard, salad dressings, roasts, ragouts, butters, shellfish, certain cheeses and vegetables, and olives.

Thyme

Thymus vulgaris

Parsley, sage, rosemary, and thyme—a magical combination and a very popular culinary blend. Thyme has a sweet, pleasantly pungent aroma with a faint clove aftertaste. Originally grown in Europe, Australia, and northern Asia, it is now cultivated in France, Germany, Spain, Italy, and other parts of Europe as well as in England, North Africa, Canada, and the United States. The dried leaves and flowering tops are used.

Uses: Dressings, sausages, cream cheese, tomato soups, juice, clam chowder, soups, stocks, vegetable dishes, beans, and lentils.

Turmeric

Curcuma domestica

Turmeric is the dried, boiled, cleaned, and polished rhizome used as whole pieces or ground. A spice greatly appreciated in the Asiatic countries, it is used not only for its important role in curry dishes, but also as a textile dye and in medicines and cosmetics. It is even considered sacred by Hindus.

Uses: Meat and fish preparations, in curry powder, cheese, as a coloring for cakes, jellies, and fruit drinks.

Vanilla

Vanilla fragrans

Vanilla pods are the cured seedpods of the vanilla vine, a member of the orchid family. Vanilla originated on the Atlantic coast from Mexico to Brazil, and cultivation spread to other countries after the discovery of America. The important vanilla-producing countries are Madagascar, Mexico, Tahiti, Reunion, and Indonesia. The world production of cured vanilla is about 1,230 tons. The most important quality attributes of cured vanilla beans for grading purposes are: length of beans, aroma, color, flexibility, luster, and freedom from blemishes, mildew, and insect infestation, not to mention the fact that the very finest-quality beans show much less vanillin content. The cost of natural vanilla extract is about twenty times that of the synthetic vanilla seasoning.

Uses: Seasoning for many sweetened foods, in the manufacture of chocolates, food products, liquor, ice creams, soft drinks, sweets, tobacco, baked goods, cakes, and cookies.

HERBS, SPICES, AND WINES

You may be wondering as you read this book: *Who sits down to a plate of coriander? Or a bowl of asparagus?* According to my guidelines so far, we would need a different wine for each foodstuff and each spice on the plate—which would bring a typical Sunday lunch up to a grand total of about fifteen different wines. . . . But the point is that although we may not be eating a dish of bay leaves, we understand that when they are the dominant flavor of the dish, they have a specific effect. And as for the asparagus, when in a tart with Parmesan . . . it dominates, and so we need to know what to drink!

Herbs add to the savory dimension of a dish and make the dish a little more interesting for the wine. Many wines even have spicy or herbal notes to them and thus are natural accompaniments. Obviously the amount of the herb used will determine the extent of its flavoring. The way in which it is used is also important. If the herbs are used in a *bouquet garni* and infused in a big pot of stock, then the flavors will gently permeate whatever you are cooking. But if you take the same *bouquet garni* and roast it alongside your meat, then their influence becomes much heavier and you will need a more assertive and up-front wine, less complex and subtle than that you would use for the former dish.

Herbs and spices can also alter the taste and texture of wine, and that's where the matching comes in. Some clash with tannins or oaks, while others—such as chili, mustard, or horseradish—simply blitz the palate and numb the taste buds, let alone what they might do to the wine. Another factor to consider is that a lot of the spices and herbs used in international cuisine are from countries where wine is not produced, so it is no wonder that finding a suitable match might be difficult. Although this book is about food and wine, do not be shy if you prefer beer with your Thai, tequila with your Mexican, or vodka with your Russian.

MATCHING HERBS, SPICES, AND WINES

Spice or Herb	Wine Type	Wine Example
Basil	Fruity, acidic red, or crisp, dry white (no oak)	Chianti, Nebbiolo, Orvieto, Soave
Bay	Young red	Barbera, Chianti
Capers	Dry, acidic, slightly sweet white	Riesling, Sauvignon Blanc

Spice or Herb	Wine Type	Wine Example
Chilies	Fruity, low-tannin, and low-oak reds	Beaujolais, Dolcetto, Merlot
Cinnamon	Spicy, warm, mature red	Merlot, Pomerol, Pinot Noir, Shiraz
Coriander	Fresh, green, crisp white, or warm, rustic red	Sauvignon Blanc, Riesling, Syrah
Cumin seed	Fruity, aromatic white	Sauvignon Blanc, Riesling
Curry	Reds with low alcohol and tannins; spicy, floral, fruity whites are best	Rhône whites (Viognier), Gewürztraminer, Riesling, Verdicchio
Dill	Fresh, green, crisp white	Sauvignon Blanc, Soave
Fennel	Full-bodied, warm white or light, acidic red	Viognier, Barbera, St-Véran
Garlic	Dry, herby white or rosé	Côtes du Rhône, Bandol rosé
Ginger	Sweet, young white with good acids	Barsac, Gewürztraminer, Muscat
Horseradish	Fruity, lightly acidic white or light red	Sancerre, Dolcetto, Beaujolais
Juniper	Spicy, full red	Zinfandel, Mourvèdre
Mint	Minty, herby, richly fruity red	Cabernet Sauvignon
Mustard	Solid, acidic white	Sancerre, Moselle, Riesling
Nutmeg	Spicy, mature red	Burgundy, New World Pinot Noir
Oregano	Spicy, earthy red or acidic white	Sauvignon Blanc, Sangiovese
Parsley	Spicy, earthy red or acidic white	Sauvignon Blanc
Pepper	Tannic, rustic red	Cabernet Sauvignon, Côtes du Rhône
Rosemary	Robust, rustic red	Syrah, Bandol, Fitou, Barolo
Saffron	Full or sweet white or fruity red	Merlot, Barsac, Vouvray, Chardonnay
Sage	Fruity, oaky, slightly sweetish, light red	New World Merlot, Alentejo
Tarragon	Smooth, slightly sweet, oaky white	Chardonnay, Chenin Blanc
Thyme	Spicy, earthy red, or acidic white	Sauvignon Blanc
Vanilla	Sweet, spicy white	Pacherenc du Vic-Bilh, Tokaji

A BRIEF HISTORY OF AMERICAN COOKING

Not surprisingly, the roots of American cuisine originate from our indigenous populations: the Native Americans. Again, climate dictated diet—tribes of the eastern and central areas hunted bison, wild turkeys, and fish, accompanied by wild plants, berries, corn, and beans, and using honey and maple syrup for sweetening. Those in the West and Southwest relied on more exotic fare; the Pimas favored beans and potatoes in their diet and are famous for their popovers and tortillas; the Papagos were a spicier lot, preferring seasoned beans and fresh green chilies, whole wheat kernels, and cheeses; the ferocious Apaches had a protein habit of deer, cattle, and fish, the less energetic Navajos relied upon the staples of mutton, fried bread, fried potatoes, and piñon nuts, and the Hopi Indians used ground cornmeal not only as a diet mainstay, but also in their religious and cultural services. Let's not forget that most resourceful Indians knew how to create a tasty stew from coyotes, rabbits, snakes, and other beasties. The western cactus was used from everything from jelly and juice to a skin pomade.

The first settlers, being European of course, grew their own vegetables and fruits from seeds (not to mention the vine cuttings) brought with them. But with the help of the natives, they also learned to adapt traditional recipes to the local food resources. For example, before wheat was widely grown, corn became the staple grain and cornmeal replaced wheat flour. From the seventeenth century on, a steady stream of English, French, Germans, Dutch, Scandinavians, Irish, Chinese, Poles, Russians, Italians, Puerto Ricans, and Mexicans flooded into America, helping to create a plethora of ethnic influences spanning the country. Ask anyone who is not American what food they think of when they think of America and they immediately will spew the culinary caricatures of pizza, hot dogs, and hamburgers. Even worse, they may insist that there *is* no "American" cuisine and that it is simply a hodgepodge mixture of all the different ethnic groups. This is true: Pizza is Italian, hot dogs are German. Still, we must appreciate the strong creative identity that has become "American" food *in spite of,* and yet *because of,* these ethnic influences.

Furthermore, despite today's massive distribution and transportation networks, variations in regional cooking continue, depending upon which cuisine dominates the region in question. For example, English influences have remained strongest in New England and the Northeast, German cooking still prevails in parts of the Midwest and Pennsylvania (the Pennsylvania Dutch were German, not Dutch), and in the Southwest, the cuisine is largely Spanish and Mexican. The Africans, first brought as slaves to the South in the seventeenth century, have left their mark on southern cuisine. Magically mixed with the French and Spanish, their style of cooking produced the spicy Cajun and Creole cuisines for which Louisiana is famous.

Region	States	Principal Foods
The Northeast (New England)	Maine, Rhode Island, Connecticut, Vermont, New Hampshire, Massachusetts	Turkey, pumpkin, sweet corn & beans (succotash), wild berries (cranberries), lobster, beans
Middle Atlantic States	New York, Pennsylvania, New Jersey, Maryland, Delaware, West Virginia	Apples (for applesauce cake or *schnitz un knepp,* a dish of ham, apples, and dumplings brought to Pennsylvania by the German settlers), waffles, pancakes, cookies (from the Dutch, who colonized New Jersey from 1655), spicy beef pastrami and bagels (introduced by Jewish immigrants)
The South	Virginia, North and South Carolina, Kentucky, Georgia, Mississippi, Tennessee, Alabama, Louisiana, Florida	Rice, sorghum, peanuts, soybeans, corn, tobacco, corn bread, southern fried chicken, black-eyed peas and rice, pecan pie, fish, prawns, oysters, crabs, tropical fruit and bacon (in Virginia and the Carolinas), peaches and peanuts (Georgia), freshwater crayfish, yams, eggplant, squash, Creole and Cajun versions of gumbo (seafood or meat soup thickened with okra), jambalaya (like Spanish paella)
The Midwest and Great Lakes	Michigan, Ohio, Indiana, Illinois, Missouri, Iowa, Minnesota, Wisconsin	The English pasty (brought by Cornish miners), beef (Illinois), trout, perch, bass, wild rice (first cultivated by the American Indians of Minnesota), cheese (began by Swiss and German immigrants), beer (brewed by German immigrants), hamburgers and hot dogs (originated in Missouri), game, mushrooms, perch, salmon, sturgeon, and pike (Great Lakes)
The Great Plains	North and South Dakota, Nebraska, Kansas, Arkansas, Oklahoma	Bison, wheat and grain
Rocky Mountain region	Colorado, Wyoming, Montana, Idaho, Nevada, Utah	Beef, lamb, game, wildfowl, and berries (from Spanish fur trappers who settled), meat loaf, spareribs, steaks, fish (poached in wine or stuffed with fresh herbs), beans, peaches and melons, corn, chilies and coriander (Mexican settlers' influence)

Region	States	Principal Foods
The Southwest	Arizona, New Mexico, Texas	Tex-Mex (mixture of Mexican and Texan cookery), sweet corn and beans, chili peppers, corn bread, tortillas and tacos, cumin, pecans and pine nuts, fish and seafood, barbecued foods (from the cowboys who drove the great herds of cattle)
The West Coast	California, Oregon, Washington	Seafood, game, mushrooms, berries, olive groves, vineyards and orchards (Spanish missionaries), peaches, plums, figs, tomatoes, avocados, artichokes, asparagus, salmon, halibut, flounder, herring, rockfish, cod, prawns, crabs, clams, and other shellfish, trout, pike, and perch, apples, pears, berries, and wheat
	Alaska	Salmon, cod, rockfish, tuna, and shellfish (fishing industry established by Gold Rush settlers), game, wildfowl, fruits and vegetables, sourdough bread or waffles, pirozhki (crisp filled pastry cases with crab or salmon, introduced by Russian settlers)
	Hawaii	Fish, coconuts, yams, sweet potatoes, bananas, pigs, chickens (brought by the earliest settlers from the southern Polynesian islands in about the eighth century), pineapple, sugarcane, rice, coffee, exotic fruits (native crops), sweet-and-sour stir-fries (in the mid-nineteenth century, many Chinese worked on the big plantations), pork dishes (Portuguese influence)

THE DIVERSITY OF INTERNATIONAL CUISINES

We know to look to regional wines to match our food in countries like France, Italy, and Germany. The exercise is also viable when extended to the New World—but the rules change a bit, for not only is the wine "new" in these countries, so is the culinary scene, insofar as they are cultural melting pots. Immigration, emigration, foreign travel, and other factors have all made for original and fresh cuisines, and they have produced a whole new genre of cuisine with myriad exotic spices, textures, and flavors called Mediterrasian, Modern British, Fusion, or Pacific Rim. Still, we have no problem figuring out that red Burgundy would suit a *coq au vin;* a Californian red

Zinfandel would beautifully complement a venison steak with juniper and sweet potatoes; and a Chilean Merlot would make a great companion for empanadas.

But what about those countries that either do not produce their own wines or produce too little to be relevant outside the specific regions? (You won't find a bottle of Chinese Rkatsiteli on the shelf at your local A&P!) Sadly, their cuisine is sometimes relegated to the category of takeout, but these cuisines are as multidimensional, complex, and diverse as those with which we are most familiar. China, for example, is a vast country with indigenous cooking styles in its many different regions. It, too, has its Alsace, Burgundy, and Bordeaux, even though the average consumer only knows of the stereotyped, generic favorites. Authentic Chinese dishes are a riot of texture, color, and contrasting flavors, and we can often find a whole range of taste sensations in a single dish.

What follows is a brief overview of the dominant flavors in the dishes of these countries. For specific dishes and their wine matches, see part 3.

In general, Oriental dishes are hot (using chilies and peppers); salty (from the soy and oyster sauces); sweet (with sugar and honey); and bitter (from the use of vinegar). Pick out the dominant flavor in the dish and match that to the dominant characteristics in the wine. You will find, however, that often even spicy or bitter dishes have a sweetish backbone and need wines with low tannins; this is why whites work so well. Also try dry rosés and sparkling wines.

Serving Wine During a Meal

Here are some guidelines on how to serve wines from different regions at the same meal.

- Chilled wines come before room-temperature wines.
- Younger wines are served before older ones.
- Lighter wines come before heavier, coarser ones.
- White wine before red.
- Red wine before sweet white wines (unless the sweet white wine has been served as an aperitif or with a first course like foie gras)

Wines served from the same wine region should be served in order of vintage, the younger before the old, even if the younger is a better growth—although there may of course be a few exceptions to this. The idea is to save the heaviest, most complex wines for last so as not to spoil the palate for lighter wine.

Chinese Food

Chinese food is a lot more than chicken chow mein and crispy noodles. The dominant flavors are ginger, garlic, spring onions, soy sauce, salt, sugar, pepper, chilies, sesame oil, oyster sauce, and coriander. The resulting sauces are sweet and sour, peanut, ginger, and oyster—all of which fall into either the sweet or salty taste groups.

This means that your best matches are going to be sweetish, spicy, or fruity white wines with a bit of residual sugar. If reds are matched, choose low-tannin, unoaked reds (especially with duck dishes), because salty foods make a wine's tannins taste more bitter. Acidic wines are also a bad idea unless you have a fatty duck dish that can take it. And oaked wines are not a good idea unless the dish contains smoked meats. A slightly oaked Chardonnay would, however, work with sesame-seed-based sauces or a peanut sauce. Or try an Alsatian Gewürztraminer with the ginger and peanut sauces, and a slightly sweet Vouvray, New World Chardonnay, or Sémillon with most others. Light, crisp rosés and sparkling wines also are a very good match, as their texture can either cut through any heaviness in a dish, or underline the delicacy of the more fragile ones, such as wontons and other steamed dumplings.

China has about ninety wineries and the recent focus, after decades of sweet white wines made from unpronounceable hybrids, is medium-dry whites for domestic and foreign consumption.

Japanese Food

The overall flavors of Japanese cuisine are bitter and vinegary: Think of wasabi (green horseradish), vinegar, soy sauces, and onions. When serving wine with Japanese food, avoid acidic wines and go for chilled, off-dry, fruity white wines and any sparkling wines with most dishes like sashimi or sushi. For the slightly heavier dishes, such as tempura or yakitori (grilled chicken and chicken livers with spring onions), choose fuller, fruitier styles: Red Chinon, Saumur, or Sancerre would work. Again, good brut Champagne will always save the day. White wine grapes (Koshu) have been grown near Mount Fuji since 1186! But the rest of Japan's annual 7,220,000 cases are a an odd mix of European-styled wines from European varieties that sadly tend to be characterless and diluted due to the heavy rainfall in the region. Worth trying, however, is Suntory's Château Lion, a sweet white of botrytized Sémillon.

Thai Food

Thai food uses more aromatic, spicy flavors, and its playful contrasting tastes make it very difficult to match indeed. Thai food indulges in generous heaps of fresh chilies, lime leaves, lemongrass, citrus juices, coriander, ginger, and basil, just to name a few. The antidote here is crisp, dry whites, not spicy, slightly sweet ones. Try New World Sauvignon Blanc, Marsanne, or Chardonnay for creamy curries, biranis, and even meat satays. A fruity, robust Shiraz will do very nicely with chili and beef dishes. My favorite—as you may have already guessed—is a brut Champagne.

Mexican Food

Another very difficult cuisine to match with wine, Mexican food is chili-dominated—the Aztecs' love of beans, chili, and corn inspired modern Mexican cooking—and everyone will tell you that chili does not affect the wine, only your palate, burning it until you cannot tell water from molasses.

Very hot and spicy foods need equally spicy wines with a touch of residual sugar to counteract the spice. Try chilled, fruity whites and acidic rosés to temper all that heat. Low-tannin reds that are fruity and spicy like New World Merlot or Pinot Noir, or a good Beaujolais Cru, will also work. Apart from the chilies, the Mexican diet seems to contain a lot of corn flour and beef—tamales, chili con carne, chili con queso, carnitas. Mexicans usually accompany their meals with beer, tequila, or chocolate drinks.

The irony of Mexico is that it has been producing wine since the end of the nineteenth century—but because it was considered too hot for wine, 80 percent of the harvest goes directly into brandy and vermouth production. You might be surprised to know that international companies such as Domecq, Freixenet, Hennessy, Martell, Suntory, Seagram, and Cinzano have all heavily invested in Mexico for their brandy trade. Despite this, the wines have become more serious since 1980 and are increasingly being relocated to cooler plateaus or coastal regions.

Indian Food

Think Indian, and you think curry, curry, and more curry. The basic staple of Indian cuisine is the rice and wheat for the doshai, chapatis, and paratha breads. There is also a great variety of vegetables and fruit, as well as coconuts for both their milk and their flesh. And while, yes, curry seems to be a common denominator, let's not forget chili, turmeric, coriander, mustard seeds, ginger, cloves, cinnamon, pepper, cumin, lime, tamarind, cardamom, and fennel.

All these spices, which are usually incorporated in a creamy yogurt- or milk-based sauce, need wines of low alcohol and tannin content that are fruity and sweet—and with definitely no oak. Straightforward Merlots, Zinfandels, and Syrahs can work. Try a full-bodied rosé from Bordeaux with samosas and pakoras, or Gewürztraminer with tandoori. Try full-bodied sparkling wines—rosé Champagne for example. If you can find it, try Indian sparkling wine.

Middle Eastern Food

The exotic perfumes of figs, raisins, cinnamon, nuts, and turmeric are warm and sweet. Soft, fruity reds and whites complement Middle Eastern flavors best, and although our rule of matching sweet food with sweet wine still applies, it needs to be done carefully. The texture and weight of Middle Eastern food can render some sweet wines too heavy; the entire meal loses its nuances and becomes sickeningly sweet. Try Beaujolais and New World Pinot Noir and Château Mûsar, Lebanon's masterpiece of Cabernet Sauvignon/Cinsault. Recently, a friend made delectable pork marinated in pistachios, raisins, rosewater, lavender, and more. We drank a hugely aromatic Amarone with it: perfect.

Mediterrasian, Pacific Rim, Modern British Food, Street Food

These trendy cuisines are rather easier to match with wine than you might think. Certainly there are no safe local or regional wines to refer to, and every single spice and condiment imaginable can be used in a same dish, sometimes in a very confrontational manner. The goal is to surprise, wake up, and startle.

As the UK editor of the Paris wine magazine *Vintage International*, I was able to participate in food and wine experiments as research for our cuisine articles, usually by Elizabeth de Meurville, the French food writer. She would call a chef and explain what she wanted to experiment with: oysters and wines at Cap Vernet, Côtes du Rhônes chez Guy Savoy, or Loires chez Jean Bardet in Tours. It was strenuous, believe it or not, keeping up with her and the magical combinations placed before us, but we were up to the challenge. She has taught me a great deal about food. I had always ignored it, paying homage only to the wine . . . I was missing the whole point.

Here are just a few of the pairings that helped me begin to understand the chemistry and magic:

Coquilles St-Jacques des Côtes d'Armor aux senteurs pérogourdines (layers of scallops, foie gras, and truffles in filo pastry) with Chablis Premier Cru Côte de l'Chetî 1990 (Tirel-Guérin Restaurant, Saint-Meloir des Ondes, St. Malo)

Risotto aux morilles (wild mushroom risotto) with Bandol Rouge Château Pibarnon 1985 (prepared by and enjoyed with Alain Ducasse at the Louis IV, Monte Carlo)

Saumon mi-fumé, poêlé sur barbe de capucin, vinaigrette au jus de betteraves (partially smoked salmon pan-fried on a bed of nasturtium and a beetroot juice vinaigrette) with Château de France Bordeaux Blanc 1993 (Hôtel Ritz, Paris)

Gâteau de pommes de terre au foie gras (potato pancakes with foie gras) with Château Lascombes 1985 and 1992 (Carré des Feuillants, with Alain Dutournier)

Blanquette de sole coquilles St-Jacques au jus de cerfeuil, concombre, et gingembre (blanquette of sole and scallops with a chervil, cucumber, and ginger sauce) with Champagne Gosset Celebris (Hotel de Brissac, Paris)

Wine and Food Pairing Rules

Here are a few simple rules to help you make the perfect matches with your food and wine.

- Rule number one: When in doubt, drink Champagne!
- Follow nature as your guide. Learn and rely upon regional associations: Sancerre and Crottin de Chavignol, for example.
- Follow the dominant flavor of the dish as your guide: The tapenade sauce on a white fish for example, will allow a light red wine rather than a white.
- Always opt for a dry white or sweet white with your cheese: Red wine with cheese is a myth!
- Match food and wine flavors: Herbal Sauvignon Blancs match vegetables; peppery Cabernet Sauvignons match steak in pepper sauce; buttery, oaky Chardonnays match fish and pasta in creamy sauces.
- Match food and wine textures: The sweet, unctuousness of Sauternes matches foie gras; crisp, lively Sancerre matches oysters.
- Match food and wine weights: again, Sauternes and foie gras match in richness; heavy Barolos match robust game dishes; light, poached fish match light dry wines.
- But . . . try the alternative approach and remember that opposites can also attract: As in sweet and sour sauce, a sweet wine balances an acidic or sour food.
- Strive for balance and respect between wine and food: An older, more complex wine takes center stage and should be served with very simple foods—not heavy sauces that will drown it.
- Always cook with wine that you would also drink, or drink the same wine that was used in the food's preparation.
- Pacific Rim and Mediterrasian cooking goes well with New World varietals.
- Remember that there are wine types that will go with just about everything, just as there are foods that will go with almost any wine, like roast chicken.
- Keep in mind the cooking method of the dish as well as the winemaking technique.

Not much room for a wine in all of that, you might say. But the best complements to all of these outspoken dishes are the equally outspoken and up-front New World varietals. The new style is to take the Old World classic staples and "sunkiss" them to the extreme: We want everything to taste, look, and smell as though it has just been picked under a high-noon sun . . . to zap the taste buds.

I like to think that the popularity of this cuisine, along with the revival of ethnic cuisine, is in response to our modern culture and the fact that our attention spans have seriously lessened. We are, and you've surely heard this before, the generation of instant gratification. After four bites (one = inquiry, two = confirmation, three = satisfaction, four = indulgence), we want to move on to something else. Ethnic foods, with their varied spices and numerous small dishes (think Spanish tapas), fit the bill perfectly. Ask someone to dig their way through a bowl of game casserole and they lose interest halfway through. The idea is to take the basics of a traditional cuisine

and simplify yet magnify the dominant flavors. The Americans have per-
fected the technique with Italian food and call it "Cal-Ital." We seem to have
embraced the entire Mediterranean basin, so the obvious vinous mate will
be the big, obvious, exaggerated, hot-climate varietals: Syrah, Merlot, Sangiovese, Primitivo, Cabernet Sauvignon, Chardonnay or Sauvignon Blanc,
Viognier, and so on.

MATCHING FOOD AND WINE

If I may, I wish to quote Matt Kramer (*Making Sense of Wine*) quoting Rich-
ard Olney (1986 interview in the *Wine Spectator*): "The general mode of
thinking always leans on the cliché and on the abstract. People do not return
to their palates. People are afraid that they do not know how to taste. They
prefer to lean on rules. With rules you don't have to think; you don't have to
taste. You just have to follow the rules—and they'll destroy you every time."
Was he talking only of food and wine?

What an appropriate way in which to begin the section on food and
wine pairing guidelines. Can we really say that there are no rules? I don't
think so. Perhaps what might best be said is that taste is subjective, so that
a combination that a certain individual might put together because he or
she likes it is then, by definition, an acceptable pairing. Because putting
personal, subjective taste aside, there are rules. Nobody sat down and wrote
them up; they are simply objective laws of nature, of chemistry. Acid and
bitter tastes reinforce each other. Sweet tastes change acidic and bitter tastes,
as well as salty tastes. (Sweet wines with salty foods work—whereas tannic
or alcohol reds with salty foods taste bitter.) The bitterness and acidity of a
tannic red wine will make fish or creamy cheese taste metallic. Now, if you
happen to enjoy the taste of a copper penny on your tongue—go to it. Because Mr. Olney is quite right in that you should taste something for yourself
rather than let someone decide for you.

If in a match, both personalities are distinct yet compatible, success has
been achieved, and if in a match, both personalities not only are distinct and
compatible but also draw out the hidden tastes or qualities of the other, then
we have nirvana. In fact, matching food and wine is very much analogous to
finding one's soul mate. Not an easy task, but certainly an enjoyable exercise.

Food as an Enemy

When we say that a particular food item or dish is an enemy to wine, we
mean that it alters detrimentally the taste of a wine. From one of my oldest
copies of the *Larousse Gastronomique* in its original French: *"Nous n'indiquons
de vins ni pour les potages ni pour les oeufs; seuls conviennent de petits vins de carafe.*

Avec les crudités et les salades, il est préférable de boire un verre d'eau fraîche." In other words, soups and eggs only merit carafe wines, and a glass of fresh water is the only solution for raw vegetables and salads.

Not true, not true! Where is their imagination? There is always a solution to these culinary quandaries, and at the risk of repeating myself, there is always Champagne!

What follows are some guidelines to some classic friends and foes of wine. For specific recipe and wine matches, refer to part 3.

Grilled and Poached Seafood or Shellfish

Dry whites are the perfect match in texture, weight, and flavor to poached seafood or shellfish, while dry rosés are perfect for the grilled dishes. Try whites such as Entre-Deux-Mers, Graves, Chablis, Pouilly-Fuissé, Soave for poached fish, and slightly more flavorful whites such a Condrieu (Viognier), New Zealand Sauvignon Blanc, Californian Chardonnay, or Orvieto for those that are grilled. Tasty rosés such as Tavel, Cassis, Bandol, or Lirac are also good, slightly heavier or more full-bodied matches.

Fish in Sauce

For fish in sauces, the same matches as above still apply. But if the sauce has a bit of personality and spice in it, you will need whites that also have a bit more character, such as Meursault, white Hermitage, Riesling, Pinot Grigio, and again, most of the New World Chardonnays and Sauvignon Blancs. If the sauce is a bit sweet, a Vouvray, Coteaux du Layon, or Monbazillac can be spectacular. Fish in a red wine sauce works if the fish is meaty, like monkfish, tuna, or swordfish, and if the red wine is light- or medium-bodied, like a Merlot or an Italian Barbera.

Oysters

If ever there was an unlikely, fraught relationship, this is it. With their high levels of salt and acid, and pronounced flavor of the sea, oysters have a reputation for killing wines. Oysters, like wines, have producers and growths (think of Bordeaux). Furthermore, their taste can vary enormously depending on their size (and therefore age) and, especially, on the *terroir* and the method used to raise them. Oysters can vary quite a bit in texture and taste: They can be salty and wiry, sweet and fleshy, or meat-like and complex. Good oysters, like good wine, are not even commercialized until they are three years old. And unlike other food and wine matches, it is the oyster that might dominate a wine.

The predictable conclusion in this match is to not serve oysters with a very expensive *grand vin* but rather with a well-made and sufficiently powerful wine, such as a Sancerre, Greco di Tuffo, or Orvieto—nothing too floral.

Expensive wines are too refined and subtle to emerge unscathed from such an encounter with the flavor of the ocean. The Sauvignon Blanc stands up to the opponent beautifully. Other perfect matches are Muscadet or Riesling (a crisp, fresh one), or a white Bordeaux, such as a Graves. What shouldn't you drink? White Côtes du Rhône, Sylvaner, and Chardonnays seem to go flat and bitter.

Grilled White Meats

Grilled white meats like chicken breast, turkey, or pork, need smooth reds that are not coarse or rustic. Try a Saumur-Champigny or Chinon (Loire), a Volnay or Beaune (Burgundy), Bardolino, or a Médoc. This is because although a white meat may take a white wine, the cooking method means that the dish can move up to a red, but only if it is soft, smoothly textured, and of low tannin content. Rustic, big, tannic reds would dominate the white meat, even if grilled. And, of course, if you are accompanying the meat with a cream-based sauce, you need to consider whites.

White Meats in White Wine Sauce

Ideally, make your sauce using the same wine you serve with the meal. White wines that lend themselves to creamy, mushroom sauces for meat are Champagne, Meursault, Graves, Sauternes, or Riesling. A trick might be to use a reasonably priced, good-quality Chardonnay for the cooking, but a better Burgundy, like the Meursault, for the drinking.

White Meats in Red Wine Sauce

Fruity, moderately tannic, and moderately alcoholic reds work best with white meats: Chambertin (Pinot Noir), Beaujolais, Chinon, and Bourgueil (Cabernet Francs), St-Emilion (Merlots), and Chianti (Sangiovese) all work well. As you can see, the common denominator is not the grape variety. It has more to do with the fruitiness and slightly acidic background that keeps the texture and flavors light enough for the meat.

Grilled or Roasted Red Meats

Grilled or roasted red meats are not difficult to match. Think Sunday roast and July barbecues; think full, ripe, and mature; think Pomerol, New World Cabernet Sauvignons and Syrahs, Cornas, Hermitage, Châteauneuf-du-Pape, St-Emilion, Barolo, Negroamaro, Nero de Troia, Primitivo, and Zinfandel. Both the red meat and the methods of grilling and roasting can take heavier textures and weights, so bring on the tannins, acids, and ripe fruit. No fresh, young things allowed here!

Stews and Casseroles

Stews and casseroles can handle the same sort of reds as grilled red meat, only there is a slight nuance to respect. Long, slow cooking really seals in the flavor of the meat and whatever flavorings are used, changing the texture of the meat. Stews have more complex flavoring and texture, and therefore your red wine should be a bit more coarse or rustic. Try a Bordeaux Supérieur, Fronsac, or Cahors instead of a St-Emilion or Pomerol; a Santenay or Mercurey instead of a Beaune; a Côtes du Rhône instead of a Hermitage or Châteauneuf-du-Pape. New World reds might be too fruity and one-dimensional for a stew, which would render them thin and weak—stick to inexpensive classics from southwest France.

Salad with Vinegar-Based Dressing

The solution here is to use lemon juice instead of vinegar in the dressing and add protein ingredients such as cheese and nuts to balance the wine. But if you have made the salad and are staring at a plate of vinegar, remember to match a fruity, aromatic, but lightly dry white wine with equal acidity to the dressing. Sauvignon Blanc, either as a New World varietal or in the guise of a Loire Valley wine, will do nicely. So do many Italian whites: Greco di Tuffo, Orvieto, Soave, Trebbiano, Verdicchio, Pinot Grigio, et cetera. When making your own salad, remember to choose the young leaves of the salad, as the older leaves will dominate the wine. The salad leaves you choose will also have an effect. Bitter salad leaves, such as arugula, need more acidic wines than, say, iceberg lettuce. Again, the ingredients, as well as the dressing will have a lot to do with the wine you choose, as you will see in part 3.

Eggs

While we may not wish to drink a glass of wine at 9 AM with our boiled egg and bread soldiers, by 12 PM our eggs Benedict, quiche, soufflés, and egg-based béarnaise or hollandaise are all crying out for some vinous sustenance. This is not such an enemy as you might think. Sparkling wine is perfect for the soft texture of most egg dishes, and it won't overpower their subtle, delicate flavors.

Smoked Foods

When foods are correctly smoked, their personalities are not extinguished (excuse the pun!); the smoke simply adds another texture and flavor dimension. Even the type of wood should be considered, and oak seems to be preferred because it best lends itself to the subtleties of most foods and wines. The two methods, cold smoking or hot smoking, give entirely different tastes.

Cold smoking, or curing, is when the smoke simply coats the food and the food is not allowed to cook. Hot smoking, on the other hand, cooks the food and gives it a smoky flavor by raising the temperature. The thinly sliced smoked salmon that we are all most familiar with should be cold smoked and does very well with an unoaked Chardonnay, such as a steely Chablis. Actually, most smoked food is ideal with very lightly oaked or unoaked wines. Smoked shellfish is still rather unusual. You really have to acquire a taste for it—and wouldn't we rather eat fresh, anyway? That said, if you find that a Scottish smoked oyster has found its way on to your plate, wash it down with a grassy New World Sauvignon Blanc.

Meat and poultry are often marinated before being smoked, so it is a good idea to find out what was used for the marinade. If that is not possible, try a Pinotage, Zinfandel, or Shiraz, as the more subtle flavors of a more complex blend would be completely dominated. Smoked cream cheese is one of my favorites, and although I might put a rich white wine with a cream cheese, I wouldn't when it is smoked. The rich blackcurrant and gentle tannins of mature and classic Bordeaux would be perfect.

But if I took that smoked cream cheese and wrapped some smoked salmon around it, as I am wont to do, then a white wine is needed again.

Mushrooms

What we have to assume here is that we are eating the mushrooms on their own as a separate side dish. If the mushrooms are in a wine sauce, the wine in the sauce would give us our lead. If I knew my mushrooms a bit better, I would have an easier time marrying them to dishes and wines for sauces. There are so many different sorts of mushrooms, and you just know that I am going to mention the words *terroir* and *climate* again. I am, and I am going to add another: *season*. Are we eating morels in the spring, girolles (a highly prized form of the chanterelle mushroom) and meadow agaric in summer, or ceps, field mushrooms (agaric), craterelles, pieds-de-mouton, lactarius, royal agaric (Caesar's mushroom), and other wild treasures in the autumn? Not to mention the various cousins that are at their peak, year-round!

With mushrooms, cooking method can greatly alter taste and texture. There are as many different ways of preparing and serving them as there are varieties: fricasseed, with garlic or shallots, gilded in butter, draped in cream, fried, steamed, chopped, sliced, pureed, in soup, in pastry, in quiches, as a garnish for meat or fish, as part of the sauce for chicken, liver, or kidneys, or in an omelet or scrambled eggs. Then there are the varied textures of plumpness and tenderness, the intensity of one variety or the delicacy of another, the sharpness of some types, the earthiness of very lightly cooked young mushrooms, the fleshy aromas of riper mushrooms. The flavors are infinite and the choice of wine depends very much on the particular dish. Another factor to be considered is the style of the meal. Is it a rustic family dinner or a sophisticated soiree?

Use the cooking method (mushrooms fried in a quick cream sauce versus mushrooms cooked overnight in a stew) as your first guide, then spices as your second. Generally, mushrooms require an elegant wine, despite the dish or preparation method. A robust red wine whose tannins are silky is the best idea. There are a few whites that might work: ones of character, strength, and a certain distinctiveness such as a Jura, an Arbois Vin Jaune, a white Côtes du Rhône, or a mature, full-bodied Meursault or other white Burgundy.

MUSHROOMS AND WINE

Mushroom	Wine Style
Ceps/boletus/porcini	Tannic, dry reds (Bordeaux, Gattinara)
Chanterelles	Light reds (Loire, Barbera)
Chestnut	Dry, acidic whites (Arneis, Chablis, Sauvignon Blanc)
Girolles	Rustic reds (Bergerac)
Matsutake	Spicy, aromatic whites (Viognier, Gewürztraminer)
Morels (morilles)/oyster	Fat, oaked whites (Burgundys or Champagne)
Pleurottes	Acidic reds (Arbois, Mercurey and other Pinot Noirs, Barbera)
Portobello/crimini	Fruity reds (Syrah, Rioja)
Shiitake	Low-tannin reds (Merlot, Beaujolais)
Truffles	Earthy, full-bodied reds (Rhône Valley, Piedmont's Barolo, Barbera, Barbaresco)

Cheese

There are so many different flavored and textured cheeses that it is impossible to make a blanket wine suggestion. Fruity red wines kill the flavorful hard cheeses, while tannic red wines kill the creamier cheeses. The best choice will almost always be a white wine, either dry or sweet. It is very difficult to convince people of this fact! Try dry whites with goat cheese and sweet whites with blue cheese. If I had to offer any rule of thumb, I would suggest matching cheese to its local wines, as cheese is very faithful to its home *terroir* and climate.

CHEESE AND WINE

Cheese	Region of Origin	Wine Matches
Appenzell	Switzerland	Syrah, Zinfandel, Chasselas, Grüner Veltliner
Asiago d'Allevo	Veneto/Trentino, Italy	Chardonnay, Pinot Grigio, Chianti
Banon	Provence, France	Bandol, Provençal rosé, Barbera, Pinot Blanc, Pinot Grigio
Bavarian Blue (Cambozola)	Bavaria, Germany	Dry Riesling, sweet whites, Grüner Veltliner
Beaufort	Haute Savoie, France	Lightly oaked Chardonnay, Meursault, Chasselas, Taurasi
Beenleigh Blue	Devon, England	Port, or sweet white
Bel Paese	Lombardy, Italy	Chardonnay or Barbera
Bleu d'Auvergne	Auvergne, France	Sauternes, Touraine Sauvignon
Bleu de Bresse	Burgundy, France	Light to medium reds, Fleurie, Mâcon
Bleu de Gex Haut Jura	Jura, France	White Burgundy, Arbois, Ponsard
Bonchester	Scotland	Merlot, Right Bank Bordeaux (Merlot-dominant)
Boursault	Normandy, France	White Rioja
Brebis	Pyrénées, France	Cahors, Buzet, Pacherence du Vic-Bihl
Bridamour	Corsica, France	Provence red
Brie	Seine et Marne, France	Chardonnay, German dessert wines, Pomerol, Barbera, Pinot Blanc
Brillat Savarin	Normandy, France	Champagne
Cabrales	Spain	Oloroso sherry, red or white Rioja
Caerphilly	Wales	Sweet whites, Rioja
Camembert	Normandy, France	Normandy cider, Médoc, Côtes du Rhône, Corbières, Bandol, Pinot Blanc
Cantal	Auvergne, France	Rioja, Côtes de Provence rosé, St-Pourçain
Cashel Blue	Ireland	Light fruity red
Cave Cheese	Denmark	White mature Burgundy
Chabichou du Poitou	Loire, France	New World Sauvignon Blanc, spicy Cabernet Franc
Chaource	Champagne, France	Champagne, Cadillac, white Burgundies (Chardonnay)
Cheddar	England	Periquita, Zinfandel, Gewürztraminer VT, Pinot Noir
Chesire	England	Meursault, sweet whites, Greco di Tufo

Cheese	Region of Origin	Wine Matches
Chèvre	France	Sancerre, Riesling, Crémant d'Alsace, Pinot Gris, Trebbiano
Colby/Longhorn	Wisconsin	Zinfandel
Comté	Haute-Savoie, France	Chianti Classico, Arneis, Chasselas, Chardonnay
Cornish Yarg	Cornwall, England	Mature red Bordeaux or Burgundy
Coulommiers	Coulommiers (Seine-et-Marne), France	Côtes du Rhône, unoaked Chardonnay
Crottin de Chavignol	Central France	Sancerre, white Bordeaux, Entre-Deux-Mers (Sauvignon Blanc), Graves
Danish blue	Denmark	Schnapps, Sauternes
Edam	Netherlands	Syrah, Zinfandel, Pauillac
Emmental	Switzerland	Côtes du Rhône, Shiraz, Primitivo
Epoisses	Burgundy, France	Mature red or white Burgundy
Esrom	Denmark	Valpolicella
Etorki	Pays-Basque, France	Irouléguy, Txakoli
Feta	Greece	Ouzo, Chardonnay
Fontina	Northwest Italy	Barbaresco, Barbera, Chianti, Pinot Grigio
Fourme d'Ambert	Central France	Côtes du Rhône, port, l'Etoile
Gaperon	Auvergne, France	Tokaji, vodka
Gjetost	Norway	Madeira, sweet white
Gloucester	England	Zinfandel, Barolo, white Burgundy
Gorgonzola	Northern Italy	Barolo, sweet white, Gigondas, Tocai Friulano
Gouda	Netherlands	Primitivo, Amarone, Chardonnay, Chinon
Grana Padano	Northern Italy	Amarone, Barbera, Vino Nobile di Montepulciano
Gruyère	Switzerland	Bordeaux, Chasselas, Alsace Pinot Gris, Merlot
Gubbeen	Southern Ireland	Oaky, mature white Burgundy
Halloumi	Cyprus	Pinot Noir, Mavro, Gewürztraminer
Havarti	Denmark	Barbera, Chianti
Idiazabal	Northern Spain	White Rioja
Jarlsberg	Norway	Primitivo, Sagrantino
Kefalotiri	Greece	Bordeaux, Mavro
Lanark Blue	Scotland	Sauternes

Cheese	Region of Origin	Wine Matches
Lancashire	England	Burgundy (Pinot Noir), Barbera, Gewürztraminer
Langres	Champagne-Ardennes, France	Mature red Burgundy, Champagne
Leicester	England	Red Provence, rustic reds
Limburg	Germany	Garrafeira red, Tokay Pinot Gris
Livarot	Normandy, France	Ste-Croix-du-Mont, Bonnezeaux
Mahón	Spain	Rioja, sherry, oaked Chardonnays
Manchego	Spain	Amontillado, Malbec
Maroilles	Northern France	Pacherence du Vic-Bihl, Tokaji
Monterey Jack	California	New World Chardonnay, Pinot Blanc
Morbier	Jura, France	Arbois white, Gevrey-Chambertin (red Burgundy)
Mozzarella	Campania, Italy	Chablis, Orvieto, Soave, Pinot Grigio
Muenster	Alsace, France	Gewürztraminer, Loupiac, Coteaux du Layon
Nokkelost (kuminost)	Norway	Pinot Blanc, Gewürztraminer, white Burgundy
Ossau-Iraty	Pays-Basque, France	Irouléguy, Txakoli, Pinot Blanc
Parmigiano-Reggiano	Northern Italy	Barolo, Barbaresco, Taurasi, Amarone
Pecorino	Italy	Primitivo, Chianti, White Burgundy
Pont l'Evèque	Normandy, France	Mature red and white Burgundys, Bourgueil, Pinot Blanc
Port Salut	Brittany, France	Bergerac, red Burgundy
Provolone	Italy	Young Chianti, Bardolino, Dolcetto d'Alba
Raclette	Switzerland	Chasselas, Chablis, Côtes de Duras, Chenin Blanc
Reblochon	Savoie, France	Chardonnay, Crépy, Lirac, Sancerre
Ricotta	Italy	Pinot Grigio, Montepulciano d'Abruzzo
Robiola	Lombardy/Piedmont, Italy	Prosecco, Arneis
Roquefort	Roquefort-sur-Soulzon, France	Sauternes, port, Châteauneuf-du-Pape, Vin de Paille
Selles-sur-Cher	Central France	Sancerre, Romorantin, Reuilly
Shropshire Blue	England	White Bordeaux, Cadillac, other sweet whites

Cheese	Region of Origin	Wine Matches
Ste-Maure	Loire, France	Chinon, Sancerre, Coteaux du Layon, Alsace Pinot Gris
Stilton	England	Port, Sauternes, Ste-Croix-du-Mont, Monbazillac
St-Nectaire	Auvergne, France	Côtes du Rhône, Sancerre, Fronsac, Mâcon, Pinot Gris
Taleggio	Northern Italy	Barbaresco, Soave, Chianti, Greco di Tufo
Tête de Moine	Switzerland	Côtes du Rhône, mature white Burgundy
Tetilla	Spain	Cava, white Rioja
Tilsit	Germany	Gewürztraminer
Tomme de Savoie	France	Beaujolais, Varois
Vacherin Mont d'Or	Savoie, France	Tokay Pinot Gris, Chablis, Corton, Barsac
Wensleydale	England	Montepulciano d'Abruzzo, Chianti

Fresh Fruit

Fruits that are high in acid can make wines taste metallic and thin. In general, drink sweet whites, especially botrytized, late-harvest, or sparkling wines. These are the best solutions for fruit, whether it be in a salad or as part of a dessert. Actually, sweet white wines and proper Champagnes can take a meal from appetizers to dessert: Try it sometime.

Chocolate

Faced with such an aromatic prospect as chocolate, the task of finding a suitable wine seems daunting. A general rule, however, is that a good port or Banyuls with most chocolate desserts, or chocolate alone, does well. With a very dark and strong chocolate, try a Mas Amiel (Maury). To accompany milk chocolate desserts or fruit and chocolate deserts, try a Gewürztraminer *vendanges tardives,* or a Muscat de Beaumes-de-Venise. Dry red wines such as a Bordeaux like St-Julien, or a Rasteau or Côtes du Rhône, can also work, especially with high-quality bitter dark chocolate that has had spices such as rosemary, cumin, or saffron added . . . or sea salt . . . or hazelnut . . . pistachio . . .

Some Classic Food and Wine Combinations

Aged Parmigiano with mature Barolo or Amarone
Bäckeofe with Pinot Gris
Bagna cauda with Barbera d'Alba
Barbecued ribs with Zinfandel
Bollito misto with Barbaresco
Brasato al Barolo with Barolo
Brie with Meursault
Caviar with Champagne
Charcuterie with Beaujolais Crus
Crottin de Chèvre with Sancerre
Farmhouse Cheddar with sweet Jurançon
Foie gras with Sauternes
Gazpacho with Fino sherry
Goulash with Egri Bikavér (Bull's Blood)
Insalata di Mare with Soave Classico
Jambon Persillé with Pouilly-Vinzelles

Moussaka with Mavroudi
Onion tart with Sylvaner d'Alsace
Oysters with Muscadet sur Lie
Panforte with Vin Santo Toscano
Ratatouille with Côtes de Provence rosé
Roast spring lamb with Pauillac
Roquefort with Sauternes
Salted cod balls with chilled white Port
Saltimbocca with Est! Est!! Est!!!
Sauerbraten with Riesling
Sole with white Burgundy
Stilton with vintage port
St-Maure with Vouvray
Stuffed cabbage with Hárslevelü
Stuffed vine leaves with Retsina
Weiner schnitzel with Grüner Veltliner
Zabaione with Moscato

ALSACE: PORTRAIT OF A REGION

Alsace is a perfect French region in which to study food and wine matches, as it makes wine varietals, and not blends. There is also a very strong regional cuisine.

Sylvaner

Fresh, fruity, and light, Sylvaner is ideal to accompany oysters and other shellfish, snails, fish, quiche Lorraine, and delicatessen platters. It is heavenly with a *salade Vosgienne* (mushrooms, red potatoes, Muenster cheese, cumin, smoked lardons, croutons, and poached eggs), with their famous onion and béchamel sauce tart, or with *flammenküeche* (a thin, flat bread dough rectangle filled with lightly fried onions, cream, and smoked bacon).

Riesling

The pride of Alsace, with its delicate fruit and subtle bouquet, Riesling is perfect with fish, shellfish (especially lobster and crab), white meats, and, of course, *choucroute* (a dish of sauerkraut, boiled meats, and potatoes). Its perfect mate, however, is a *kougelhopf* (or savory brioche) of salmon and pike.

Kougelhopf can, in fact, be either savory or sweet, but is always made in the shape of a large brioche.

Gewürztraminer

This noble, full-bodied, and structured nectar is ideal with exotic, spicy dishes and strong cheeses, as well as with desserts such as crème brûlée, or alone as an aperitif. Try it with a *brioche de foie gras* (duck pâté en croûte) instead of the usual Sauternes. It works beautifully with pork tenderloin in a sweet and sour sauce—and, of course, with the local *grumbeerekiechle* (potato pancakes) with salmon and horseradish and their *tarte aux pommes à l'alsacienne* (apple tart with ground almond filling).

Pinot Blanc

Fresh and supple, Pinot Blanc marries well with almost everything, but does better with fish, especially trout or sole with dill seed, and shellfish, especially oysters.

Tokay Pinot Gris

A grape variety that fits in somewhere between the steely crispness of a Riesling and the sweeter opulence of a Gewürztraminer. It complements foie gras and most fowl (turkey, goose, *magret de canard,* sweetbreads in cream and morel mushrooms) and game (venison or wild boar). Also try it with mussels and lobster tails in a saffron and cream sauce. My favorite match is with *baeckaoffa* (a slow-cooked marinated meat stew with onions, potatoes, and seasoning).

Pinot Noir

Not to be confused with the Burgundian style of Pinot Noir, here it is lighter (it is often a rosé) and fruitier. It goes very well with lamb and other red meats, delicatessen platters, and cheeses such as goat cheese (but not fresh) and Cheddar. Try it with gamier poultry with tarragon sauce or turkey stuffed with ceps and ground veal and pork.

Crémant d'Alsace

Like Champagne, this goes with everything, although a heavy game dish might overpower it. Otherwise try it with foie gras or a sweet *kougelhopf.* This is often a better accompaniment than the heavy, classic Sauternes or

Gewürztraminer. Then drink it throughout the rest of the meal with the seafood, cheese, dessert, and, of course, long into the night.

A special treat, Clos de Zahnacker is the deliciously unique concoction of Riesling, Tokay Pinot Gris, and Gewürztraminer (produced by the Caves de Ribeauvillé in Ribeauvillé) with a *presskopf* (a sort of terrine) of fresh wild salmon, lobster, and oysters in a creamy sauce of caviar, parsley, tarragon, and chives.

PROVENCE: PORTRAIT OF A REGION

Garlic, basil, olive oil, ripe plum tomatoes—delicious. Just mention the word Provence and my mouth waters. I think if I had to say that I learned to taste wines while living in Paris, it was living in Nice for a couple of years that taught me how to cook and eat, and seriously shop for fresh, quality ingredients.

There are eight AOC appellations in Provence: Côtes de Provence, Coteaux d'Aix-en-Provence, Coteaux d'Aix-en-Provence les Baux, Palette, Bandol, Cassis, Bellet, and the Coteaux Varois.

The reds and rosés are mostly composed of Mourvèdre (robust and aromatic), Grenache (full-bodied and vital), Cinsault (fresh and fruity), Syrah (rich and spicy), Tibouren (fine and elegant), and Cabernet Sauvignon, apart from Bellet, which is principally of Braquet, Folle Noir, and Cinsault. The whites are herby brews of Bourboulenc, Clairette, Ugni Blanc, Sauvignon Blanc, Marsanne, Rolle, and Sémillon. Their aromas vary from pears and lemons to roses and lavender with hints of exotic spices.

Here are some good pairings . . .
- *Légumes farcies* (meat-filled vegetables) with a rosé from Bandol or Bellet
- *Tapenade* (anchovy, garlic, and olive spread) with a fruity rosé
- *Anchoîade* (puree of anchovies, olive oil, and seasonal vegtables) with a light, fruity Côtes de Provence rosé
- *Pan bagna* (bread coated in olive oil, garlic, and tomatoes) with a red Côtes de Provence or Cassis
- *La tourte de blette* (a savory tart of chard leaves and zucchini) with an herby, substantial white Bandol
- *La bouillabaisse* (a medley of fish and seafood cooked in a sauce of white wine, olive oil, tomatoes, garlic, saffron, parsley, and herbs) with a Côtes de Provence rosé
- *Ravioli Niçoise* (ravioli filled with the juice of daube de boeuf) with a red Bandol

- *La daube de boeuf* (beef braised in red wine and herb sauce) with a red Côtes de Provence or Coteaux d'Aix-en-Provence
- *Ratatouille Niçoise* (onions, zucchini, eggplant, peppers, and tomatoes in olive oil and herbs) with Côtes de Provence rosé or white
- *Salade Niçoise* (tomatoes, cucumber, broad beans, peppers, onion, eggs, anchovies, olives, olive oil, garlic, and basil) with rosés from Bellet, Palette, Cassis, or Bandol
- *Fromage Mont-Vento* (a hard, local cheese) with whites from Côtes de Provence or Palette
- *Le socca* (a chickpea cake) with sweet and fruity rosés
- Crystallized fruits and *fougasse* (a fruitcake-like bread) with Muscat de Beaumes-de-Venise

PIEDMONT: PORTRAIT OF A REGION

Barbaresco, Barolo, Barbera d'Alba, Barbera d'Asti, Boca, Bramaterra, Brachetto d'Acqui—bbbeautiful! Why is it that the names of most of my favorite Italian wines begin with the letter *B* and are from Piedmont? Bordering France and Switzerland, nestled at the foot of the Alps and the Apennines (hence the name Piemonte, or "foot of the mountain"), this region is only seventh among Italy's regions in terms of total production, but it has the most DOC and DOCG quality designation zones and the most vineyards dedicated to classified production.

Almost all of these classified wines are issued from indigenous grape varieties such as Nebbiolo, Barbera, Freisa, Grignolino, and Brachetto: But Nebbiolo is the king. They are elaborate, sensual, complex, stunning, sometimes fresh (Freisa), sometimes slightly acidic (Barbera), but on the whole thoroughly succulent wines. And they are perfect mates for the region's equally ample cuisine: game, buttery sauces, polenta, white truffle, risotto. Where else would you find a fondue dish served with two kinds of pasta, wheat-based and potato-based (gnocchi), in the same meal? My kind of country. For the more timid, Piedmont also has the fruity, gentle Dolcetto grape, and an entire gamut of whites.

- *Brasato al Barolo* (braised beef) with a Barolo, naturally
- *La bagna caoda* (anchovy dip with hot oil for vegetables) with a Freisa or a Barbera
- *Bollito* (boiled meats with spicy hot sauces) with Barolo or Barbaresco
- *Fonduta* (melted Fontina cheese, butter, and eggs over polenta or pasta) with a Dolcetto, Barbera, or Barolo
- *Carbonata* (rich beef stew with polenta) with a Barolo

- *Vitello tonnato* (veal in a tuna and anchovy sauce) with Grignolino d'Asti or Dolcetto or Arneis
- *Uova alla Piemontese con Tartufo Bianco* (eggs with white truffle) with Arneis.
- *Risotto alla Piemontese* with Barolo or Barbaresco
- *Carne Cruda all'Albese* (steak tartare with truffles) with Barbera d'Alba.
- *Lepre in salmi Val d'Aosta* (hare casserole in Barbera) with a mature Barbera
- *Bonét Piemontese* (amaretto biscuit and egg custard pudding) with Asti Spumante

PART THREE

Wines and Foods

The following food-to-wine cross-reference is not meant to be finite and all-encompassing. Indeed, such a feat would be beside the point, as the idea is not to create a gustatory dictate or dictionary, but rather, a guide to pleasurable frolicking for your taste buds.

The foods and wines listed are an odd mix from the very general to the very specific, hoping to capture larger flavor groups as well as more specific and illustrative examples. These matches are a smattering of ideas meant to get your own taste buds activated and to be used to invent your own taste pairings. Do not consider the suggestions to be exhaustive or inflexible— just because Chilean Chardonnay is matched to carrot soup does not mean that this is the only Chardonnay that will do. I have used it as an example either because I personally find a certain *je ne sais quoi* in the combination, or because I am trying to represent equally the geographic distribution of the world's Chardonnay production.

I have included some wines that may be more expensive or more difficult to find, if I felt that they were the very best example I could give, but all the wines listed should be available in the United States. If you do find the wine listed is too expensive or hard to come by, you can buy the New World version for everyday and save the real thing for special occasions.

"Why so much detail on specific wines?" I hear you ask. Well, if when cooking your Sunday roast, you choose your spices, gravy, and vegetables with care, then the natural evolution is to include the wine in the equation in the same way. Consider the wine as something on your plate and not in the glass next to the plate—it is part of the meal, not an adjunct.

There are enough wines listed to be able to extrapolate a taste theme. When the European wines are cited, you can use the Which Grapes Make

Which Wines? table on page 00 to find New World grape variety substitutes. For example, the Rhône Valley's Condrieu is issued from the white grape variety Viognier—so you can eat your ceviche just as pleasurably with a Viognier grown elsewhere—variations on its theme, assumed and permitted.

Old World appellation and vineyard subtleties are slightly bowed to, yet it would be a bit too restrictive to insist that only a Gevrey-Chambertin could do the trick and that a Chambertin just couldn't possibly. There are also occasional references to a wine's classification, such Villages, Premier Cru, or Grand Cru. As we move up to the next quality classification, we are looking for a more serious version bearing greater weight and concentration, which is a result of the more attentive viticultural and viniculture practices (such as lower yields, less oak, and so on, as discussed in part 1).

When discussing varietals such as Chardonnay and Cabernet Sauvignon, the term New World is used to signify that most exported versions of a particular European variety will do very nicely in that particular case. To be honest, I find the nuances among the New World exports becoming less significant as clean winemaking techniques still dominate, despite the recent trends in Europe, finally, for more traditional wines. Just note that most New World versions tend to taste oakier, sweeter, and monolithic, whereas their Old World counterparts are (or should be) more subtle, dry, and complex, becoming more opulent with age. Hence the New World wines match the bold, spicy New World cuisine and the Old World wines are best with their corresponding regional cuisines. Although this is not to say that European wine and food lacks boldness and spice—don't confuse subtle with boring.

Finally, these culinary couplings are a mixture of the "tried and true" as well as those from years of my tasting notes gleaned from the back of lipstick-stained dinner napkins. I know that it is hard to please all of the people all of the time, and I would be quite happy to please somebody just once. In that light, I supplied, if applicable, wines for each food entry that were New World and Old World, sweet and dry, red, white, and rosé. I did not always list and match all of a wine's types. For example, I mention red Dão but not white. However, again, if you refer to the Which Grapes Make Which Wines? index on page 00, you will find a complete listing of wine styles.

The second half of this cross-reference, the wines to foods section, was tricky, as there are many more dishes to a wine than there are wines to a dish—so again, for space and clarity, the wine guide is not exhaustive. The point of the exercise is not to tell you what and how to eat and drink, but to provide a quick and easy guide as well as to present a springboard of ideas for your own adventures.

Bon appétit!

FOOD TO WINE INDEX

FOOD	WINE NAME	REGION/COUNTRY	WINE STYLE
Acras	Champagne	Champagne	Sparkling
	Riesling VT	Alsace	Medium-dry white
	Port	Portugal	Fortified white
	Vouvray	Loire	Medium-dry white
Aioli	Bordeaux rosé	Bordeaux	Dry rosé
	Palette rosé	Provence	Dry rosé
	Soave	Italy	Dry white
Almonds, grilled and salted			
	Chablis Grand Cru	Burgundy	Dry white
	Fino sherry	Spain	Fortified white
	Moscatel de Setúbal	Portugal	Sweet white
Almonds, walnuts, hazelnuts, peanuts			
	Amontillado	Spain	Fortified red
	Madeira	Spain	Fortified red
	Manzanilla	Spain	Fortified white
	Port	Portugal	Fortified white
	Samos	Greece	Sweet white
Anchovies or anchovy paste (anchoiade)			
	Bandol rosé	Provence	Dry rosé
	Fino sherry	Spain	Fortified white
	Greco di Tufo	Campania	Dry white
	Saumur	Loire	Dry white
	Sylvaner	Alsace	Dry white
	Tavel	Rhône	Dry rosé
Andouillette	Arbois	Jura	Dry white
	Grenache	France or New World	Dry red
	Minervois	Languedoc	Dry red
	Palette	Provence	Dry red
Antipasti	Bardolino	Veneto	Dry red
	Dolcetto d'Alba	Piedmont	Dry red
	Falerno del Massico	Campania	Dry red
	Torgiano	Umbria	Dry white
	Verdicchio	Italy	Dry white
Apple (see DESSERTS with a base of Apples)			
	Pineau des Charentes	Cognac	Vin de liqueur
	Vin de Paille	Jura	Vin doux naturel
	Vouvray	Loire	Sweet white

FOOD	WINE NAME	REGION/COUNTRY	WINE STYLE
Apricot (see DESSERTS with a base of Apricot)			
	Blanquette de Limoux	Languedoc	Sparkling
	Côteaux du Layon	Loire	Sweet white
	Muscat de Rivesaltes	Roussillon	Vin doux naturel
	Vin de Paille	Jura	Vin doux naturel
Artichokes	Chardonnay (unoaked)	Burgundy or New World	Dry white
	Rully	Burgundy	Dry white
	Sauvignon Blanc	New Zealand	Dry white
	Viognier	Rhône or New World	Dry white
Asparagus	Bourgueil	Loire	Dry red
	Chinon	Loire	Dry red
	Gewürztraminer	Alsace	Dry white
	Muscat (dry)	Alsace	Dry white
	Sauvignon Blanc	New Zealand	Dry white
	Arneis	Piedmont	Dry white
Asparagus in hollandaise sauce			
	L'Etoile	Jura	Dry white
	Meursault	Burgundy	Dry white
	Muscat	Alsace	Dry white
	Petit Chablis	Burgundy	Dry white
Asparagus in vinaigrette sauce			
	St-Véran	Burgundy	Dry white
	Arneis	Piedmont	Dry white
	Tavel	Rhône	Dry rosé
	Pinot Grigio	Italy	Dry white
Avocado	Chablis	Burgundy	Dry white
	Champagne (brut)	Champagne	Sparkling
	Sauvignon Blanc	New Zealand	Dry white
	Sancerre	Loire/Centre	Dry white
Bacon	Beaujolais	Burgundy	Dry red
	Chardonnay	Burgundy	Dry white
	Pinot Noir	New World	Dry red
	Riesling	Alsace	Dry white
Baklava	Beaumes-de-Venise	Rhône	Vin doux naturel
	Moscatel du Setubal	Portugal	Sweet white
	Samos	Greece	Sweet white
Bagels with salmon and cream cheese			
	Chablis	Burgundy	Dry white
	Champagne	Champagne	Sparkling
	Pinot Noir	Alto Adige	Dry red
Baked beans	Bourgueil	Loire	Dry red
	Cabernet Franc	New World	Dry red
	Merlot	France or New World	Dry red
	Zinfandel	California	Dry red

FOOD	WINE NAME	REGION/COUNTRY	WINE STYLE
Barbecued meats	Cabernet Sauvignon/Cinsault	Lebanon	Dry red
	Gewürztraminer	Alsace	Dry white
	Lirac	Rhône	Dry red
	Mourvèdre	France	Dry red
	Shiraz	Australia	Dry red
	Zinfandel	California	Dry red
Barbecued fish	Bordeaux Sec	Bordeaux	Dry white
	Entre-Deux-Mers	Bordeaux	Dry white
	Sémillon	Australia	Dry white
Bass, grilled	Chardonnay	France or New World	Dry white
	Pouilly-Fuissé	Burgundy	Dry white
	Tocai Friulano Collio	Italy	Dry white
Basque chicken	Châteauneuf-du-Pape	Rhône	Dry red
	Corbières	Languedoc	Dry red
	Fronsac	Bordeaux	Dry red
	Madiran	SW France	Dry red
Bean and pasta soup			
	Bergerac	SW France	Dry red
	Buzet	SW France	Dry red
	Côte-Rôtie	Rhône	Dry red
	Shiraz	Australia	Dry red
Béarnaise sauce	Frascati Superiore	Italy	Medium-dry white
	Riesling Kabinett	Germany	Dry white
	Sancerre	Loire/Centre	Dry white
	Vouvray	Loire	Medium-dry white
Beef bourguignon			
	Barolo	Piedmont	Dry red
	Brouilly	Beaujolais	Dry red
	Clos de Vougeot	Burgundy	Dry red
	Gigondas	Rhône	Dry red
	Kékfrankos	Hungary	Dry red
	Saumur	Loire	Dry red
Beef dishes	Barolo	Piedmont	Dry red
	Cabernet Sauvignon/Cinsault	Lebanon	Dry red
	Corbières	Languedoc	Dry red
	Gigondas	Rhône	Dry red
	Juliénas	Beaujolais	Dry red
	Pomerol	Bordeaux	Dry red
	Taurasi	Campania	Dry red
Beef potpie	Rioja	Spain	Dry red
	St-Emilion	Bordeaux	Dry red
	Zinfandel	California	Dry red

FOOD	WINE NAME	REGION/COUNTRY	WINE STYLE
Beef Stroganoff	Bordeaux rosé	Bordeaux	Dry rosé
	Kékfrankos	Hungary	Dry red
	Mavrud	Bulgaria	Dry red
	Merlot	New World	Dry red
	Meursault	Burgundy	Dry white
	Vacqueyras	Rhône	Dry red
Beef tacos	Riesling	Alsace or New World	Dry white
	Zinfandel	California	Dry red
Beef Wellington	Champagne (brut)	Champagne	Sparkling
	Malbec	Argentina	Dry red
	Merlot	New World	Dry red
	St-Emilion	Bordeaux	Dry red
Blackened fish	Chardonnay	Chile	Dry white
	Entre-Deux-Mers	Bordeaux	Dry white
	Sémillon	Australia	Dry white
Black pudding	Côtes de Provence	Provence	Dry white
	Côtes du Rhône	Rhône	Dry red
	Dolcetto d'Alba	Piedmont	Dry red
	Fronsac	Bordeaux	Dry red
Blanquette de veau			
	Côtes de Provence rosé	Provence	Dry rosé
	Minervois rosé	Languedoc-Roussillon	Dry rosé
	Muscadet	Loire	Dry white
	Riesling	Alsace	Dry white
Blinis	Champagne	Champagne	Sparkling
	Crémant de Bourgogne	Burgundy	Sparkling
Blue cheese dip	Aligoté	Burgundy	Dry white
	Cadillac	Bordeaux	Sweet white
	Champagne	Champagne	Sparkling
Boeuf en daube	Bandol	Provence	Dry red
	Barolo	Piedmont	Dry red
	Gattinara	Piedmont	Dry red
	Hermitage	Rhône	Dry red
	Shiraz	Australia	Dry red
	Vin de Corse	Corsica	Dry red
Borscht	Chianti	Tuscany	Dry red
	Copertino	Puglia	Dry red
	Kékfrankos	Hungary	Dry red
Bouillabaisse	Riesling	Alsace	Dry white
	Tavel	Provence	Dry rosé
	Vin de Corse	Corsica	Dry white

FOOD	WINE NAME	REGION/COUNTRY	WINE STYLE
Bread and butter pudding			
	Côtes de Provence	Provence	Dry white
	Loupiac	Bordeaux	Sweet white
	Monbazillac	SW France	Sweet white
	Pacherenc du Vic-Bilh	SW France	Sweet white
	Sauternes	Bordeaux	Sweet white
Bresaola	Chianti	Tuscany	Dry red
	Sangiovese	California	Dry red
	Valpolicella	Veneto	Dry red
Brie (see Cheese and Wine on page 102)			
Brown sugar (as a principal ingredient or dominant flavor)			
	Gewürztraminer	Alsace	Sweet white
	Riesling Auslese	Germany	Sweet white
	Barsac	Bordeax	Sweet white
	Vosne-Romanée	Burgundy	Dry red
Brownies (see DESSERTS with a base of Chocolate)			
Brunswick stew	Bergerac	SW France	Dry red
	St-Véran/Mâcon	Burgundy	Dry white
	Zinfandel	California	Dry red
Bolognese sauce (see also SAUCES)			
	Cabernet Sauvignon	Australia	Dry red
	Merlot	Chile	Dry red
	Montepulciano d'Abruzzo	Italy	Dry red
	Rosso Cònero	Italy	Dry red
Bruschetta	Chardonnay	Chile	Dry white
	Soave	Veneto	Dry white
	Vernaccia di San Gimignano	Italy	Dry white
Brussels sprouts	Pinot Grigio	Italy	Dry white
	Pinot Blanc	Alsace	Dry white
	Riesling	Alsace	Dry white
Buffalo wings	Buzet	SW France	Dry red
	Côtes du Roussillon	Roussillon	Dry red
	Zinfandel	California	Dry red
Buttermilk pancakes			
	Champagne	Champagne	Sparkling
	Crémant du Loire	Loire	Sparkling
	Sauternes	Bordeaux	Sweet white
Cabbage, stuffed	Bourgueil	Loire	Dry red
	Crozes-Hermitage	Rhône	Dry red
	Shiraz	Australia	Dry red

FOOD	WINE NAME	REGION/COUNTRY	WINE STYLE
Caesar salad (see also SALADS)			
	Champagne	Champagne	Sparkling
	Chardonnay	Chile	Dry white
	Rully	Burgundy	Dry white
Cajun-style meats	Pommard	Burgundy	Dry red
	Syrah	New World	Dry red
	Zinfandel	California	Dry red
Calamari (see Squid)			
Camembert (see Cheese and Wine on page 102)			
Carp, grilled	Pouilly-Fumé	Loire	Dry white
	Sauvignon Blanc	France or New World	Dry white
	Trebbiano	Italy	Dry white
	Ugni Blanc	New World	Dry white
Carpaccio	Champagne (rosé)	Champagne	Sparkling
	Chianti	Tuscany	Dry red
	Reguengos	Portugal	Dry red
	Sangiovese	California	Dry red
Carrot cake	Crémant du Bourgogne	Burgundy	Sparkling
	Meursault	Burgundy	Dry white
	Tokaji	Hungary	Dry white
Carrot soup	Chablis Grand Cru	Burgundy	Dry white
	Chardonnay	California	Dry white
	Viognier	Italy	Dry white
Cassoulet	Barbaresco	Italy	Dry red
	Cahors	SW France	Dry red
	Corbières	Languedoc	Dry red
	Mourvèdre	France or New World	Dry red
	Shiraz	Australia	Dry red
	Zinfandel	California	Dry red
Caviar	Champagne (non-vintage)	Champagne	Sparkling
	Châteauneuf-du-Pape	Rhône	Dry white
	Puligny-Montrachet	Burgundy	Dry white
	Pinot Gris	Alsace	Dry white
Ceviche (raw fish marinated in lemon juice)			
	Condrieu	Rhône	Dry white
	Sauvignon Blanc	Chile	Dry white
	Vinho Verde	Portugal	Dry white
Charcuterie	Bardolino	Italy	Dry red
	Beaujolais	Burgundy	Dry red
	Cabernet Sauvignon	Chile	Dry red
	Chinon	Loire	Dry red
	Côtes du Rhône	Rhône	Dry red
	Rully	Burgundy	Dry red

FOOD	WINE NAME	REGION/COUNTRY	WINE STYLE
Châteaubriand	Barolo	Piedmont, Italy	Dry red
	Echezeaux	Burgundy	Dry red
	Margaux	Bordeaux	Dry red
	Recioto della Valpolicella	Veneto	Dry red
Cheese (see Cheese and Wine on page 102)			
Cheese fondue (match the cheese)			
	Chardonnay	California	Dry white
	Chasselas	Alsace or Switzerland	Dry white
	Côtes du Rhône	Rhône	Dry red
	Mâcon	Burgundy	Dry white
	Patrimonio	Corsica	Dry white
Cheesecake	Cadillac	Bordeaux	Sweet white
	Champagne	Champagne	Sparkling
	Coteaux du Layon	Loire	Sweet white
	Monbazillac	SW France	Sweet white
	Pacherenc du Vic-Bihl	SW France	Sweet white
Chef's salad (with eggs, tomatoes, and cheese)			
	Chardonnay	California	Dry white
	Soave	Veneto	Dry white
	Viognier	California	Dry white
Chicken, plain roast			
	Bergerac	SW France	Dry red
	Bordeaux Supérieur	Bordeaux	Dry red
	Chardonnay (oaked)	New World	Dry white
	Pinot Noir	New World	Dry red
	Torgiano	Umbria	Dry red
Chicken Basque	Chateauneuf-du-Pape	Rhône	Dry red
	Corbières	Languedoc	Dry red
	Fronsac	Bordeaux	Dry red
Chicken chasseur	Bourgueil	Loire	Dry red
	Entre-Deux-Mers	Bordeaux	Dry white
	Médoc	Bordeaux	Dry red
	Savigny-lès-Beaune	Burgundy	Dry red
	Sémillon	California	Dry white
Chicken in cream and morel sauce			
	Chablis Premier Cru	Burgundy	Dry white
	Chardonnay	New World	Dry white
	Corbières	Languedoc	Dry white
	Pinot Noir	Oregon	Dry red
	Riesling	Alsace	Dry white
Chicken, Creole	Gewürztraminer	Alsace	Dry white
	Sancerre	Loire/Centre	Dry white
	Sauvignon Blanc	New Zealand	Dry white
	Savennières	Loire	Dry white

FOOD	WINE NAME	REGION/COUNTRY	WINE STYLE
Chicken, curry	Arbois	Jura	Dry white
	Chardonnay	New World	Dry white
	Côtes du Rhône	Rhône	Dry red
	Morgon	Beaujolais	Dry red
	Pinot Gris	Alsace	Dry white
	St-Emilion	Bordeaux	Dry red
Chicken korma	Chardonnay	California	Dry white
	Chenin Blanc	California	Dry white
	Sémillon	New World	Dry white
Chicken, lemon	Champagne rosé	Champagne	Sparkling
	Chenin Blanc	South Africa	Dry white
	Falanghina	Campania, Italy	Dry white
Chicken paprika	Kékfrankos	Hungary	Dry red
	Shiraz	Australia	Dry red
	Zinfandel	California	Dry red
Chicken piri-piri (a Portuguese dish with chilies)			
	Periquita	Portugal	Dry red
	Renguengos	Portugal	Dry red
	Sauvignon Blanc	France or New World	Dry white
	Vinho Verde	Portugal	Dry white
Chicken salad	Beaujolais	Burgundy	Dry red
	Bordeaux rosé	Bordeaux	Dry rosé
	Chardonnay	California	Dry white
	Sauvignon Blanc	New Zealand	Dry white
Chicken in sweet and sour sauce			
	Gewürztraminer VT	Alsace	Medium-dry white
	Muscat de Rivesaltes	Roussillon	Vin doux naturel
	Pomerol	Bordeaux	Dry red
	Sylvaner	Alsace	Dry white
Chicken, tarragon	Arnies	Piedmont, Italy	Dry white
	Cahors	SW France	Dry red
	Chardonnay (oaked)	Australia	Dry white
Chicken teriyaki	Sancerre	Loire/Centre	Dry white
	Sauvignon Blanc	New Zealand	Dry white
	Soave	Italy	Dry white
Chicken tikka masala (see Indian food)			
Chili con carne	Cabernet Sauvignon	Argentina or Chile	Dry red
	Côtes du Rhône	Rhône	Dry red
	Pinotage	South Africa	Dry red
	Shiraz	Australia	Dry red
	Zinfandel	California	Dry red

FOOD	WINE NAME	REGION/COUNTRY	WINE STYLE
Chili sauce	Côtes de Provence rosé	Provence	Dry rosé
	Côtes du Rhône	Rhône	Dry red
	Fitou	Languedoc	Dry red
	Shiraz	Australia	Dry red
Chinese food	Champagne (non-vintage)	Champagne	Sparkling
	Chasselas	Switzerland	Dry white
	Gewürztraminer VT	Alsace	Medium-dry white
	Riesling VT	Alsace	Dry to medium white
	Riesling Spätlese	Germany	Sweet white
	Grüner Veltliner Beerenauslese	Austria	Sweet white
Chorizo	Chacoli de Guetaria	Spain	Dry white
	Corbières	Languedoc	Dry red
	Irouléguy	SW France	Dry red
	Navarra	Spain	Dry red
	Pinotage	South Africa	Dry red
	Zinfandel	California	Dry red
Choucroute garni	Chablis (unoaked)	Burgundy	Dry white
	Crozes-Hermitage	Rhône	Dry white
	Pinot Blanc	Alsace	Dry white
	Riesling	Austria	Dry white
Christmas pudding			
	Asti Spumante	Italy	Sparkling
	Banyuls	Roussillon	Vin doux natural
	Champagne	Champagne	Sparkling
	Sauternes	Bordeaux	Sweet white
	Tokaji Aszú	Hungary	Sweet white
Chutney	Bellet rosé	Provence	Dry rosé
	Champagne	Champagne	Sparkling
	Gewürztraminer	Alsace	Dry white
	Zinfandel	California	Dry red
Clam chowder	Chablis Grand Cru	Burgundy	Dry white
	Chardonnay	Long Island	Dry white
	L'Etoile	Jura	Dry white
	Riesling	Alsace	Dry white
	Pinot Gris	Alsace	Dry white
Cod	Côtes de Provence	Provence	Dry rosé
	Mâcon	Burgundy	Dry white
	Sylvaner	Alsace	Dry white
Confit du canard	Cahors	SW France	Dry red
	Merlot	New World	Dry red
	Pommard	Burgundy	Dry red
	St-Emilion	Bordeaux	Dry red
	Saumur-Champigny	Loire	Dry red

FOOD	WINE NAME	REGION/COUNTRY	WINE STYLE
Coq au vin	Châteauneuf-du-Pape	Rhône	Dry red
	Corbières	Languedoc	Dry red
	Côtes du Rhône	Rhône	Dry red
	Gevrey-Chambertin	Burgundy	Dry red
	Pinot Noir	California	Dry red
Coquilles St-Jacques (see Scallops)			
Corn bread	Chardonnay	California	Dry white
	Côtes du Jura	Jura	Dry red
	Merlot	New World	Dry red
	Vin de Corse	Corsica	Dry red
Corn chowder	Chardonnay	California	Dry white
	Meursault	Burgundy	Dry white
	Rully	Burgundy	Dry white
Corn-on-the-cob	Chardonnay	California	Dry white
	Pinot Gris	Alsace	Dry white
Cornish pasties	Côtes du Rhône	Rhône	Dry white
	Sangiovese	California	Dry red
	Viognier	California	Dry white
Couscous	Cabernet Sauvignon/Cinsault	Lebanon	Dry red
	Navarra	Spain	Dry red
	Pinotage	South Africa	Dry red
	Shiraz	Australia	Dry red
Crab	Chablis	Burgundy	Dry white
	Crépy	Savoie	Dry white
	Crozes-Hermitage	Rhône	Dry white
	Entre-Deux-Mers	Bordeaux	Dry white
	Muscadet	Loire	Dry white
Cranberry sauce	Mouvèdre	France or New World	Dry red
	Riesling Kabinett	Germany	Dry white
	Shiraz	Australia	Dry red
Crème caramel or brûlée			
	Champagne (demi-sec)	Champagne	Sparkling
	Gaillac	SW France	Dry white
	Sauternes	Bordeaux	Sweet white
	Baumes-de-Venise	Rhône	Sweet white
Crêpes, savory	Chardonnay	Alto Adige, Italy	Dry white
	Bordeaux Supérieur	Bordeaux	Dry red
	Pinot Blanc	Alsace	Dry white
	Rully	Burgundy	Dry white
	St-Amour	Beaujolais	Dry red

FOOD	WINE NAME	REGION/COUNTRY	WINE STYLE
Crêpes, sweet	Champagne (demi-sec)	Champagne	Sparkling
	Muscat de Rivesaltes	Roussillon	Vin doux naturel
	Vin de Paille	Jura	Vin doux naturel
	Vouvray	Loire	Sparkling (mousseux)
Croque Monsieur or Madame			
	Anjou Gamay	Loire	Dry red
	Bordeaux	Bordeaux	Dry red
	Chardonnay	Australian	Dry white
	Sylvaner	Alsace	Dry white
Crudités	Gros Plant	Loire/Nantes	Dry white
	Pinot Blanc	Alsace	Dry white
	Pinot Grigio	Italy	Dry white
Curried tomato soup			
	Crozes-Hermitage	Rhône	Dry white
	Gewürztraminer	Alsace	Dry white
	Marsanne	New World	Dry white
	Rioja Reserva	Spain	Dry red
Curry sauces	Condrieu	Rhône	Dry white
	Marsanne	New World	Dry white
	Viognier	Rhône	Dry white
DESSERTS with a base of Apples			
	Pineau des Charentes	Cognac	Vin de liqueur
	Vin de Paille	Jura	Vin doux naturel
	Vouvray	Loire	Sweet white
DESSERTS with a base of Apricots			
	Blanquette de Limoux	Languedoc	Sparkling
	Côteaux du Layon	Loire	Sweet white
	Muscat de Rivesaltes	Roussillon	Vin doux naturel
	Vin de Paille	Jura	Vin doux naturel
DESSERTS with a base of Bananas			
	Crémant de Bourgogne	Burgundy	Sparkling
	Monbazillac	SW France	Sweet white
	Muscat de Beaumes-de-Venise	Rhône	Vin doux naturel
DESSERTS with a base of Caramel			
	Barsac	Bordeaux	Sweet white
	Champagne (demi-sec)	Champagne	Sparkling
	Moscatel de Setúbal	Portugal	Sweet white
DESSERTS with a base of Cassis			
	Bergerac	SW France	Dry white
	Champagne (rosé)	Champagne	Sparkling rosé
	Muscat de Rivesaltes	Roussillon	Vin doux naturel

FOOD	WINE NAME	REGION/COUNTRY	WINE STYLE
DESSERTS with a base of Cherry			
	Black Muscat	California	Sweet white
	Blanquette de Limoux	Languedoc	Sparkling
	Côteaux du Layon	Loire	Sweet white
	Riesling Beerenauslese	Germany	Sweet white
DESSERTS with a base of Chestnuts			
	Asti Spumante	Italy	Sparkling
	Chenin Blanc	Loire	Dry white
	Loupiac	Bordeaux	Sweet white
DESSERTS with a base of Chocolate			
	Banyuls	Roussillon	Vin doux naturel
	Champagne (Noir de Noirs)	Champagne	Sparkling
	Muscatel du Setúbal	Portugal	Sweet white
	Pineau des Charentes	Cognac	Vin de liqueur
	Port	Portugal	Fortified red
	Sauternes	Bordeaux	Sweet white
DESSERTS with a base of Cinnamon			
	Gevrey-Chambertin	Burgundy	Dry red
	Ste-Croix-du-Mont	SW France	Sweet white
	Sauternes	Bordeaux	Sweet white
	Volnay	Burgundy	Dry red
	Pinot Nero	Alto Adige	Dry red
DESSERTS with a base of Coconut			
	Champagne	Champagne	Sparkling
	Chardonnay	New World	Dry white
	Gewürztraminer VT	Alsace	Medium-dry white
	Marsanne	France	Dry white
	Sémillon	France or New World	Dry white
DESSERTS with a base of Coffee			
	Banyuls	Roussillion	Vin de liqueur red
	Champagne (brut)	Champagne	Sparkling
	Vin Santo	Tuscany	Sweet white
	Vosne-Romanée	Burgundy	Dry red
DESSERTS with a base of Cognac			
	Arbois	Jura	Dry white
	Pineau de Charentes	Cognac	Vin de liqueur white
DESSERTS with a base of Cointreau			
	Champagne	Champagne	Sparkling
	Sauternes	Bordeaux	Sweet white

FOOD	WINE NAME	REGION/COUNTRY	WINE STYLE
DESSERTS with a base of Fruit			
	Asti Spumante	Italy	Sparkling
	Barsac/Sauternes	Bordeaux	Sweet white
	Beaumes de Venise	Rhône	Vin doux naturel
	Coteaux du Layon	Loire	Sweet white
	Quarts de Chaume	Loire	Sweet white
DESSERTS with a base of Ginger			
	Muscat	France	Sweet white
	Muscat de Beaumes-de-Venise	Rhône	Vin doux naturel
	Sauvignon Blanc	France or New World	Dry white
DESSERTS with a base of Honey			
	Black Muscat	California	Sweet white
	Montrachet	Burgundy	Dry white
	Muscat de Beaumes-de-Venise	Rhône	Vin doux naturel
DESSERTS with a base of Lemon			
	Hermitage	Rhône	Dry white
	Sauternes	Bordeaux	Sweet white
	Vouvray	Loire	Sweet white or sparkling
DESSERTS with a base of Mint			
	Asti Spumante	Italy	Sparkling
	Muscat de Beaumes-de-Venise	Rhône	Vin doux naturel
DESSERTS with a base of Orange			
	Muscat de Rivesaltes	Roussillon	Vin doux naturel
	Ste-Croix-du-Mont	SW France	Sweet white
DESSERTS with a base of Pineapple			
	Cadillac	Bordeaux	Sweet white
	Champagne (demi-sec)	Champagne	Sparkling
	Muscat de Rivesaltes	Roussillon	Vin doux naturel
	Orvieto	Umbria	Dry white
	Pacherenc du Vic-Bihl	SW France	Sweet white
DESSERTS with a base of Raspberry			
	Beaujolais-Villages	Beaujolais	Dry red
	Champagne (demi-sec)	Champagne	Sparkling
	Coteaux du Layon	Loire	Sweet white
	Loupiac	Bordeaux	Sweet white
	Monbazillac	SW France	Sweet white
	Riesling	Alsace	Dry white
	Saumur-Champigny	Loire	Dry red
DESSERTS with a base of Strawberry			
	Banyuls	Roussillon	Vin doux naturel
	Champagne	Champagne	Sparkling
	Monbazillac	SW France	Sweet white
	Saumur-Champigny	Loire	Dry red

FOOD	WINE NAME	REGION/COUNTRY	WINE STYLE
Duck, roast	Bonnes-Mares	Burgundy	Dry red
	Châteauneuf-du-Pape	Rhône	Dry red
	Madiran	SW France	Dry red
	Pomerol	Bordeaux	Dry red
	Pommard	Burgundy	Dry red
	Zinfandel	California	Dry red
Duck à l'orange	Cahors	SW France	Dry red
	Côtes de Provence	Provence	Dry red
	Gewürztraminer	Alsace	Dry white
	Graves	Bordeaux	Dry red
	Riesling Auslese	Germany	Sweet white
	Rosso Cònero	Italy	Dry red
	Shiraz	Australia	Dry red
Eels, smoked	Bourgeuil	Loire	Dry red
	Sancerre	Loire	Dry white
	Sauvignon Blanc	New Zealand	Dry white
Eels with a creamy herb sauce			
	Pouilly-Fumé	Loire	Dry white
	Riesling	Alsace	Dry white
	Sancerre	Loire/Centre	Dry white
Eggplant	Corbières	Languedoc	Dry red
	Dão	Portugal	Dry red
	Vin de Corse	Corsica	Dry red
	Zinfandel	California	Dry red
Eggplant with Parmesan			
	Barbaresco	Piedmont	Dry red
	Barolo	Piedmont	Dry red
	Brunello di Montalcino	Tuscany	Dry red
Eggs (general)	Brouilly	Beaujolais	Dry red
	Muscadet	Loire	Dry white
	Sauvignon Blanc	France or New World	Dry white
	Arneis	Piedmont, Italy	Dry white
Eggs Benedict	Champagne	Champagne	Sparkling
	Chardonnay (unoaked)	New World	Dry white
	Pinot Blanc	Alsace	Dry white
Empanadas	Malbec	Argentina	Dry red
	Merlot	Chile	Dry red
	Zinfandel	California	Dry red
Escargots	Bourgueil	Loire	Dry red
	Chablis	Burgundy	Dry white
	Champagne	Champagne	Sparkling
	Côtes du Roussillon	Roussillon	Dry red
	Vacqueyras	Rhône	Dry red

FOOD	WINE NAME	REGION/COUNTRY	WINE STYLE
Fettuccine Alfredo	Bardolino	Veneto	Dry red
	Chardonnay	Alto Adige	Dry white
	Frascati Superiore	Italy	Dry white
	Rully	Burgundy	Dry white
Fish (white)	Chardonnay	California	Dry white
	Muscadet sur Lie	Loire	Dry white
	Sauvigon Blanc	New World	Dry white
	Vouvray	Loire	Dry white
Fish (fried)	Bergerac	SW France	Dry red
	Pinot Grigio	Italy	Dry white
	Verdicchio	Italy	Dry white
Fish (grilled)	Chenin Blanc	New World	Dry white
	Riesling	Alsace	Dry white
Fish (smoked)	Riesling Auslese	Germany	Sweet white
	Gewürztraminer VT	Alsace	Sweet white
Fish cakes	Chardonnay	Chile	Dry white
	Muscadet	Loire	Dry white
	Sancerre	Loire/Centre	Dry white
	Sauvignon Blanc	New Zealand	Dry white
	Vouvray	Loire	Dry white
Fish in red wine	Barbaresco	Italy	Dry red
	Bardolino	Italy	Dry red
	Graves	Bordeaux	Dry red
Foie gras	Champagne (Blanc de Blancs)	Champagne	Sparkling
	Corton-Charlemagne	Burgundy	Dry red
	Monbazillac	SW France	Sweet white
	Pineau des Charentes	Cognac	Vin de liqueur
	Pinot Gris VT	Alsace	Dry to medium white
	Riesling Auslese	Germany	Sweet white
	Ste-Croix-du-Mont	SW France	Sweet white
	Sauternes/Barsac	Bordeaux	Sweet white
	Vin de Paille	Jura	Vin doux naturel
Fruit-based desserts (general)			
	Asti Spumante	Italy	Sparkling
	Barsac/Sauternes	Bordeaux	Sweet white
	Champagne (Blanc de Blancs)	Champagne	Sparkling
	Coteaux du Layon	Loire	Sweet white
	Loupiac	Bordeaux	Sweet white
	Monbazillac	SW France	Sweet white
	Muscat de Beaumes-de-Venise	Rhône	Vin doux naturel
	Quarts de Chaume	Loire	Sweet white
	Vouvray	Loire	Sweet white/ sparkling

FOOD	WINE NAME	REGION/COUNTRY	WINE STYLE
Fondue (à la bourguignonne)			
	Bordeaux	Bordeaux	Dry red
	Côte de Beaune	Burgundy	Dry red
	Côtes du Rhône	Rhône	Dry red
	Saumur	Loire	Dry white
	Shiraz	Australia	Dry red
Fruit compote or salad			
	Muscat de Rivesaltes	Roussillon	Vin doux naturel
	Moscato Spumante	Italy	Sparkling
	Loupiac	Bordeaux	Sweet white
	Champagne (rosé)	Champagne	Sparkling rosé
	Ste-Croix-du-Mont	SW France	Sweet white
Game	Barolo	Piedmont	Dry red
	Bonnes-Mares	Burgundy	Dry red
	Clos de Vougeot	Burgundy	Dry red
	Corton	Burgundy	Dry red
	Echezeaux	Burgundy	Dry red
	Shiraz	Australia	Dry red
	Syrah	New World	Dry red
	Nero d'Avola	Sicily	Dry red
Gazpacho	Buzet	SW France	Dry red
	Rioja	Spain	Dry white
	Soave	Veneto	Dry white
	Sancerre	Loire	Dry white
	Viognier	Rhône/New World	Dry white
Goose	Champagne	Champagne	Sparkling
	Châteauneuf-du-Pape	Rhône	Dry red
	Chianti Classico	Tuscany	Dry red
	Margaux	Bordeaux	Dry red
	Shiraz	Australia	Dry red
	Vouvray	Loire	Demi-sec white
Gougère	Chablis	Burgundy	Dry white
	Côtes du Rhône	Rhône	Dry red
	Pinot Gris	Alsace	Dry white
	Pouilly-Fuissé	Burgundy	Dry white
Goulash	Gigondas	Rhône	Dry red
	Mavrud	Bulgaria	Dry red
	Penedès	Spain	Dry red
	Zinfandel	California	Dry red
Gravlax	Champagne (Blanc de Blancs)	Champagne	Sparkling
	Chardonnay	Australia	Dry white
	Riesling Kabinett	Germany	Dry white

FOOD	WINE NAME	REGION/COUNTRY	WINE STYLE
Greek food	Naoussa	Greece	Dry red
	Rioja	Spain	Dry red
	Shiraz	Australia	Dry red
	Zinfandel	California	Dry red
Grouse	Barolo	Italy	Dry red
	Chambertin	Burgundy	Dry red
	Hermitage	Rhône	Dry red
	Richebourg	Burgundy	Dry red
Guacamole	Champagne	Champagne	Sparkling
	Chardonnay	California	Dry white
	Meursault	Burgundy	Dry white
	Pinot Grigio	Italy	Dry white
Guinea fowl	Chambertin	Burgundy	Dry red
	Fronsac	Bordeaux	Dry red
	Pauillac	Bordeaux	Dry red
	Falerno del Massico	Campania	Dry red
Ginger (see DESSERTS with a base of Ginger)			
Haddock	Arbois	Jura	Dry red
	Graves	Bordeaux	Dry white
	Riesling	Alsace	Dry white
	Sauvignon Blanc	France or New World	Dry white
Haggis	Baden Spätburgunder	Germany	Dry red
	Bordeaux Supérieur	Bordeaux	Dry red
	Cabernet Sauvignon	New World	Dry red
	Bairrada	Portugal	Dry red
Ham, baked	Beaujolais	Burgundy	Dry red
	Chinon	Loire	Dry red
	Pinot Noir	New World	Dry red
Ham, baked with pineapple			
	Bourgueil	Loire	Dry red
	Côtes de Montravel	SW France	Dry white
	Saumur	Loire	Medium-dry white
Ham, smoked	Chardonnay (oaked)	New World	Dry white
	Pacherenc du Vic-Bihl	SW France	Sweet white
	Riesling Spätlese	Germany	Sweet white
	Riesling VT	Alsace	Sweet white
Hamburgers	Beaujolais	Burgundy	Dry red
	Cabernet Sauvignon	California	Dry red
	Chianti	Tuscany, Italy	Dry red
	Shiraz	Australia	Dry red
	Zinfandel	California	Dry red

FOOD	WINE NAME	REGION/COUNTRY	WINE STYLE
Hare	Bonnes-Mares	Burgundy	Dry red
	Canon-Fronsac	Bordeaux	Dry red
	Cornas	Rhône	Dry red
	Minervois	Languedoc-Roussillon	Dry red
Hare, potted or jugged			
	Bergerac	SW France	Dry red
	Buzet	SW France	Dry red
	Corbières	Languedoc	Dry red
Herbs and spices (see part 2)			
Herring	Corbières	Languedoc	Dry white
	Entre-Deux-Mers	Bordeaux	Dry white
	St-Véran	Burgundy	Dry white
Hummus	Furmint	Hungary	Dry white
	Pinot Grigio	Italy	Dry white
	Zitsa	Greece	Dry white
Ice cream	Champagne	Champagne	Sparkling
	Muscat de Beaumes-de-Venise	Rhône	Vin doux naturel
	Vin Santo	Tuscany	Vin doux naturel
Iles flottantes	L'Etoile	Jura	Dry white
	Loupiac	Bordeaux	Sweet white
	Muscat de Rivesaltes	Roussillon	Vin doux naturel
	Vouvray	Loire	Semi-sec white
Indian food with spicy yogurt sauces			
	Bordeaux rosé	Bordeaux	Dry rosé
	Champagne (non-vintage)	Champagne	Sparkling
	Chardonnay	California	Dry white
	Chenin Blanc	Loire or New World	Dry white
	Gewürztraminer VT	Alsace	Medium-dry white
	Orvieto Abboccato	Italy	Medium-dry white
	Sémillon	New World	Dry white
	Viognier	New World	Dry white
Jambalaya	Poulsard	Jura	Dry red
	Sancerre	Loire	Dry white
	Sauvignon Blanc	New Zealand	Dry white
Jambon persillé	Chablis	Burgundy	Dry white
	Chardonnay	Chile	Dry white
	Puilly-Fumé	Loire	Dry white
	Rully	Burgundy	Dry white
	Sauvignon Blanc	Chile	Dry white

FOOD	WINE NAME	REGION/COUNTRY	WINE STYLE
Japanese food	Champagne (Blanc de Noirs)	Champagne	Sparkling
	Pomerol	Bordeaux	Dry red
	Pouilly-Fuissé	Burgundy	Dry white
	Riesling	Austria	Dry white
Kidneys	Beaujolais	Beaujolais	Dry red
	Cabernet Sauvignon	New World	Dry red
	Pommard	Burgundy	Dry red
Kangaroo	Cabernet Sauvignon	Australia	Dry red
	Chardonnay	Australia	Dry white
	Shiraz	Australia	Dry red
Kebabs	Arbois	Jura	Dry red
	Côtes de Provence rosé	Provence	Dry rosé
	Patrimonio	Corsica	Dry red
	St-Joseph	Rhône	Dry red
Kedgeree	Champagne	Champagne	Sparkling
	Chardonnay	New World	Dry white
	Pinot Blanc	Alsace	Dry white
Kippers	Champagne	Champagne	Sparkling
	Corbières	Languedoc	Dry white
	Entre-Deux-Mers	Bordeaux	Dry white
Kleftiko (kebabs)	Bairrada	Portugal	Dry red
	Cabernet Franc	New World	Dry red
	Nemea	Greece	Dry red
	Periquita	Portugal	Dry red
	Poulsard	Arbois	Dry red
Kougelhopf	Riesling SGN	Alsace	Sweet white
	Pinot Gris VT	Alsace	Semi-sweet white
	Quarts de Chaume	Loire	Sweet white
Lamb (general)	Malbec	Argentina	Dry red
	Médoc	Bordeaux	Dry red
	Navarra	Spain	Dry red
	Pauillac	Bordeaux	Dry red
	Rioja	Spain	Dry red
Lamb chops, grilled			
	Côtes de Provence rosé	Provence	Dry rosé
	Lirac rosé	Rhône	Dry rosé
	Pomerol	Bordeaux	Dry red
	Saumur-Champigny	Loire	Dry red

FOOD	WINE NAME	REGION/COUNTRY	WINE STYLE
Lamb crown roast	Ajaccio	Corsica	Dry red
	Barolo	Piedmont	Dry red
	Pauillac	Bordeaux	Dry red
	St-Julien	Bordeaux	Dry red
Lamb curry	Gewürztraminer	Alsace	Dry white
	Pinot Noir	California	Dry red
	Savigny-lès-Beaune	Burgundy	Dry red
	Shiraz	Australia	Dry red
Lamb with Herbes de Provence			
	Cinsault or Mourvèdre	France	Dry red
	Colli Orientali del Friuli	Italy	Dry red
	Côtes de Provence rosé	Provence	Dry rosé
	Dão	Portugal	Dry red
	St-Emilion	Bordeaux	Dry red
Lamb, roast with mint sauce			
	Champagne (rosé)	Champagne	Sparkling rosé
	Kékfrankos	Hungary	Dry red
	Margaux	Bordeaux	Dry red
	Mavrud	Bulgaria	Dry red
	Pommard	Burgundy	Dry red
	Vino Nobile di Montepulciano	Tuscany	Dry red
Lamb shoulder	Bordeaux Supérieur	Bordeaux	Dry red
	Côtes de Bourg	Bordeaux	Dry red
	Hermitage	Rhône	Dry red
	St-Emilion	Bordeaux	Dry red
Lancashire hotpot	Bergerac	SW France	Dry red
	Cabernet Sauvignon	New World	Dry red
	Fitou	Languedoc	Dry red
	Montepulciano d'Abruzzo	Abruzzo	Dry red
Lasagne	Barberai d'Asti	Piedmont	Dry red
	Chianti	Tuscany	Dry red
	St-Amour	Beaujolais	Dry red
Lemon chicken	Champagne (rosé)	Champagne	Sparkling rosé
	Chenin Blanc	Northwest	Dry white
	Saumur-Champigny	Loire	Dry red
	Vouvray	Loire	Dry white
Linguine (see PASTAS)			
Liver	Champagne (Blanc de Blancs)	Champagne	Sparkling
	Côtes de Provence rosé	Provence	Dry rosé
	Médoc	Bordeaux	Dry red
	Rioja	Spain	Dry red

FOOD	WINE NAME	REGION/COUNTRY	WINE STYLE
Lobster	Bordeaux sec	Bordeaux	Dry white
	Champagne	Champagne	Sparkling
	Condrieu	Rhône	Dry white
	Meursault	Burgundy	Dry white
Lobster bisque (see clam chowder)			
Lotte	Champagne	Champagne	Sparkling
	Muscadet	Loire	Dry white
	Orvieto	Umbria	Dry white
Macaroni and cheese			
	Dolcetto	Piedmont	Dry red
	Chianti	Tuscany	Dry red
	Soave	Veneto	Dry white
Mackerel with butter and spring onions			
	Chablis (oaked)	Burgundy	Dry white
	Gaillac	Rhône	Dry white
	Graves	Bordeaux	Dry white
	Sémillon	New World	Dry white
Mackerel with green gooseberry sauce			
	Gros Plant	Loire/Centre	Dry white
	Muscadet	Loire	Dry white
	Sancerre	Loire/Centre	Dry red
	Vinho Verde	Portugal	Dry white
Meat loaf	Bordeaux Supérieur	Bordeaux	Dry red
	Cabernet Sauvignon	California	Dry red
	Pinot Noir	New World	Dry red
	Zinfandel	California	Dry red
Melanzane alla Parmigiana			
	Primitivo	Italy	Dry red
	Nero d'Avola	Sicily	Dry red
	Nero de Troia	Puglia	Dry red
	Rosato di Salento	Puglia	Dry red
Melon with Parma ham			
	Bardolino	Italy	Dry red
	Bergerac	SW France	Dry red
	Bianco di Scandiano	Italy	Dry white
	Chinon	Loire	Dry red
	St-Joseph	Rhône	Dry red
Melon with port	Monbazillac	SW France	Sweet white
	Pineau des Charentes	Cognac	Vin de liqueur

FOOD	WINE NAME	REGION/COUNTRY	WINE STYLE
Merguez sausage	Grenache	New World	Dry red
	Rioja	Spain	Dry red
	Shiraz	Australia	Dry red
Meringues	Asti Spumante	Italy	Sparkling
	Champagne	Champagne	Sparkling
	Muscat de Rivesaltes	Roussillon	Vin doux naturel
Mexican food	Cahors	SW France	Dry red
	Côtes du Rhône	Rhône	Dry red
	Fitou	Languedoc	Dry red
	Valpolicella	Veneto	Dry red
Mille feuilles	Champagne	Champagne	Sparkling
	Pacherenc du Vic-Bihl	SW France	Sweet white
Mince pies	Pacherenc du Vic-Bihl	SW France	Sweet white
	Port	Portugal	Fortified red
	Vouvray	Loire	Sweet white or sparkling
Minestrone	Alenquir	Portugal	Dry white
	Barbera d'Alba	Piedmont	Dry red
	Chianti	Tuscany	Dry red
	Corbières	Languedoc	Dry red
Monkfish	Chardonnay	Chile	Dry white
	Puligny-Montrachet	Burgundy	Dry white
	Sémillon	Australia	Dry white
Moûles et frites	Muscadet	Loire	Dry white
	Sancerre	Loire	Dry white
	Verdicchio	Italy	Dry white
Moûles Mariniers	Chablis	Burgundy	Dry white
	Entre-Deux-Mers	Bordeaux	Dry white
	Pouilly-Fumé	Loire	Dry white
	Riesling	Alsace	Dry white
Moussaka	Côtes du Rhône	Rhône	Dry red
	Dão	Portugal	Dry red
	Kékfrankos	Hungary	Dry red
	Naoussa	Greece	Dry red
	Nemea	Greece	Dry red
	Pinotage	South Africa	Dry red
	Rioja	Spain	Dry red

Mushrooms (see Mushrooms and Wine on page 101)

Mussels (see Moûles)

FOOD	WINE NAME	REGION/COUNTRY	WINE STYLE
Octopus	Bellet	South of France	Dry white
	Fiano	Campania	Dry white
	Rioja	Spain	Dry red
Olives	Amontillado	Spain	Fortified red
	Côtes de Provence	Provence	Dry white
	Manzanilla	Spain	Fortified white
	Riesling	Alsace	Dry white
	Sherry	Spain	Fortified red
Oxtail	Brunello di Montalcino	Tuscany, Italy	Dry red
	Châteauneuf-du-Pape	Rhône	Dry red
	Periquita	Portugal	Dry red
Omelet	Brouilly	Beaujolais	Dry red
	Champagne	Champagne	Sparkling
	Pinot Blanc	Alsace	Dry white
	Sancerre	Loire/Centre	Dry white
Omelet with bacon			
	Chardonnay	New World	Dry white
	Pinot Gris	Alsace	Dry white
Omelet with cheese			
	Chardonnay	New World	Dry white
	Pinot Blanc	Alsace	Dry white
	Torgiano	Umbria	Dry white
	Vosne-Romanée	Burgundy	Dry red
Omelet with mushrooms			
	Côtes du Rhône	Rhône	Dry red
	Dolcetto d'Alba	Piedmont	Dry red
	Petit Chablis	Burgundy	Dry white
	Saumur-Champigny	Loire	Dry red
Omelet with tomato			
	Beaujolais	Burgundy	Dry red
	Chianti	Italy	Dry red
	Vermentino	Liguria	Dry white
Omelet with truffles			
	Chambolle-Musigny	Burgundy	Dry red
	Champagne (Blanc de Blancs)	Champagne	Sparkling
Onions, creamed	Gewürztraminer	Alsace	Dry white
	Palette	Provence	Dry white
	Riesling	Alsace	Dry white

Orange (see DESSERTS with a base of Orange)

FOOD	WINE NAME	REGION/COUNTRY	WINE STYLE
Osso Buco	Barbera	Piedmont	Dry red
	Dolcetto d'Alba	Piedmont	Dry red
	Refosco	Grave del Friuli	Dry red
	Valpolicella	Veneto	Dry red
Oxtail	Brunello di Montalcino	Tuscany	Dry red
	Châteauneuf-du-Pape	Rhône	Dry red
	Lagrein	Alto Adige	Dry red
	Periquita	Portugal	Dry red
Oysters	Champagne	Champagne	Sparkling
	Entre-Deux-Mers	Bordeaux	Dry white
	Gavi	Italy	Dry white
	Muscadet	Loire	Dry white
	Sancerre	Loire	Dry white
Paella	Côtes de Provence rosé	Provence	Dry rosé
	Penedès	Spain	Dry white
	Pouilly-Fumé	Loire	Dry white
	Rioja	Spain	Dry red
Pancakes with maple syrup			
	Champagne	Champagne	Sparkling
	Riesling Beerenauslese	Germany	Sweet white
	Vouvray	Loire	Sparkling (mousseux)
Partridge	Barolo	Piedmont	Dry red
	Châteauneuf-du-Pape	Rhône	Dry red
	Pomerol	Bordeaux	Dry red
PASTAS with carbonara sauce			
	Barbera	Piedmont	Dry red
	Bardolino	Veneto	Dry red
	Chardonnay	Alto Adige	Dry white
	Mâcon or St-Véran	Burgundy	Dry white
PASTAS with clam sauce			
	Chablis (unoaked)	Burgundy	Dry white
	Fiano	Campania	Dry white
	Pinot Grigio	Italy	Dry white
	Vermentino	Liguria	Dry white
PASTAS with cream sauce			
	Bianco di Custoza	Veneto	Dry white
	Orvieto	Umbria	Dry white
	Meursault	Burgundy	Dry white
PASTAS with pesto			
	Barbera d'Asti	Piedmont	Dry red
	Chardonnay	New World	Dry white
	Soave	Veneto	Dry white

FOOD	WINE NAME	REGION/COUNTRY	WINE STYLE
Pasta primavera	Pinot Grigio	Italy	Dry white
	Sauvignon Blanc	New World	Dry white
	Verdicchio	Italy	Dry white
Pâté (see Foie gras)			
Pea and ham soup			
	Chardonnay	Chile	Dry white
	Pinotage	South Africa	Dry red
Pecan pie	Champagne	Champagne	Sparkling
	Moscatel de Valencia	Spain	Sweet white
	Sauternes	Bordeaux	Sweet white
Peking duck	Gewürztraminer VT	Alsace	Medium-dry white
	Pinot Noir	Australia	Dry red
	Rioja	Spain	Dry white
	St-Emilion	Bordeaux	Dry red
Peppers (roasted or stuffed)			
	Bandol rosé	Provence	Dry rosé
	Beaujolais	Beaujolais	Dry red
	Mâcon	Burgundy	Dry white
Pesto Sauce (see PASTAS with pesto)			
Pheasant	Barolo	Italy	Dry red
	Chambolle-Musigny	Burgundy	Dry red
	Crozes-Hermitage	Rhône	Dry red
	Pomerol	Bordeaux	Dry red
	St-Emilion	Bordeaux	Dry red
Pigeon	Amarone della Valpolicella	Piedmont	Dry erd
	Buzet	SW France	Dry red
	Crozes-Hermitage	Rhône	Dry red
	Pinotage	South Africa	Dry red
	Salice Salento	Puglia	Dry red
	St-Emilion	Bordeaux	Dry red
Pissaladière (onion, olive, and anchovy tart)			
	Bellet rosé	South of France	Dry rosé
	Tavel	Rhône	Dry red
	Corbières	Languedoc	Dry white
	Côtes de Provence	Provence	Dry white
	Pinot Blanc	Alsace	Dry white
	Pinot Gris	Alsace	Dry white
	Tavel	Rhône	Dry rosé
Pike with garlic	Riesling	Austria	Dry white
	Sauvignon Blanc	Australia	Dry white
	Sylvaner	Alsace	Dry white

FOOD	WINE NAME	REGION/COUNTRY	WINE STYLE
Piperada	Bandol rosé	Provence	Dry rosé
	Chacoli de Guetaria	Spain	Dry white
	Champagne (rosé)	Champagne	Sparkling rosé
	Irouguley	Basque	Dry red
	Pacherenc du Vic-Bihl	SW France	Dry white
Pizza	Barbera d'Asti	Piedmont	Dry red
	Chianti	Tuscany	Dry red
	Greco di Tufo	Campania	Dry white
	Zinfandel	California	Dry red
Pizza, seafood	Bianco	di Custoza, Italy	Dry white
	Pouilly-Fumé	Loire	Dry white
	Fiano	Campania	Dry white
Plaice	Chablis	Burgundy	Dry white
	Orvieto	Italy	Dry white
	Riesling	Alsace	Dry white
Polenta	Ajaccio rosé	Corsica	Dry rosé
	Barbera d'Alba	Piedmont	Dry red
	Chianti	Tuscany	Dry red
	Côtes de Provence rosé	Provence	Dry rosé
Pork chops, grilled	Corbières	Languedoc	Dry red
	Côtes de Duras	SW France	Dry red
	Pinot Gris	Alsace	Dry white
	Pinot Noir	New World	Dry red
Pork, roast	Bairrada	Portugal	Dry red
	Chablis Grand Cru	Burgundy	Dry white
	Chianti Classico	Tuscany	Dry red
	Riesling Spätlese	Germany	Sweet white
	Rioja	Spain	Dry red
Pork, roast with mustard sauce or stewed fruit			
	Gewürztraminer VT	Alsace	Sweet white
	Riesling Spätlese	Germany	Sweet white
Pot-au-feu	Anjou	Loire	Dry red
	Bergerac	SW France	Dry red
	St-Emilion	Bordeaux	Dry red
Pot roast	Riesling	Alsace	Dry white
	Gewürztraminer	Alsace	Dry white
	St-Emilion	Bordeaux	Dry red
Potato Salad (see SALAD, potato)			

FOOD	WINE NAME	REGION/COUNTRY	WINE STYLE
Prawns	Champagne	Champagne	Sparkling
	Chassagne-Montrachet	Burgundy	Dry white
	Sauvignon Blanc	New Zealand	Dry white
	Sauvignon Colli Orientali del Friuli	Italy	Dry white
	Sancerre	Loire	Dry white
	Soave	Veneto	Dry white
Prawn cocktail	Bergerac	SW France	Dry white
	Muscadet	Loire	Dry white
	Sauvignon Blanc	France or New World	Dry white
Prosciutto	Barbera d'Asti	Piedmont	Dry red
	Pinot Grigio	Italy	Dry white
	Salice Salento	Puglia	Dry red
	Valpolicella Classico	Veneto	Dry red
Pumpkin pie	Monbazillac	SW France	Sweet white
	Savennieres	Loire	Dry white
	Sémillon	New World	Sweet white
Quail	Champagne	Champagne	Sparkling
	Pinot Nero	Alto Adige	Dry red
	Saumer-Champigny	Loire	Dry red
	Volnay	Burgundy	Dry red
Quail eggs	Champagne	Champagne	Sparkling
	Crémant de Bourgogne	Burgundy	Sparkling
Quiche Lorraine	Bergerac	SW France	Dry white
	Bianco di Custoza	Italy	Dry white
	Chinon	Loire	Dry red
	Pinot Gris	Alsace	Dry white
	Riesling	Alsace	Dry white
Rabbit	Côtes de Duras	SW France	Dry red
	Brunello di Montalcino	Tuscany	Dry red
	Lagrein	Alto Adige	Dry red
	Pinot Noir	New World	Dry red
	Refosco	Grave del Friuli	Dry red
	St-Estèphe	Bordeaux	Dry red
Raclette	Chasselas	Switzerland	Dry white
	Côtes du Rhône	Rhône	Dry red
	Pinot Gris	Alsace	Dry white
	Refosco	Grave del Friuli	Dry red
	Valpolicella Classico	Italy	Dry red

FOOD	WINE NAME	REGION/COUNTRY	WINE STYLE
Ratatouille (or caponata)			
	Corbières	Languedoc	Dry red
	Minervois	Languedoc	Dry red
	Nero d'Avola	Sicily	Dry red
	Taurasi	Campania	Dry red
	Zinfandel	California	Dry red
Raspberry-based desserts (see DESSERTS with a base of Raspberry)			
Red mullet	Bordeaux rosé	Bordeaux	Dry rosé
	Mercurey	Burgundy	Dry red
	Sancerre	Loire/Centre	Dry white
Risotto alla Milanese			
	Bardolino	Veneto	Dry red
	Pinot Grigio	Italy	Dry white
	Gattinara	Piedmont	Dry red
	Salice Salento	Puglia	Dry red
	Soave	Veneto	Dry white
	Trebbiano d'Abruzzo	Abruzzo	Dry white
Risotto all Parmigiana (see also Cheese and Wine on page 104)			
	Bardolino	Veneto	Dry red
	Chianti	Tuscany	Dry red
	Dolcetto d'Alba	Piedmont	Dry red
Roquefort (see Cheese and Wine on page 104)			
Sachertorte	Champagne	Champagne	Sparkling
	Muscat de Beaumes-de-Venise	Rhône	Vin doux naturel
	Riesling Trockenbeerenauslese	Germany	Sweet white
SALAD, chef's (with eggs, tomatoes, and cheese)			
	Chardonnay	California	Dry white
	Soave	Veneto	Dry white
	Viognier	California	Dry white
SALAD, chicken	Beaujolais	Burgundy	Dry red
	Bordeaux rosé	Bordeaux	Dry rosé
	Chardonnay	California	Dry white
	Sauvignon Blanc	New Zealand	Dry white
	Torgiano	Umbria	Dry white
SALAD, green, with oil and vinegar dressing			
	Aligoté	Burgundy	Dry white
	Cheverny	Loire	Dry white
	Muscadet	Loire	Dry white
	Sancerre	Loire/Centre	Dry white
	Vinho Verde	Portugal	Dry white

FOOD	WINE NAME	REGION/COUNTRY	WINE STYLE
SALAD, potato	Bordeaux rosé	Bordeaux	Dry rosé
	Côtes de Provence	Provence	Dry rosé
SALAD, seafood	Soave	Veneto	Dry white
	Verdicchio	Italy	Dry white
SALAD, tomatoes	Barbera	Piedmont	Dry red
	Côtes de Provence	Provence	Dry rosé
	Sancerre	Loire	Dry white
SALAD, tuna (see Salade Niçoise)			
SALAD, Waldorf	Beaumes-de-Venise	Roussillon	Sweet white
	Chablis	Burgundy	Dry white
	Riesling VT	Alsace	Sweet white
SALADE, Niçoise	Bandol	Provence	Dry red or rosé
	Bellet	South of France	Dry red
	Côtes de Provence	Provence	Dry red or rosé
	Mourvèdre	France	Dry red
Salami	Barbera d'Asti	Italy	Dry red
	Bardolino	Italy	Dry red
	Montepulciano d'Abruzzo	Italy	Dry red
	Rosso Cònero	Italy	Dry red
	Tavel	Rhône	Dry rosé
	Zinfandel	California	Dry red
Salmon, cooked, cold			
	Chardonnay	Long Island	Dry white
	Coteaux d'Aix en Provence	Provence	Dry rosé
	Pinot Noir	Alsace	Dry red
Salmon and cream cheese bagels			
	Chablis	Burgundy	Dry white
	Champagne (brut)	Champagne	Sparkling
	Pinot Noir	Romania	Dry red
Salmon, poached, steamed, or lightly grilled			
	Chablis	Burgundy	Dry white
	Chinon	Loire	Dry red
	Condrieu	Rhône	Dry white
	Sancerre	Loire/Centre	Dry white
Salmon, smoked	Chablis (oaked)	Burgundy	Dry white
	Champagne (brut)	Champagne	Sparkling
	Chardonnay (oaked)	Long Island	Dry white
	Riesling	Alsace	Dry white
	Rully	Burgundy	Dry white

FOOD	WINE NAME	REGION/COUNTRY	WINE STYLE
Salt cod balls, deep-fried			
	Chinon	Loire	Dry red
	Port (white and chilled)	Portugal	Fortified white
	Rioja	Spain	Dry white/ red
Salt cod with garlic, oil, and cream			
	Côtes de Provence rosé	Provence	Dry rosé
	Mâcon	Burgundy	Dry white
	Sylvaner	Alsace	Dry white
Saltimbocca alla Romana			
	Barbera d'Asti	Piedmont	Dry red
	Rosso Cònero	Marches	Dry rosé
	Sangiovese	California	Dry red
Salsa (red and green)			
	Rioja	Spain	Dry white
	Sauvignon Blanc	New World	Dry white
	Vinho Verde	Portugal	Dry white
Sandwiches (see principal ingredient)			
Sardines, grilled	Gaillac	SW France	Dry white
	Greco di Tufo	Campania	Dry white
	Irouléguy	Basque	Dry red
	Orvieto	Italy	Dry white
	Vinho Verde	Portugal	Dry white
Sashimi	Riesling Kabinett	Germany	Dry white
	Sancerre	Loire	Dry white
	Sauvignon Blanc	New Zealand	Dry white
Satay	Pinot Gris	Alsace	Dry white
	Rully	Loire/Centre	Dry white
	Taurasi	Campania	Dry red
SAUCE, béarnaise	Frascati	Italy	Demi-sec white
	Riesling Kabinett	Germany	Dry white
	Sancerre	Loire/Centre	Dry white
	Vouvray	Loire	Demi-sec white
SAUCE, Bolognese	Cabernet Sauvignon	Australia	Dry red
	Merlot	Chile	Dry red
	Montepulciano d'Abruzzo	Abruzzo	Dry red
	Rosso Cònero	Marche	Dry red
SAUCE, chasseur (see Chicken chasseur)			
SAUCE, chili	Chardonnay (oaked)	New World	Dry white
	Côtes du Rhône	Rhône	Dry red
	Fitou	Languedoc	Dry red
	Shiraz	Australia	Dry red

FOOD	WINE NAME	REGION/COUNTRY	WINE STYLE
SAUCE, hollandaise			
	Bâtard-Montrachet	Burgundy	Dry white
	Chablis Grand Cru	Burgundy	Dry white
	Champagne	Champagne	Sparkling
SAUCE, horseradish			
	Riesling	Alsace	Dry white
	Sancerre	Loire	Dry white
	Shiraz	Australia	Dry red
SAUCE, mayonnaise			
	Arneis	Piedmont	Dry white
	Chablis (unoaked)	Burgundy	Dry white
	Champagne	Champagne	Sparkling
	Chardonnay (unoaked)	New World	Dry white
	Fiano	Campania	Dry white
SAUCE, mint	Champagne rosé	Champagne	Sparkling rosé
	Kékfrankos	Hungary	Dry red
	Margaux	Bordeaux	Dry red
	Mavrud	Bulgaria	Dry red
	Pommard	Burgundy	Dry red
	Vino Nobile di Montepulciano	Tuscany	Dry red
SAUCE, mustard	Chardonnay	Chile	Dry white
	Riesling	Alsace	Dry white
	(Tokay) Pinot Gris	Alsace	Dry white
SAUCE, peanut	Gewürztraminer	Alsace	Dry white
	Muscat	Alsace	Dry white
	Pinot Gris	Alsace	Dry white
SAUCE, pepper	Mourvèdre	SW France	Dry red
	Pomerol	Bordeaux	Dry red
	Pommard	Burgundy	Dry red
	Shiraz	Australia	Dry red
	Valpolicella	Veneto	Dry red
	Zinfandel	California	Dry red
SAUCE, red wine (use the same wine or grape that is being served with the dish)			
SAUCE, sweet and sour			
	Gewürztraminer	Alsace	Dry white
	Pinot Gris VT	Alsace	Dry white
	Taurasi	Campania	Dry red
	Vouvray	Loire	Semi-dry white
SAUCE, tomato	Bardolino	Veneto	Dry white
	Chianti	Tuscany	Dry red
	Malbec	Chile	Dry white
	Merlot	New World	Dry red

FOOD	WINE NAME	REGION/COUNTRY	WINE STYLE
SAUCE, vinaigrette	Arneis	Piedmont	Dry white
	Reuilly	Loire/Centre	Dry white
	Vinho Verde	Portugal	Dry white
SAUCE, white wine (use same wine or grape that is being served with the dish)			
Sauerbraten	Baden Spätburgunder	Germany	Dry red
	Barbaresco	Piedmont	Dry red
	Morgon	Beaujolais	Dry red
	Pinot Nero	Alto Adige	Dry red
Sausage and mash	Corbières	Languedoc	Dry red
	Fitou	Languedoc	Dry red
	Gigondas	Rhône	Dry red
	Kékfrankos	Hungary	Dry red
	Zinfandel	California	Dry red
Scallops, grilled	Graves	Bordeaux	Dry white
	Muscadet	Loire	Dry white
	Savennières	Loire	Dry white
Scallops in cream and tarragon sauce			
	Bâtard-Montrachet	Burgundy	Dry white
	Champagne	Champagne	Sparkling
	Meursault	Burgundy	Dry white
	Sauvignon Blanc	New Zealand	Dry white
Scrambled eggs with smoked salmon			
	Cava	Spain	Sparkling
	Champagne (rosé)	Champagne	Sparkling rosé
	Chardonnay (oaked)	Chile	Dry white
	Petit Chablis	Burgundy	Dry white
Seafood dishes	Bianco di Custoza	Veneto	Dry white
	Sancerre	Loire/Centre	Dry white
	Sauvignon Blanc	France or New World	Dry white
	Verdicchio	Italy	Dry white
	Vermentino	Liguria	Dry white
Shepherd's pie	Bourgueil	Loire	Dry red
	Buzet	SW France	Dry red
	Pomerol	Bordeaux	Dry red
Shrimp cocktail	Bergerac	SW France	Dry white
	Muscadet	Loire	Dry white
	Sauvignon Blanc	New World	Dry white
Snails (see Escargots)			
Sole meunière	Bellet	Provence	Dry white
	Chablis	Burgundy	Dry white
	Condrieu	Rhône	Dry white
	Riesling	Alsace	Dry white

FOOD	WINE NAME	REGION/COUNTRY	WINE STYLE
Sorbets (see also DESSERTS with the appropriate fruit base)			
	Champagne	Champagne	Sparkling
	Pineau des Charentes	Cognac	Vin de liqueur
Soufflé, broccoli and cheese			
	Champagne	Champagne	Sparkling
	Muscadet sur Lie	Loire	Dry white
	Rully	Burgundy	Dry white
	Sauvignon Blanc	New Zealand	Dry white
Soufflé, seafood (see Seafood dishes)			
Soufflé, spinach	Champagne (Blanc de Blancs)	Champagne	Sparkling
	Chardonnay	New World	Dry white
	Frascati Superiore	Italy	Dry white
	Mâcon	Burgundy	Dry white
	St-Véran	Burgundy	Dry white
	Vin du Jura	Jura	Dry white
Southern fried chicken			
	Bordeaux Supérieur	Bordeaux	Dry red
	Buzet	SW France	Dry red
	Shiraz	Australia	Dry red
Spices and herbs (see part 2)			
Squid cooked in their own juices			
	Ajaccio	Corsica	Dry red
	Côtes de Bordeaux	Bordeaux	Dry white
	Gaillac	France	Dry white
	Mâcon	Burgundy	Dry white
	Torgiano	Umbria	Dry white
	Valdepeñas	Spain	Dry red
Steak, sirloin	Barolo	Piedmont	Dry red
	Cabernet Sauvignon	California	Dry red
	Chianti Classico	Tuscany	Dry red
	Merlot	New World	Dry red
	Pomerol	Bordeaux	Dry red
	Shiraz	Australia	Dry red
	Torgiano	Umbria	Dry red
Steak, sirloin, with wild mushrooms			
	Cabernet Sauvignon	California	Dry red
	Chinon	Loire	Dry red
	Mercurey	Burgundy	Dry red
	Merlot	New World	Dry red
	Pomerol	Bordeaux	Dry red
Steak and kidney pie			
	Buzet	SW France	Dry red
	Cahors	SW France	Dry red
	Beaujolias	Burgundy	Dry red
	Valpolicella	Veneto	Dry red

FOOD	WINE NAME	REGION/COUNTRY	WINE STYLE
Steak tartare	Cahors	SW France	Dry red
	Cornas	Rhône	Dry red
	Crozes-Hermitage	Rhône	Dry red
	St-Amour	Beaujolais	Dry red
	St-Véran	Burgundy	Dry red
Stews and casseroles, red meat			
	Amarone della Valpolicella	Veneto	Dry red
	Brunello di Montalcino	Tuscany	Dry red
	Cahors	SW France	Dry red
	Copertino	Italy	Dry red
	Cornas	Rhône	Dry red
	Pauillac	Bordeaux	Dry red
	Periquita	Portugal	Dry red
	Salice Salento	Puglia	Dry red
	Shiraz	Australia	Dry red
	Vino Nobile di Montepulciano	Tuscany	Dry red
Stilton (see Cheese and Wine on page 105)			
Stir-fries	Pinot Grigio	Italy	Dry white
	Rieslinsg	Alsace	Dry white
	Sauvignon Blanc	New Zealand	Dry white
Sushi	Riesling	Alsace/Germany	Dry white
	Rioja	Spain	Dry white
	Sancerre	Loire	Dry white
	Viognier	Rhône	Dry white
Sweetbreads	Côte de Beaune	Burgundy	Dry red
	Côtes de Provence rosé	Provence	Dry rosé
	Sylvaner	Alsace	Dry white
Sweet potatoes, candied			
	Crozes-Hermitage	Rhône	Dry white
	Monbazillac	SW France	Sweet white
	Viognier	California	Dry white
Swordfish	Chardonnay	New World	Dry white
	Côte-Rôtie	Rhône	Dry white
	Marsanne	New World	Dry white
	Meursault	Chablis	Dry white
Tabbouleh	Bandol rosé	Provence	Dry rosé
	Bellet rosé	Provence	Dry rosé
	Côtes du Jura	Jura	Dry red
Tandoori	Cabernet Sauvignon	California	Dry red
	Gewürztraminer	Alsace	Dry white
	Shiraz	Australia	Dry red

FOOD	WINE NAME	REGION/COUNTRY	WINE STYLE
Tapas	Amontillado	Spain	Fortified red
	Bandol rosé	Provence	Dry rosé
	Fino sherry	Spain	Fortified white
	Sancerre	Loire/Centre	Dry white
Tapenade	Lirac rosé	Rhône	Dry rosé
	Palette	Provence	Dry red
	Patrimonio	Corsica	Dry red
	Nero di Troia	Umbria	Dry red
Taramasalata	Chablis	Burgundy	Dry white
	Muscadet	Loire	Dry white
	Patrimonio	Corsica	Dry white
	Sancerre rosé	Loire/Centre	Dry rosé
Tarte tatin (see DESSERTS with a base of Apple)			
Tempura	Sancerre	Loire/Centre	Dry white
	Chablis	Burgundy	Dry white
	Orvieto	Italy	Dry white
Thai food	Chablis	Burgundy	Dry white
	Colombard	New World	Dry white
	Gewürztraminer VT	Alsace	Medium-dry white
	Sauvignon Blanc	France or New World	Dry white
	Tokaji	Hungary	Dry white
	Vin de Paille	Jura	Vin doux naturel
Tiramisu (see also DESSERTS with a base of Coffee)			
	Muscat de Rivesaltes	Roussillon	Vin doux naturel
	Passito	Italy	Sweet white
	Sauternes	Bordeaux	Sweet white
Toad-in-the-hole	Merlot	France or New World	Dry red
	Periquita	Portugal	Dry red
	Navarra	Spain	Dry red
	Shiraz	Australia	Dry red
Tongue	Bergerac	SW France	Dry red
	Cahors	SW France	Dry red
	Chardonnay	Chile	Dry white
Treacle tart	Champagne	Champagne	Sparkling
	Monbazillac	SW France	Sweet white
	Moscatel de Valencia	Spain	Sweet white
Trifle	Cadillac	Bordeaux	Sweet white
	Crémant de Bourgogne	Burgundy	Sparkling
	Sémillon	New World	Sweet white

FOOD	WINE NAME	REGION/COUNTRY	WINE STYLE
Tripe	Meursault	Burgundy	Dry white
	Pacherenc du Vic-Bihl	SW France	Dry white
	Pouilly-Fumé	Loire	Dry white
Trout	Entre-Deux-Mers	Bordeaux	Dry white
	Riesling	Alsace	Dry white
	Rully	Burgundy	Dry white
Truffles, black and white			
	Barbaresco	Italy	Dry red
	Cahors	SW France	Dry red
	Champagne (Blanc de Blancs)	Champagne	Sparkling
	Chassagne-Montrachet	Burgundy	Dry white
	Echezeaux	Burgundy	Dry red
	Pomerol	Bordeaux	Dry red
	Vosne-Romanée	Burgundy	Dry red
Tuna	Côtes du Jura	Jura	Dry white
	Côtes de Provence rosé	Provence	Dry rosé
	Merlot	New World	Dry red
	Saumur	Loire	Dry red
Turbot	Chablis	Burgundy	Dry white
	Graves	Bordeaux	Dry white
	Minervois	Languedoc-Roussillon	Dry red
	Pinot Gris	Alsace	Dry white
	Sauvignon Blanc	New World	Dry white
Turkey, roast with all the trimmings			
	Chardonnay	California	Dry red
	Châteauneuf-du-Pape	Rhône	Dry red
	Vosne-Romanée	Burgundy	Dry red
	Zinfandel	California	Dry red
Vanilla (see DESSERTS with a base of Vanilla)			
	Arbois	Jura	Dry rosé
	Bergerac	SW France	Dry white
	Muscat de Rivesaltes	Roussillon	Vin doux natural
Veal, roast or veal cutlets			
	Côte de Beaune	Burgundy	Dry red
	Graves	Bordeaux	Dry white
	Lagrein	Alto Adige	Dry red
	Margaux	Bordeaux	Dry red
	Pinot Gris	Alsace	Dry white
	Riesling	Alsace	Dry white
Vegetables, grilled or roasted			
	Beaujolais-Villages	Burgundy	Dry red
	Cassis	Provence	Dry white
	Corbières	Languedoc	Dry white
	Palette	Provence	Dry white
	Rueda	Spain	Dry white
	St-Joseph	Rhône	Dry white

FOOD	WINE NAME	REGION/COUNTRY	WINE STYLE
Vegetables, raw	Bardolino	Veneto	Dry red
	Beaujolais	Burgundy	Dry red
	Pinot Blanc	Alsace	Dry white
	Pinot Grigio	Italy	Dry white
	Sauvignon Blanc	France or New World	Dry white
Venison with cranberries or juniper berries			
	Amarone della Valopolicella	Veneto	Dry red
	Bandol	Provence	Dry red
	Cabernet Sauvignon/Cinsault	Lebanon	Dry red
	Chambertin	Burgundy	Dry red
	Mourvèdre	New World	Dry red
	Shiraz	Australia	Dry red
	Zinfandel	California	Dry red
Vichyssoise	Bergerac	SW France	Dry white
	Sancerre	Loire/Centre	Dry white
	Vacqueyras	Rhône	Dry white
White fish	Chardonnay (oaked)	California	Dry white
	Chassagne-Montrachet	Burgundy	Dry white
	Muscadet sur Lie	Loire	Dry white
	Sauvignon Blanc	France or New World	Dry white
	Vouvray	Loire	Dry white
White fish, grilled	Chenin Blanc	New World	Dry white
	Orvieto	Umbria	Dry white
	Riesling	Alsace	Dry white
	Trebbiano	Italy or New World	Dry white
	Viognier	Rhône, Italy	Dry white
Wild boar	Bandol	Provence	Dry red
	Cabernet Sauvignon/Cinsault	Lebanon	Dry red
	Gigondas	Rhône	Dry red
	Pomerol	Bordeaux	Dry red
	Pommard	Burgundy	Dry red
	Shiraz	Australia	Dry red
	Vino Nobile de Montepulciano	Tuscany	Dry red
Wiener schnitzel	Chinon	Loire	Dry red
	Grüner Veltliner	Austria	Dry white
	Sancerre	Loire	Dry white
	Weissburgunder	Germany	Dry red

WINE TO FOOD INDEX

WINE	REGION	WINE STYLE	FOOD MATCHES
Ajaccio	Corsica	Red	Lamb crown roast, Roast pork, Spicy sausages, Squid cooked in their own juices
		Rosé	Polenta, Bouillabaisse, Ratatouille
Alenquir	Portugal	Dry white	Grilled sardines, Minestrone, Salt cod balls, Tapas
Aligoté	Burgundy	Dry white	Cod, Blue cheese dip, Escargots à la bourguignonne, oysters and mussels, Green salad with oil and vinegar dressing, Tomato-sauce-based dishes, Trout
Amarone della Valpolicella	Veneto, Italy	Dry red	Rissotto alla Parmigiana, Red meat stews and casseroles
Amontillado sherry	Spain	Fortified red	Almonds, walnuts, hazelnuts, and peanuts, Chorizo, Manchego cheese and ewe's milk cheeses, Olives and tapas, Wild boar
Anjou	Loire, France	Dry red	Bacon and ham dishes, Charcuterie, Pot-au-feu, White meats
Arbois	Jura, France	Red Rosé White	Game, Spicy meat dishes, Sushi Chutney, Lamb dishes, Onion tart Andouillette, grilled with mustard, Brussels sprouts, Cauliflower cheese, Chicken curry, Cognac-based desserts, Haddock and white fish dishes, Kebabs
Asti Spumante	Italy	Sparkling	Chestnut-, mint-, or fruit-based desserts, Christmas pudding, Meringues
Baden Spätburgunder	Germany	Dry red	Goulash, Beef stews and casseroles, Sauerbraten
Bairrada	Portugal	Dry red	Garlic-based sauces, Haggis, Roast pork, Roast vegetables in oil and herbs

WINE	REGION	WINE STYLE	FOOD MATCHES
Bandol	Provence	Red	Barbecued meats, Boeuf en daube, Ravioli Niçoise, Roasted vegetables, Venison with cranberries or juniper berry sauce, Wild boar
		Rosé	Anchovies or anchovy paste, Fish-and-chips, Roasted or stuffed peppers, Pipperada, Salade Niçoise, Tabbouleh, Tapas
Banyuls	Roussillon	Vin doux naturel	Chocolate-, coffee-, or strawberry-based desserts, Christmas pudding
Barbaresco	Piedmont, Italy	Dry red	Cassoulet, Eggplant with Parmesan, Fish in red wine and red wine sauce dishes, Sauerbraten, Truffles, black and white
Barbera d'Asti	Piedmont, Italy	Dry red	Anchovy paste and dips, Bolognese sauce, lasagne and pizza, Osso buco, Pasta with carbonara or pesto sauce, Pasta with meat and béchamel sauce, Prociutto, Risottos, especially mushroom, Salami-based dishes, Saltimbocca alla Romana, Tomato salad
Bardolino	Veneto, Italy	Dry red	Antipasti and charcuterie, Melon with Parma ham, Pasta with carbonara sauce, Pasta dishes with meat and béchamel sauce, Raw vegetables, Risotto alla Parmigiana and other risottos, Salami-based dishes
Barolo	Piedmont, Italy	Dry red	Beef bourguignon, boeuf en daube, brasato al Barolo, Eggplant with Parmesan, Game, grouse and pheasant, Sirloin steak
Barsac	Bordeaux, France	Sweet white	Caramel- and fruit-based desserts, Pâtés and terrines, Spicy ethnic foods
Bâtard-Montrachet	Burgundy, France	Dry white	Hollandaise sauce, Most butter- or cream-based sauces, Scallops in cream and tarragon sauce, White fish dishes
Beaujolais	Burgundy, France	Dry red	Bacon and ham, Charcuterie and boudin blanc (white pudding), Chicken salad, Grilled, roasted, and raw vegetables, Hamburgers, Kidneys, Macaroni and cheese, Raspberry-based desserts, Refried beans, Mexican and chili dishes

WINE	REGION	WINE STYLE	FOOD MATCHES
Bellet	Provence, France	Rosé	Pissaladière (onion, olive, and anchovy tart), Roasted or stuffed peppers, Tabbouleh
		White	Octopus, Salade Niçoise, Sole meunière
Bergerac	Southwest France	Red	Bean and pasta soup, Fried fish, Potted or jugged hare, Lancashire hotpot, Melon with Parma ham, Pot-au-feu, Roasted meats, both white and red, Tongue
		White	Cassis-based desserts, Fish-and-chips, Quiche Lorraine, Prawn cocktail, Vichyssoise
Bianco di Custoza	Italy	Dry white	Pasta with spinach and ricotta, Pizza with seafood and other seafood dishes, Quiche Lorraine, Risotto alla Parmigiana
Bianco di Scandiano	Italy	Dry white	Melon with Parma ham, Pasta with cream and cheese sauces, Poached oysters in vegetable broth, Seafood dishes
Black Muscat	California	Sweet white	Cherry-based desserts, Chocolate, Caramelized oranges
Blanquette de Limoux	Languedoc, France	Sparkling	Apricot- and cherry-based desserts, Lemon chicken, Sweet and savory soufflés
Bonnes-Mares	Burgundy, France	Dry red	Beef and chicken potpies, Dry sausages, Hare, game, grouse, and partridge, Mushroom and red wine sauces, Roast duck or goose, Savory cheese dishes
Bordeaux and Bordeaux Supérieur		Red	Barbecued red meats, Cold lamb or beef, Croque Monsieur or Madame, Meat fondue, Southern fried chicken
		Rosé	Aioli, Beef Strognanoff, Chicken salad, Indian food with spicy yogurt sauces
		White	Barbecued fish, Haggis, Light, white meat dishes, Lobster, Meat loaf, Roast chicken, Savory crêpes
Bourgueil	Loire	Dry red	Asparagus, Baked beans, Baked ham with pineapple, Chicken chasseur, Smoked eels, Escargots à la bourguignonne, Shepherd's pie, Stuffed cabbage

WINE	REGION	WINE STYLE	FOOD MATCHES
Brouilly	Beaujolais, Burgundy	Dry red	Beef bourguignon, Cold meats, Grilled and roasted vegetables, Omelet with tomato, quiches and pizzas
Brunello di Montalcino	Tuscany, Italy	Dry red	Eggplant with Parmesan, Oxtail, Red meat stews and casseroles, Red-wine-sauce-based dishes
Buzet	Southwest France	Dry red	Bean and pasta soup, Buffalo wings, Gazpacho, Pigeon, Potted or jugged hare, Shepherd's pie, Southern fried chicken, Steak and kidney pie
Cabernet Sauvignon			All beef dishes, Herbs: thyme, rosemary, and mint
	Argentina		Chili con carne, spiced pork and sausages
	Australia		Bolognese sauce, Kangaroo, Roast lamb with mint sauce
	California		Hamburgers, Meat loaf, Sirloin steak
	Chile		Charcuterie
	New World		Haggis and kidneys, Red-wine-sauce-based dishes
Cabernet Sauvignon/ Cinsault	Lebanon	Dry red	Barbecued meats, Couscous, Lamb with Herbes de Provence, Pizza bolognese, Venison with cranberry or juniper berry sauce, Wild boar
Cadillac	Bordeaux, France	Sweet white	Blue cheese dip, Cheesecake, Pineapple-based desserts, Trifle
Cahors	Southwest France	Dry red	Cassoulet, Confit du canard, Duck à l'orange, Red meat stews and casseroles, Refried beans and other Mexican dishes, Steak and kidney pie, Steak tartare, Tarragon chicken, Tongue, Truffles, black and white
Cassis	Provence, France	Dry white	Grilled and roasted vegetables, Light lamb dishes
Cava	Spain	Sparkling	Custard dessesrts, Quiches, scrambled eggs with smoked salmon, Tapas

WINE	REGION	WINE STYLE	FOOD MATCHES
Chablis	Burgundy, France	Dry white	Avocado, Bagels with salmon and cream cheese, Crab, escargots à la bourguignonne, moules marinières, Gougère, Jambon persillé, Salmon, sole meunière, plaice, and other white fish dishes, Taramasalata, Tempura, Thai food, White-wine-sauce-based dishes
		Grand Cru Premier Cru Oaked Unoaked	Almonds, Carrot soup, Clam chowder Chicken in cream and morels sauce Smoked salmon Mayonnaise, Choucroute garni
Chacoli de Guetaria	Spain	Dry white	Chorizo and other dried spicy sausages, Pipperada, Spicy casseroles
Chambertin	Burgundy, France	Dry red	Grouse and guinea fowl, Venison with cranberry or juniper berry sauce
Chambolle-Musigny	Burgundy, France	Dry red	Meat and mushroom dishes, Pheasant, Omelet with truffles
Champagne	Champagne, France	Sparkling	Everything! Acras, Bagels with salmon and cream cheese, Blinis and buttermilk pancakes, Caesar salad, Cheesecake, Cheeses, especially blue and goat, Chocolate-, coffee-, Cognac-, and fruit-based desserts, Christmas pudding, Guacamole, Ice cream and sorbets, Indian food, Japanese food, Kedgeree, Kippers, Lobster, prawns, and scallops in cream and tarragon, Omelets, eggs Benedict, and quail eggs, Quail, Red cabbage with apples, Soufflés with broccoli and cheese, spinach, and chocolate, Truffles, black and white
		Blanc de Blancs Brut	Escargots, Foie gras, Liver Avocado, Beef Wellington, Smoked salmon
		Demi-sec Non-vintage Rosé	Caramel-based desserts, Sweet crêpes Caviar, Chinese food, Indian food Carpaccio, Cassis-based desserts, Lamb with mint sauce, Lemon chicken, Scrambled eggs with smoked salmon
Chardonnay Oaked		Dry white	Kippers, Roast chicken, Smoked salmon, White fish dishes

WINE	REGION	WINE STYLE	FOOD MATCHES
Chardonnay cont'd.			
Burgundy			Artichokes, Asparagus, Bacon, Carrot soup and pea and ham soup, Chef's salad and chicken salad, Cheese fondue, Chicken in cream and morel sauce, Cold salmon and smoked salmon, Croque Monsieur or Madame, Omelet with cheese and eggs Benedict, Pasta with clam sauce, Roast pork, Tongue, Soufflé with spinach, White-sauce-based dishes
New World			Blackened fish, Bruschetta, Caesar salad, Clam chowder, Corn bread, corn chowder, and corn-on-the-cob, Fish cakes and grilled bass, Guacamole, Indian food, Kangaroo, Lancashire hotpot, Lobster dishes, Mayonnaise, Mustard sauce, Pesto sauce, Scrambled eggs with smoked salmon
Chassagne-Montrachet	Burgundy, France	Dry white	Mushrooms, Prawns and delicate seafood dishes, Tarragon, Truffles, black and white, White sauces
Chasselas	Alsace or Switzerland	Dry white	Cheese fondue, Chinese food, Crab, Mild curry dishes, Pasta with clam sauce, Raclette
Châteauneuf-du-Pape	Rhône, France	Dry red	Basque chicken and coq au vin, Caviar, Goose stuffed with prunes, Gratin dauphinois, Oxtail, Partridge, Roast duck, Roast turkey with traditional trimmings
Chénas	Burgundy	Dry red	See **Beaujolais**
Chenin Blanc	Loire or New World	Dry white	Chestnut-based desserts, Grilled fish, Indian food, Lemon chicken and other poultry dishes, Oriental dishes containing soy sauce, garlic, ginger, and honey, Vegetable and fruit salads
Cheverny	Loire	Dry white	Green salad with oil and vinegar dressing, Salade Niçoise, Vinaigrette sauce
Chianti	Tuscany, Italy	Dry red, Red	Borscht, Bresaola and carpaccio, Goose stuffed with prunes or other fruit, Hamburgers, Lasagne, Omelet with tomato, Pizza Bolognese, Roast pork, Sirloin steak

WINE	REGION	WINE STYLE	FOOD MATCHES
Chianti cont'd.		White	Chicken dishes, Light pasta dishes, Minestrone, Pasta with spinach and ricotta
Chinon	Loire, France	Dry red	Asparagus, Baked ham and charcuterie, Melon with Parma ham, Poached, steamed, or lightly grilled salmon, Quiche Lorraine, Salt cod balls, Sirloin steak with wild mushrooms, Wiener schnitzel
Chiroubles	Burgundy, France	Dry red	See **Beaujolais**
Clos de Vougeot	Burgundy, France	Dry red	Beef bourguignon, Châteaubriand, Game
Colli Berici Pinot Bianco	Italy	Dry white	Pasta with spring vegetables, Seafood dishes
Colli Orientali del Friuli	Italy	Dry red	Lamb with Herbes de Provence, Lemon chicken, Light pasta dishes
Colombard	France	Dry white	Melon with Parma ham, Poached white fish dishes, Most salads, Thai food
Condrieu	Rhône, France	Dry white	Ceviche, Curry, Indian food, Lobster, Poached, steamed, or lightly grilled salmon, Sole meunière
Copertino	Puglia, Italy	Dry red	Borscht, Heavy pasta dishes, Red meat stews and casseroles, Spicy and dried sausages
Corbières	Languedoc, France	Dry red	Cassoulet, Chicken in cream and morel sauce, Basque chicken, and coq au vin, Chorizo, Eggplant, Hare, Herring, Kippers, Minestrone, Onion tart, Pork chops, Ratatouille, Roasted meats, especially beef, Sausage and mash
Cornas	Rhône, France	Dry red	Hare, Red meat stews and casseroles, Steak tartare
Corton	Burgundy, France	Dry red	Duck, Game, Red meat dishes, Red-wine-sauce-based dishes
Corton-Charlemagne	Burgundy, France	Dry red	Foie gras, Scallops, Veal dishes, White oily fish dishes, White wine sauces with morels

WINE	REGION	WINE STYLE	FOOD MATCHES
Côte de Beaune	Burgundy, France	Dry red	Meat fondue, Sweetbreads, Pizza Bolognese, Veal dishes
Côte de Brouilly	Burgundy, France	Dry red	See **Beaujolais**
Côte-Rotie	Rhône, France	Dry red	Bean and pasta soup, Roasted meats, game, and poultry, Smoked meats
Coteaux d'Aix en Provence	Provence, France	Dry rosé or white	Cold salmon, Lamb chops, Red mullet, Salade Niçoise
Coteaux du Layon	Loire, France	Sweet white	Boudin blanc (white pudding), Cheesecake, Fruit-based desserts and fruit salad
Côtes de Bourg	Bordeaux, France	Dry red	Casseroles and stews, Heavy bean and rice dishes, Lamb shoulder, Pasta in tomato and meat sauces
Côtes de Duras	Southwest France	Dry red	Casseroles and stews, Rabbit and hare, Roast pork dishes
Côtes du Jura	Jura, France	Red	Corn bread and cornmeal-based dishes, Roasted meats, especially lamb and game, Tabbouleh
		White	Soufflé with spinach
Côtes de Provence	Provence	Red	Anchovy and olive pastes, Brussels sprouts and baked or roasted vegetable dishes, Duck à l'orange, Mediterranean dishes
		Rosé	Blanquette de veau, Kebabs, Lamb chops and lamb with Herbes de Provence, Liver and sweetbreads, Paella, Polenta, Potato and tuna salad, Ratatouille, Salt cod with garlic, oil, and cream, Seafood pizza
		White	Black pudding, Olives
Côtes du Rhône	Rhône, France	Dry red	Black pudding, Charcuterie, Cheese fondue and raclette, Chicken curry and coq au vin, Chili con carne, Cornish pasties, Meat fondue, Gougère, Mexican food, Moussaka, Omelet with mushrooms, Red-wine-sauce-based dishes, Risotto alla Milanese, Salade Niçoise

WINE	REGION	WINE STYLE	FOOD MATCHES
Côtes du Roussillon	Roussillon	Dry red	Buffalo wings, Escargots à la Bourguignonne
Crémant de Bourgogne	Burgundy	Sparkling	Banana-based desserts, Blinis, Carrot cake, Trifle
Crémant de Loire	Loire	Sparkling	Buttermilk pancakes, Creamy fish dishes, Custard-based dishes
Crépy	Savoie	Dry white	Cheese fondue and raclette, Chinese food, Crab, Mild curry dishes, Pasta with clam sauce
Crozes-Hermitage	Rhône	Red White	Pigeon and pheasant, Steak tartare, Stuffed cabbage, Tarragon chicken Candied sweet potatoes, Choucroute garni, Crab, Curried tomato soup, Osso buco
Dão	Portugal	Dry red	Lamb with Herbes de Provence, Moussaka and eggplant dishes, Pork dishes
Dolcetto d'Alba	Piedmont, Italy	Dry red	Antipasti, Black pudding, Fonduta, Osso buco, Pasta with meat sauces, Risotto alla Parmigiana
Echezeaux	Burgundy	Dry red	Venison, game, and roasted meats, Mushrooms and mushroom sauces, Rich wine sauces, Truffles, black and white. See also **Vosne-Romanée**
Entre-Deux-Mers	Bordeaux	Dry white	Barbecued and blackened fish, Chicken chasseur, Crab, Herring, Kippers, Moules marinières and oysters
L'Etoile	Jura	Dry white	Asparagus in cream sauce, Clam chowder, Gratin dauphinois, Iles flottantes
Falerno del Massico	Campania, Italy	Dry white	Antipasti, Pasta with Parmesan sauce, Veal dishes
Fino sherry	Spain	Fortified white	Almonds, Anchovies or anchovy paste, Olives, Tapas
Fitou	Languedoc	Dry red	Andouillette, Chili sauce and Mexican dishes, Lancashire hotpot, Sausage and mash

WINE	REGION	WINE STYLE	FOOD MATCHES
Fleurie	Burgundy	Dry red	See **Beaujolais**
Frascati Superiore	Italy	Demi-sec white	Béarnaise sauce, Fettuccine Alfredo, Soufflé with spinach
Fronsac	Bordeaux	Dry red	Black pudding, Basque chicken, Guinea fowl, Hare
Furmint	Hungary	Dry white	Curry dishes, Goulash, Houmus, Poultry casseroles
Gaillac	Southwest France	Dry white	Crème caramel or brûlée, Grilled sardines, Mackerel with butter and spring onions, Squid cooked in their own juices
Gavi	Italy	Dry white	Creamy pasta dishes, Mushroom risotto, Oysters
Gevrey-Chambertin	Burgundy	Dry red	Coq au vin, Mint sauce, Mushroom soufflés, tarts, and risottos, Roast duck and duck à l'orange
Gewürztraminer Vendanges Tardives	Alsace	Semi-sec white	Baeckaoffa, Barbecued meats, Brown-sugar-based desserts, Chinese food, especially chicken or other meats in sweet and sour sauce, Creamed onions, Curried tomato soup, Duck à l'orange, Indian food, especially lamb curry, Pot roast, Red cabbage with apples, Roast pork in mustard sauce, Sauerbraten, Smoked fish, Thai food
Gigondas	Rhône, France	Dry red	Beef bourguignon and goulash, Goose stuffed with prunes, Octopus, Osso buco, Sausage and mash, Wild boar
Grave del Fruili	Italy	Sparkling	Light pasta dishes, especially cream- or cheese-based, Seafood dishes
Graves	Bordeaux	Dry red, Red White	Duck à l'orange, Fish in red wine, Roast beef or steak, Steak and kidney pie Grilled scallops, Haddock, Mackerel with butter and spring onions, Veal, White-wine-sauce-based dishes
Greco di Tufo	Campania, Italy	Dry white	Anchovies or anchovy paste, Green salad, Olives and olive paste, Pasta in tomato and cheese sauce, Risotto

WINE	REGION	WINE STYLE	FOOD MATCHES
Grenache	France or New World	Dry red	Andouillette and Merguez sausages, Beef casseroles, Chili con carne and other spicy meat dishes, Steak tartare
Gros Plant	Loire/Nantes	Dry white	Avocados or guacamole, Mackerel with green gooseberry sauce and other oily fish dishes, Raw vegetables and salads, Sashimi
Grüner Veltliner	Austria	Sweet white	Chinese food, Roast pork, Wiener schnitzel
Hermitage	Rhône	Dry red	Beef Wellington, Boeuf en daube and other red meat stews and casseroles, Grouse, Lamb shoulder
Irouléguy	Southwest France	Dry red	Barbecued meats, Basque chicken, Chorizo
Juliénas	Burgundy	Dry red	See **Beaujolais**
Kékfrankos	Hungary	Dry red	Beef bourguignon and beef Stroganoff, Moussaka, Sausage and mash
Lirac	Rhône	Red Rosé	Barbecued meats Lamb chops, Tapenade
Loupiac	Bordeaux	Sweet white	Bread and butter pudding, Chestnut-, fruit-, and raspberry-based desserts and fruit salad or compote, Iles flottantes
Mâcon	Burgundy	Dry white	Cheese fondue, Fish-and-chips, Pasta with carbonara sauce, Roasted or stuffed peppers, Salt cod with garlic, oil, and cream, Squid cooked their own juices
Madeira	Spain	Fortified red	Almonds, walnuts, hazelnuts, and peanuts, Christmas pudding, Marzipan desserts
Madiran	Southwest France	Dry red	Basque chicken, Pea and ham soup, Roast duck
Malbec	Bordeaux and New World	Dry red	Beef Wellington, Empanadas, Roast lamb
Manzanilla sherry	Spain	Fortified white	Almonds, walnuts, hazelnuts, and peanuts, Garlic-based sauces, Gazpacho, Olives

WINE	REGION	WINE STYLE	FOOD MATCHES
Margaux	Bordeaux	Dry red	Châteaubriand, Goose stuffed with prunes or other fruit, Roast lamb with mint sauce, Veal dishes
Marsanne	Rhône Valley and New World	Dry white	Coconut-based dishes, Curry dishes and curried tomato soup, White fish in creamy sauces
Mavrud	Bulgaria	Dry red	Beef Stroganoff, goulash, hotpots, and casseroles, Roast lamb with mint sauce
Médoc	Bordeaux	Dry red	Chicken chasseur, Grilled meats, Lamb dishes, Liver, Roast pork and chicken
Mercurey	Burgundy	Dry red	Charcuterie, Ham and bacon dishes, Macaroni and cheese, Red mullet, Sirloin steak with wild mushrooms, Toad-in-the-hole
Merlot	Bordeaux and New World	Dry red	Beef Stroganoff, Beef Wellington, Bolognese sauce, pizza and hearty pasta dishes, Confit de canard, Empanadas, Sirloin steak
Meursault	Burgundy	Dry white	Asparagus, Beef Stroganoff, Corn chowder, Creamy, buttery dishes, Eggs Benedict, Guacamole, Lobster dishes and scallops in cream and tarragon sauce, Tripe, White-sauce-based dishes
Minervois	Languedoc-Roussillon	Dry red	Andouillette, grilled with mustard, Blanquette de veau, Grilled meats with garlic and herbs, Hare and rabbit, Ratatouille
Monbazillac	Southwest France	Sweet white	Bread and butter pudding, Candied sweet potatoes, Cheesecake, Foie gras, Fruit-based desserts, Goat cheese and blue cheeses, Melon with port, Pumpkin pie, Thai dishes, Treacle tart
Montepulciano d'Abruzzo	Abruzzo, Italy	Dry red	Bolognese sauce, pizza, and pasta dishes with meat and béchamel sauce, Lancashire hotpot, Salami-based dishes, Toad-in-the-hole
Montravel	Southwest France	Dry white	Baked ham with pineapple, Blue cheeses, Chinese food, Honey-based sauces and desserts, Seafood dishes

WINE	REGION	WINE STYLE	FOOD MATCHES
Morgon	Burgundy	Dry red	See **Beaujolais**
Moscatel de Valencia	Spain	Sweet white	Almond biscuits, Fruit-based desserts, Treacle tart
Moulin-à-Vent	Burgundy	Dry red	See **Beaujolais**
Mourvèdre	France or New World	Dry red	Barbecued meats, Cassoulet, Cranberry sauce, Pepper sauce, Tarragon chicken, Venison with cranberry or juniper berries
Muscadet and Muscadet sur Lie	Loire	Dry white	Blanquette de veau, Crab, scallops, oysters, prawn cocktail, and moules et frîtes, Egg dishes such as soufflés and quiches, Fish cakes, Green salad with oil and vinegar dressing, Mackerel with green gooseberry sauce and other oily fish dishes, Taramasalata, White fish dishes, White-wine-sauce-based dishes
Muscat de Beaumes de Venise	Rhône	Vin doux naturel	Baclava, Chocolate-based desserts, especially sachertorte, Fruit-, ginger-, and mint-based desserts, Ice cream, Stewed fruit, Waldorf salad
Muscat de Rivesaltes	Roussillon	Vin doux naturel	Apricot-, cassis-, ginger-, orange-, and pineapple-based desserts, Chicken in sweet and sour sauce, Dried fruits such as figs and raisins, fresh grapes, and fruit compote and salad, Iles flottantes and meringues, Sweet crêpes, Tiramisu
Moscatel de Setúbal	Portugal	Sweet white	Almonds, grilled and salted, Baclava, Caramel- and chocolate-based desserts
Moscato Spumante	Italy	Sparkling	Fruit-based desserts, fruit compote and salad, Caramel- and chocolate-based desserts
Naoussa	Greece	Dry red	Eggplant puree, Greek food, especially kleftiko and moussaka
Navarra	Spain	Dry red	Chorizo, Couscous, Toad-in-the-hole
Nemea	Greece	Dry red	Eggplant purée, Greek food, especially kleftiko and moussaka

WINE	REGION	WINE STYLE	FOOD MATCHES
Oloroso Sherry	Spain	Fortified white	Christmas pudding, Nut cakes, Praline and chocolate ice cream, Treacle and chocolate puddings
Orvieto	Umbria, Italy	Dry or semi-sweet white	Creamy pasta dishes, Grilled sardines, Indian food with spicy yogurt sauces, Light fish dishes, Tempura
Pacherenc du Vic-Bihl	Southwest France	Dry to sweet white	Bread and butter pudding, Cheesecake, Chutney, Goose stuffed with prunes or other fruit, Mille feuilles, Mince pies, Pineapple-based desserts, Pipperade, Smoked ham, Tripe
Palette	Provence	Red Rosé White	Aioli, Tapenade Andouillette, grilled with mustard Creamed onions, Grilled or roasted vegetables
Passito	Italy	Sweet white	Ice cream, Italian biscuits or shortbread, Tiramisu
Patrimonio	Corsica	Red White	Cheese fondue, Kebabs, Osso buco, Tapenade Salade Niçoise, Sardines and anchovies, Taramasalata
Pauillac	Bordeaux	Dry red	Guinea fowl, pigeon, and quail, Lamb, Red meat stews and casseroles
Penedès	Spain	Dry red, Red White	Empanadas, Goulash Paella, Spanish fish stew, Spanish omelet with potatoes, garlic, and oil
Periquita	Portugal	Dry red	Chicken piri-piri, Kleftiko, Oxtail, Red meat stews and casseroles, Roast pork, Toad-in-the-hole
Pineau des Charentes	Cognac	Vin de liqueur	Apple-, chocolate-, and Cognac-based desserts, Foie gras, Melon with port, Sorbets
Pinot Blanc	Alsace	Dry white	Choucroute garnie, Eggs Benedict, cheese omelet, and other egg dishes, Kedgeree, Onion tart, Raw vegetables and salads, Savory crêpes

WINE	REGION	WINE STYLE	FOOD MATCHES
Pinot Grigio	Italy	Dry white	Fish-and-chips and other fried fish dishes, Guacamole, Hummus, Pasta with clam sauce or spring vegetables, Prosciutto, Raw vegetables, Risotto alla Milanese, Stir-fries
Pinot Gris	Alsace	Dry white	Caviar, Chicken curry, Clam chowder, Corn-on-the-cob, Gougère, Omelet with bacon and quiche Lorraine, Onion tart, Pork chops and roast pork, Raclette, Roasted or stuffed peppers, Satay, Veal dishes
		Vendanges Tardives	Foie gras, Kougelhopf, Sweet and sour sauce, White-wine-sauce-based dishes
Pinot Noir	Italy Alsace	Dry red	Cold salmon, Potato salad, Quail, Sauerbraten
	New World		Bacon and baked ham, Bagels with salmon and cream cheese, Brussels sprouts and green vegetables, Coq au vin and chicken in cream and morel sauce, Lamb curry, Meat loaf, Pork chops, Rabbit, Roast chicken
Pinotage	South Africa	Dry red	Beef Wellington, Chili con carne, Chorizo, Couscous, Moussaka, Pea and ham soup, Pigeon, Roast beef and steak
Pomerol	Bordeaux	Dry red	Beef and steak dishes, Chicken in sweet and sour sauce, Goose stuffed with prunes or other fruit, Grilled lamb chops, Mint sauce and pepper sauce, Partridge and pheasant, Roast duck, Shepherd's pie, Truffles, black and white, Wild boar
Pommard	Burgundy	Dry red	Cajun-style meats, Confit de canard, Kidneys, Pepper sauce, Roast duck and roast lamb with mint sauce, Wild boar
Port	Portugal	Fortified red	Almonds, walnuts, hazelnuts, and peanuts, Chocolate-based desserts, Melon and port, Mince pies
Pouilly-Fumé	Loire	Dry white	Eels with a creamy herb sauce, Goat cheese, Grilled carp, Jambon persillé, Moules marinières, oysters, and seafood pizza, Paella, Tripe, Vinaigrette sauce

WINE	REGION	WINE STYLE	FOOD MATCHES
Pouilly-Fuissé	Burgundy	Dry white	Cold salmon, Grilled bass, Fish terrines, Quiches and soufflés, Japanese food
Poulsard	Arbois	Dry red	Game, Jambalaya, Kleftiko, Spicy meat dishes
Puligny-Montrachet	Burgundy	Dry white	Caviar, Creamy and buttery sauces, Lobster, Monkfish, Roast veal
Quarts de Chaume	Loire	Sweet white	Chocolate-based desserts, Exotic fruit-based desserts and fruit salads, Kougelhopf
Regaleali Rosato	Italy	Dry rosé	Roasted or stuffed peppers
Regnié	Burgundy	Dry red	See **Beaujolais**
Reguengos	Portugal	Dry red	Carpaccio, Chicken piri-piri
Retsina	Greece	Dry white	Eggplant dishes, Olives and anchovies, Spicy sausages
Richebourg	Burgundy	Dry red	Calves' liver, Coffee-based desserts, Grouse, venison, and roast meats
Riesling	Alsace	Dry white	Baeckaoffa and pot roast, Blanquette de veau, Boudin blanc (white pudding), Bouillabaisse, Chicken in cream and morel sauce, Creamed onions, Horseradish sauce, Mustard sauce, Olives, Potato salad or creamy potato dishes, Quiche Lorraine, Raspberry-based desserts, Seafood in creamy sauces and moules marinières, Smoked salmon, White fish dishes
		Vendanges Tardives	Acras, Chinese food, Smoked ham, Waldorf salad
Riesling	Germany	Dry to sweet white	
		Kabinett	Béarnaise sauce, Cranberry sauce, Gravlax, Sashimi and sushi
		Spätlese	Chinese food, Roast pork with mustard sauce, Smoked ham, Tomato salad
		Auslese	Brown-sugar-based desserts, Duck à l'orange, Foie gras, Red cabbage with apples, Smoked fish
		Beerenauslese	Cherry-based desserts, Pancakes with maple syrup, Sachertorte and other chocolate-based desserts

WINE	REGION	WINE STYLE	FOOD MATCHES
Riesling	New World	Dry white	Apple-based desserts, Choucroute garnie, Curry dishes, Japanese food, Pike with garlic and poached white fish dishes
Rioja	Spain	Dry red, Red	Beef potpie, Curried tomato soup, Greek food, especially moussaka, Lamb, Liver, Merguez sausage, Roast pork
		Rosé	Paella
		White	Octopus, Roasted spicy sausages, Salt cod balls, Stuffed onions, Tapas
Rosso Cònero	Tuscany, Italy	Red	Bolognese-sauce-based dishes, Duck à l'orange, Salami and spicy meats
		Rosé	Cured meats, Saltimbocca alla Romana and other veal dishes, Roast lamb
Rueda	Spain	Dry white	Salads, Sausages, dried or smoked, Spicy meat casseroles, Grilled or roasted vegetables
Rully	Burgundy	Red	Charcuterie, Coq au vin, Roast pork, Escargots de Bourgogne
		White	Artichokes, Caesar salad, Jambon persillé, Savory crêpes, Smoked salmon, Satay, Soufflés with broccoli and cheese
St-Amour	Burgundy	Dry red	See **Beaujolais**
St-Emilion	Bordeaux	Dry red	Beef potpie, Beef Wellington, Camembert and English cheeses, Chestnut and dried fruit stuffings, Chicken curry, Confit de canard, Game and venison, Lamb with Herbes de Provence, Pasta with pesto sauce, Pheasant, pigeon, and quail, Pot roast, Pot-au-feu, Roasted meats such as chicken, turkey, and beef, Sausage and mash
St-Estèphe	Bordeaux	Dry red	Lamb with flageolets or light meat casseroles, Rabbit, Roast lamb
St-Georges-St-Emilion	Bordeaux	Dry red	See **St-Emilion**
St-Joseph	Rhône	Dry red	Boiled or roast vegetables, Grilled meats, Kebabs, Melon with Parma ham. See also **Syrah** and **Marsanne**

WINE	REGION	WINE STYLE	FOOD MATCHES
St-Julien	Bordeaux	Dry red	Lamb crown roast, Roast turkey with traditional trimmings. See also **St-Estèphe**
St-Véran	Burgundy	Dry white	Artichokes, Asparagus in vinaigrette sauce, Herring, Soufflés with spinach and cheese, Steak tartare
Ste-Croix-du-Mont	Southwest France	Sweet white	Cheeses, Foie gras and other pâtés, Fruit salad and orange-based desserts. See also **Sauternes**
Samos	Greece	Sweet white	Baclava, Nuts, almonds, and honey-based desserts, Pastries and breads
Sancerre	Loire/Centre	Dry white	Avocado, Béarnaise sauce, Creole and teriyaki chicken, Hollandaise sauce and mustard sauce, Omelets, Red mullet and fish cakes, Poached, steamed, or lightly grilled salmon, Sashimi and sushi, Seafood dishes, especially smoked eels, Taramasalata, Tomato-sauce-based dishes, Vichyssoise, Wiener schnitzel
Sangiovese	Italy and California	Dry red	Bresaola and carpaccio, Pasta dishes with meat and béchamel sauce, Cornish pasties, Pizza Bolognese, Saltimbocca alla Romana. See also **Brunello di Montalcino**
Saumur and **Saumur-Champigny**	Loire	Dry red	Anchovies or anchovy paste, Baked ham with pineapple, Beef bourginon, Confit de canard, Grilled lamb chops, Lemon chicken, Meat fondue, Quail, Raspberry- and strawberry-based desserts
Sauternes	Bordeaux	Sweet white	Bread and butter pudding, Brown-sugar-based desserts, Buttermilk pancakes, Cheeses, especially blue cheeses, Chocolate-, Cointreau-, and lemon-based desserts, Christmas pudding, Crème caramel or brûlée, Foie gras, Pecan pie, Tiramisu, Waldorf salad

WINE	REGION	WINE STYLE	FOOD MATCHES
Sauvignon Blanc	France		Artichokes, Avocado, Ceviche, Egg dishes, soufflés, and quiches, Fish-and-chips, Jambon persillé, Pike with garlic, grilled carp or haddock, Pizza with seafood, prawn cocktail, and other seafood dishes, especially scallops in cream and tarragon sauce, Smoked eels, Stir-fries, Thai food, White fish dishes, White-wine-sauce-based dishes
	New World		Asparagus, Chicken Creole, Chicken piri-piri and teriyaki chicken, Chicken salad, Fish cakes and prawns, Gazpacho, Ginger-based desserts, Jambalaya, Pasta with spring vegetables, Salsa, red and green, and other tomato-based sauces, Sashimi, Stir-fries, Tomato salad and raw vegetables
Sauvignon Colli Orientali del Friuli	Italy	Dry white	Mozzarella and ricotta cheeses, Prawns, scampi, and seafood pasta dishes. See also **Sauvignon Blanc**
Savennières	Loire	Dry white	Creole chicken, Goat cheese, Grilled scallops, Pumpkin pie. See also **Chenin Blanc**
Savigny-lès-Beaune	Burgundy	Dry red	Chicken chasseur, Lamb curry, Mushroom and red wine sauces, Tarragon chicken. See also **Pinot Noir, New World**
Sémillon	France and New World	Dry white	Barbecued and blackened fish, Blue cheeses, Chicken chasseur, Chinese food, Coconut-based desserts and savory dishes, Ham and pork dishes, Honey-based dishes, Indian food with spicy yogurt sauces, Mackerel with butter and spring onions and other oily fish dishes, Monkfish and other seafood, Pumpkin pie, Spicy white meat dishes, Trifle
Sherry	Spain	Fortified red	See **Amontillado, Fino, Manzanilla,** and **Oloroso**

WINE	REGION	WINE STYLE	FOOD MATCHES
Shiraz	Australia	Dry red	Barbecued meats, Bean and pasta soup, Boeuf en daube, cassoulet, and other red meat stews and casseroles, Chicken paprika and southern fried chicken, Chili con carne and chili sauce, Couscous, Cranberry sauce, Duck à l'orange, Game, Greek food, Hamburgers, Horseradish sauce, Lamb curry, Meat fondue, Merguez sausages, Pepper sauce, Sirloin steak, Stuffed cabbage, Toad-in-the-hole, Venison and wild boar
Soave	Veneto, Italy	Dry white	Aioli, Bruschetta, Chef's salad and other salads, Gazpacho, Macaroni and cheese, Pasta with pesto sauce, Prawns, seafood salad, and light white fish dishes, Risotto alla Milanese, Teriyaki chicken
Sylvaner	Alsace	Dry white	Anchovies or anchovy paste, Baeckaoffa, Chicken in sweet and sour sauce, Croque Monsieur or Madame, Onion tarts, Pike with garlic, Quiche Lorraine, Salt cod with garlic, oil, and cream, Sweetbreads
Syrah	New World	Dry red	Cajun-style and barbecued meats, Game, Mushroom and red wine sauces. See also **Hermitage, Cornas, Côte-Rôtie, Crozes-Hermitage,** and **St-Joseph**
Tavel	Rhône	Dry rosé	Anchovies or anchovy paste, Asparagus in vinaigrette sauce, Bouillabaisse, Onion tart, Salami-based dishes
Tempranillo	Spain	Dry red	See **Rioja**
Tokaji	Hungary	Dry to sweet white	Carrot cake, Christmas pudding, Thai food. See also **Muscat de Beaumes-de-Venise, Ste-Croix-du-Mont,** and**Sauternes**
Tokayi Aszú, 5 puttonyos	Hungary	Sweet white	Christmas pudding
Trebbiano d'Abruzzo/ Ugni Blanc	Italy or New World	Dry white	Egg dishes with ham or bacon, Creamy spinach and pasta dishes, Grilled carp, Risotto alla Milanese

WINE	REGION	WINE STYLE	FOOD MATCHES
Vacqueyras	Rhône	Dry red	Beef Stroganoff, Escargots à la bourguinonne, Pigeon. See also **Grenache**
Valdepeñas	Spain	Dry red	Squid cooked in their own juices
Valpolicella Classico	Italy	Dry red	Bresaola, Italian garlic and tomato dishes, Mexican food, Mushroom risotto, Osso buco, Proscuitto, Raclette, Tuna salad
Verdicchio	Italy	Dry white	Antipasti, Fish-and-chips and other fried fish dishes, Light, creamy pasta dishes, Moules et frîtes, Seafood salad and other seafood dishes
Vernaccia di San Gimignano	Italy	Dry white	Bouillabaisse, Bruschetta, Grilled white fish, especially bass, Pesto-based pasta dishes
Vin de Corse	Corsica	Red	Boeuf en daube, Corn bread, Eggplant, Merguez sausages, Polenta
		White	Bouillabaisse, Tabbouleh, Tuna salad
Vin de Paille	Jura	Vin doux naturel	Apple- and apricot-based desserts, Foie gras, Sweet crêpes, Thai food. See also **Pacherenc du Vic-Bihl, Tokaji**
Vinho Verde	Portugal	Dry white	Ceviche, Chicken piri-piri, Green salad with oil and vinegar dressing, Grilled sardines, Mackerel with green gooseberry sauce, Salsas, red and green, Vinaigrette sauce
Vino Nobile de Montepulciano	Tuscany, Italy	Dry red	Roast lamb with mint sauce, Red meat stews and casseroles, Wild boar. See also **Brunello di Montalcino, Sangiovese**
Viognier	Rhône, Italy, or New World	Dry white	Artichokes, Carrot soup, Chef's salad, Cornish pasties, Curry, Gazpacho, Indian food with spicy yogurt sauces. See also **Condrieu**
Volnay	Burgundy	Dry red	Mushroom and red wine dishes, Quail, Rabbit, Roast beef, Veal dishes. See also **Echezeaux**

WINE	REGION	WINE STYLE	FOOD MATCHES
Vosne-Romanée	Burgundy	Dry red	Brown-sugar-based desserts, Coffee-based desserts, Game, Roast turkey with traditional trimmings, Truffles, black and white
Vouvray	Loire	Dry to sweet white	Acras, Apple-, fruit-, and lemon-based desserts, Béarnaise and hollandaise sauce, Goat cheese, Goose stuffed with prunes or other fruit, Quiches and soufflés, Sweet and sour sauce, White fish dishes
		Sparkling (mousseux)	Apple-, fruit-, and lemon-based desserts, Mince pies, Pancakes with maple syrup, Sweet crêpes
Weissburgunder	Germany	Dry red	Braised beef, stews, and casseroles, Roast pork, Wiener schnitzel
Zinfandel	California	Red	Baked beans, Barbecued meats, Beef potpie, Beef tacos, Buffalo wings, Cajun-style meats, Cassoulet, Chicken paprika, Chili con carne, Chorizo sausage, Eggplant-based dishes, Empanadas, Goulash, Greek food, Hamburgers, Meat loaf, Pepper sauce, Pizza Bolognese, Ratatouille, Roast duck, Roast turkey with traditional trimmings, Salads, Sausage and mash, Venison with cranberries or juniper berries
		White	Grilled white fish, Pasta dishes, Octopus, Roasted vegetables
Zitsa	Greece	Dry white	Anchovies, Hummus, Olives, Spicy sausages, Tapas

Wine Vocabulary

Acid, acetic   Acid found in all wine, though usually present in tiny quantities. Excess amounts cause the wine to turn to vinegar.

Acid, ascorbic   Acid with an antioxidizing effect, often added to wine just before bottling. It is only effective in the presence of **sulfur dioxide**.

Acid, citric   Acid found particularly in citrus fruit but also present in lesser quantities in grapes. White grapes, especially those affected by **noble rot**, contain more than red grapes. As an additive, it is strictly controlled by law.

Acid, lactic   Acid that appears during the malolactic fermentation of the wine when malic acid changes into carbon dioxide and lactic acid. Eventually this fades and becomes imperceptible in tasting.

Acid, malic   Once the grape ripens, the malic acid present at high levels in the green grapes decreases. Its tart taste of green apples makes it easily recognizable. The hotter the year, the faster it decreases during the ripening process, which is why it is more apparent when the weather has been colder.

Acid, tartaric   Regarded as the most "noble" acid, tartaric acid has more acidifying power than the other acids contained in wine, and is not commonly found in fruits other than grapes. The tartaric acid content goes down as the grape ripens, then varies depending on the weather.

Acidify   To add lemon juice or vinegar to a sauce or cooked dish.

Acidity, fixed   The total of all the acids contained in the fruit itself, such as tartaric acid, malic acid, lactic acid.

Acidity, real   Intensity of acidity, usually expressed in **pH** (potential hydrogen), is expressed on a scale from 0 to 7, with 7 representing total neutrality. The usual pH varies around 3 to 4 on this scale.

Acidity, total   Combined total of **volatile acidity** and **fixed acidity**. This naturally varies depending upon whether seasons are cold (when the grapes are too acid) or hot (when the grapes are overripe). It is on the basis of these figures and of the legal standards that the decision to acidify or disacidify a wine is made.

Acidity, volatile   In small quantities (0.3–0.4 gram per liter), excess volatile acids are strictly controlled by law. Only levels below 0.9 gram per liter (production) and 1 gram per liter (retail trade) are tolerated, quantities higher than this making the wine too sour. This acidity, mainly made up of acetic acid, increases as the wine ages.

Acidulation   Adding acid to wine made from grapes deficient in natural acid in order to bring the wine into balance. Acidulation is legal in California (where the warmer climates keep acid levels down) but illegal in France. It is interesting to note that adding sugar (**chaptalization**) is legal in France but illegal in California.

Aerate   Exposing wine to air during decanting. It allows any trapped odors to escape from an older wine and a younger wine to let off a bit of steam.

Aioli   A Mediterranean mayonnaise made with garlic, egg yolks, and oil.

Al dente   A term used for describing the perfect texture of cooked pasta: tender but still slightly firm to the bite. Because each type of pasta (lasagne, fettuccine, penne, tagliatelli, rigatoni, fusilli, et cetera) demands a different cooking time, it is essential to test pasta regularly during its preparation.

Alcohol   An essential element in wine, alcohol is produced during fermentation, when enzymes created by the yeasts change the sugar content of the grape juice into alcohol, carbon dioxide, and heat. The level of alcohol varies from less than 7°C to more than 15° degrees in wine. To obtain one degree of alcohol, eighteen grams of sugar must be added per liter for white wines and seventeen grams per liter for red.

Ample   How to describe a wine that feels full and expansive in the mouth.

Anthocyanin   The red pigments in grapes that give red wine its color. The purpley-red color of young wine is almost exclusively caused by fairly unstable anthocyanin molecules, which in the course of aging join up with **tannins** to give the wine its ruby-red color. This polymerization of tannin and anthocyanin is helped by the dissolution of oxygen in the wine, which produces stable polymers.

Appellation   The name given to a wine's official geographic origin.

AOC   *Appellation d'origine contrôlée,* a designation created by the French authorities to establish specific areas of production, grape varieties, minimum levels of sugar in the must and of alcohol in the wine, maximum yield per hectare, pruning of the vine, and cultivation and vinification methods.

Aromas   These are the scents that a wine gives off, as absorbed by the taster's nose and palate. Three levels of aromas can be distinguished: primary, or varietal aromas; secondary aromas resulting from the fermentation; and tertiary aromas, which develop as the wine ages. Together they form the wine's **bouquet**.

Aromatic esters   The term used for the compounds formed most often during fermentation by the wine's acids and alcohols.

Astringent   When a wine feels dry and tart on the upper mouth, usually due to unbalanced tannins and acidity.

Attack In French, *premier attaque* refers to the first impression a wine gives when tasting . . . literally on the tip of the tongue. Sometimes when an attack is too present, too forward, we worry that there won't be enough extracts or substance to carry the wine the rest of the way. A first attack should be in proportion to the rest of the mouth: the palate and the finish. And in fact, a subtle first attack is hopefully a sign that there is more and better to come.

Au gratin The cooking term used for dishes that are browned in the oven or under a grill. Gratins are often made with béchamel sauce, cheese, or eggs.

Auslese German white wines made from late-harvest grapes with a high sugar concentration.

Balance The harmony among the various elements of a wine, such as acidity, sweetness, alcohol, and tannin content.

Barrel fermented Wine that is fermented in oak barrels as opposed to stainless-steel tanks.

Barrique A French term for "barrel," the capacity of which may vary from one region to another: In the Bordeaux area, where it is most commonly used, it contains 225 liters (four *barriques* make one *tonneau*); in the Muscadet area, it contains 228 liters; in Touraine-Anjou it holds 232 liters. The traditional English equivalent is the hogshead. In France, other names are used depending on the region and capacity. See also: **piece, foudre, queue.**

Beerenauslese QmP German wines made from grapes affected by *Botrytis cinerea,* or **noble rot**.

Blanc, Blanco, Branco French, Spanish, Portuguese for "white."

Blanc de Blancs "White of whites," meaning a white wine made of white grapes, such as Champagne made from Chardonnay. It is also used as the names of some wineries' special blends of still white wines, ranging from dry to medium-dry.

Blanc de Noirs White wine made from red or black grapes.

Bleeding The bleeding process, or *saignee,* consists in drawing off some of the wine during fermentation. The light-colored wine drawn off is used to make rosé wines such as **Clairet** in Bordeaux and Clarete in Rioja.

Blending Blending, or *assemblage,* is the mixing of several vats of wine varieties to make a more balanced wine and is usually performed after each variety has fermented individually. For example, Bordeaux are usually a blend of Cabernet Sauvignon, Cabernet Franc, and Merlot.

Bodega An agricultural estate in Spain. However, wines labeled "bodega" do not necessarily contain grapes that all come from the estate in question.

Body Used to describe a wine with good tannic structure and good aging potential.

Botrytis A mold that attacks grapes, it manifests itself either as **gray rot,** which may then endanger the harvest; or, in certain atmospheric conditions, as **noble rot,** which is used to make dessert wines such as Sauternes, Barsac, Monbazillac, certain Anjou wines, and German wines like Auslese, Beerenauslese, or Trockenbeerenauslese, or the famous Hungarian Tokaji.

Botrytis cinerea   Literally "noble rot," *edelfäule* in German, a mold that dehydrates grapes left late on the vine and concentrates their juice.

Bottle age   This is when a wine ages in the bottle after being bottled. Some wineries hold back their wine from sale to allow this; some don't bother. Finer wines capable of bottle aging should be cellared by the consumer.

Bottle sickness   Unbalance of wine flavor after bottling or after rough travel, caused by excessive aeration; clears up when wine is allowed to rest.

Bouche   The French word for "mouth" is used to describe the body and impressions of the wine when tasting.

Bouquet   Complex emanation from a wine, perceptible in the nose, resulting from maturation and oak aging. Bouquet is more complex than and encompasses **aroma,** which is present only with young wines.

Brettanomyces   An undesirable yeast found on grapes, and therefore in wines, which produces very disagreeable odors when in excess and is a sign of poor hygiene in the winery. In small amounts it escapes unnoticed, or shows itself as an earthy, manure-like smell we sometimes appreciate.

Broker   See **courtier.**

Brut   A French term for sparkling wines, it indicates very low level of sugar (up to fifteen grams per liter). There is no sugar present in *Brut intégral* or *Brut zéro* Champagne.

Capers   The unopened flower buds of the Mediterranean caper bush, a sort of creeper. They are pickled in vinegar and used as a seasoning.

Carbonic maceration   The type of vinification during which red wine grapes are put into vats as they are, without being crushed. This used to be a natural process, with the grapes being left to ferment without interference. Now the vat is closed and filled with carbon dioxide, which causes the malic acid to break down and intracellular fermentations to take place, changing part of the sugar into alcohol. A few days later the **free-run wine** is drained off to be blended at a later stage with the **press wine**. The alcoholic fermentation is then allowed to finish. This process has proved particularly effective for Gamay wines, such as the Beaujolais Primeurs, that are sold and consumed when young.

Cask   Wooden containers much larger than barrels and used for aging or storing wine. Because it is larger, a cask imparts fewer properties from the oak, which is a good thing. A good oak program will incorporate a mixed balance of stainless-steel or new oak barrels, older barrels, and casks so to ensure that the fruit is never dominated by oak.

Castello   Italian for "château"; a winery estate.

Chaptalization   Named after Chaptal, this technique consists in adding sugar (cane or beet or rectified, concentrated must) to the must before fermentation to give the wine a higher alcoholic content. It is strictly forbidden in many countries and is usually controlled by law in those countries that permit it (in France a maximum of three kilos of sugar per hectoliter of grape juice is allowed). The new EU regulations have added to this legislation, defining certain parameters: Chaptalization should be authorized only under certain conditions relative to the degree of ripeness, the climatic conditions, and the production methods used. Chaptalization is a necessary evil in difficult years; however, in France it has become something of a habit, allowing growers to harvest maximum volume in the sure knowledge that they can boost the degree of alcohol by chaptalizing. The EU would like French growers to use only rectified concentrated musts, or RCMs, when chaptalizing. Today nuclear magnetic resonance is used to detect fraudulent chaptalization.

Château   To the northwest of Bordeaux, in the Médoc, most country residences have vineyards that have become famous. As a result, this term has come to designate the wine from a particular estate. A real château does not necessarily stand on every property.

Clairet   Light red wine obtained by **bleeding** in the course of fermentation of red wine. Not to be confused with **Claret,** the British name for the red wines of Bordeaux.

Claret   The British name for the red wines of Bordeaux.

Climat   French term originating in Burgundy to indicate a legally defined geographic area. It has nothing to do with weather. However, different *climats* can have varying weather climates in them or between them.

Clone   A subvariety of a wine grape. For example, Sangiovese has many clones. In the past Chianti producers planted high-yield clones so to increase grape production, and thus profits. But high yields equals diluted, boring wines. So they turned to Super Tuscans, abandoning Sangiovese altogether and using Cabernet Sauvignon and Merlot. These are not indigenous Italian varieties, but were well-known French varieties selling heaps in the United States. But now the region is turning back to its roots: Sangiovese-based Chiantis. Still, they want better Sangiovese and are experimenting with clones to find which produce better-quality grapes in smaller yields.

Clos   A French term that originally referred to a vine-growing parcel of land surrounded by a wall, particularly in Burgundy. Many of the original walls even on the oldest properties are still standing.

Cold stabilization   A method of clarifying wine by lowering the temperature of wine to 0°C/32°F for a short period, allowing the suspended particules to drop out.

Colheita   The Portuguese word for "vintage," or year.

Complex   The term used to describe a wine that has many different levels and layers of flavors and textures.

Concentrated   The term used to describe a wine that has a lot of extracted matter, and is intense and rich. The extract comprises the non-volatile solids of a wine: sugars, acids, minerals, phenolics, glycerol, and so on.

Corked   The expression used for a wine that has a very strong smell of rotten cork. The wine is usually undrinkable. This rather rare occurrence is caused by the development of molds on the cork.

Cosecha   The Spanish word for "vintage," or year.

Courtier   A courtier or broker is an intermediary between the grower and the **négociant.**

Cru   Literally, in French, a "growth" or tract of land such as a vineyard, the term is principally used to mean a vineyard's rank in the 1855 classification or ranking of Bordeaux vineyards and their wines into five classes or Crus. Eighty-three Médoc, Graves, and Sauternes châteaus were thus classified in 1855, but since then hundreds more around Bordeaux have classified themselves as first to fifth Crus or as Crus Exceptionnels or as Crus Bourgeois (the lesser-quality categories preceding the Crus).

Crush   The physical act of crushing the grapes, as well as the term referring to the harvest season.

Cuvaison, Cuvage   The French term for the essential stage in the making of a wine, from when the musts from the harvest are put into the fermentation vats, up to the draining off or *égouttage.*

Cuve   A vat designed to hold the fermenting musts, or to store wines. Some vats are closed with an upper lid fitted with a hatch, as in Bordeaux; others are open, as in Burgundy. The vats are made of various materials: Wooden vats were once used, but nowadays stainless-steel vats are preferred for cleanliness and, principally, temperature control.

Cuvée   A French term literally meaning a "vatful," the word signifies a specific selection of wine that may or may not have been blended. See **blending.**

Daube   A method of cooking meat, usually beef, that braises the meat in a red wine sauce, often with garden vegetables and seasonings.

Decanting   The process of separating the sediment of a wine from the clear liquid. During the decanting operation, a young wine comes into contact with the air, so that the addition of oxygen makes it more palatable. Should the wine be too old, such an operation can be disastrous, as it accelerates the process of deterioration.

Declassification   When a wine exceeds certain norms (in terms of yield), or falls short (in degree of alcohol), the wine is declassified and loses its **AOC** classification. The decision may be taken voluntarily by the winemaker. Such wine may be used to make vinegar or pure alcohol.

Dekkera   The spore-producing form of the yeast **brettanomyces.**

Demi-sec   EU classification for white wines with a sugar content of less than nine grams per liter. In Champagnes, it is one category below sec in terms of dryness, and considered the ideal accompaniment to dessert pastries.

Deposit   The sediment of solid particles found in wine that separate from the wine during fermentation and aging. In the case of white wines, these are often fragments of colorless crystalline deposits; in red wines, they are usually a combination of tannins and pigments. See **decanting.**

Dessert wine   US legal term for wines over 14 percent but not over 24 percent in alcoholic strength by volume; includes appetizer wines such as sherry.

Distillation   The operation during which the alcohol is separated by heating the alcoholic mixture, on the principle that alcohol has a boiling point lower than that of water: the first vapors to be given off are alcoholic ones that are condensed by cooling.

DO *Denominacion de origen,* the Spanish equivalent of the French **AOC.**

DOC *Denominazione di origine controllata,* the Italian equivalent of the French **AOC.** The classification underwrites the origin of the wine, but not necessarily the quality. There are more than 220 at present.

Doce, dolce, dulce "Sweet" in Portuguese, Italian, Spanish.

DOCG *Denominazione di origine controllata garantita.* An Italian guarantee that refers to testing by sensory analysis. Existing ones are Barbaresco, Barolo, Brunello, Chianti, and Vino Nobile di Montepulciano.

Dry Refers to a wine that is not sweet. In Champagne, however, it is something of a *faux-ami:* It in fact means sweet, the driest Champagnes actually being called Brut or xtra dry.

Earthy The positive characteristics of loamy topsoil, mushrooms, or truffles sometimes found in red wines.

Elevage Literally "raising," this French term describes the operations of maturing and blending young wines to attain better balance.

En primeur Rather than being sold when it is ready to drink, wine is most often offered at a much earlier stage. In Bordeaux, the Grands Crus usually sell all or part of a year's harvest (usually in September) the following March or April, in what are known as the sales *en primeur.*

Enology, oenology The science and study of winemaking.

Espumoso, Espumante Spanish and Portugese for "sparkling wine," such as Champagne.

Estate-bottled This originally meant that the wine was produced and bottled entirely at the winery adjoining the proprietor's vineyard, but amendments have broadened it to include any vineyards controlled by the same proprietor or owned by members of a cooperative winery within the same delimited viticultural area as the winery.

Esters Volatile bodies resulting from the combination of an alcohol and an organic acid. They do not have such a marked influence on the wine's bouquet as is commonly thought.

Extra dry The quality of sparkling or still wine containing between twelve and twenty grams of sugar per liter.

Fermentation, alcoholic Transformation of the sugar contained in the must into alcohol and carbon dioxide, in the presence of yeasts.

Fermentation, malolactic This follows the alcoholic fermentation. Malic acid is affected by specific bacteria and changed into lactic acid and carbon dioxide. Because lactic acid is less harsh than malic acid, the wine becomes softer and more pleasant to drink than when young.

Fining   Fining, or collage, is a way of clearing wines before they are bottled. With this method, a "colloid" is added to the wine to absorb suspended particles and to fall to the bottom of the container. Products used are beaten egg white, fish glue, casein, or bentonite, a type of clay. The wine is then drawn off and sometimes filtered before bottling.

Finish   The last impression a wine make when you taste it. You want it to last a long time, and not end mid-palate. A long finish is the sign of a mature, well-balanced, well-made wine.

Flintstone   This evokes the smell of two flints being rubbed together, characteristic of Pouilly-Fumé in the Loire Valley and some other wines, usually made from the Sauvignon grape.

Fortified wine   A wine that has alcohol added to it. This is actually how port was "invented." When red wine was shipped from Portugal to England during its warring with France, alcohol was added to the wine to help keep it from going off. The English loved the "unintentional" result.

Foxy   In general, this term describes wine with an unpleasant and aggressively gamey smell. Specifically, it refers to the red Concord grape, native of North America and belonging to the *Vitis labrusca* species (grapes from *V. vinifera* are the best for winemaking—and indeed all those varieties with which we are familiar are *V. vinifera*).

Fruity   A characteristic of a young wine, or of a wine that has retained its fruity aromas.

Garrafeira   Portuguese for a reserve wine, used for reds that will be aged in oak for at least three years and again in thebottle before being released from the winery.

Glycerine   A trialcohol with a slightly sweet flavor, one of the important constituents of wine. On the palate it is often more pronounced in wines matured in new oak.

Gnocchi   Italian potato, egg, and flour dumplings.

Gran Reserva   Spanish for reserve wines aged at least five years in oak and then in the bottle before release.

Grassy or herbaceous   Aromas and flavors resembling new-mown grass, a negative characteristic when dominant.

Graves   Soils made up of gravels and drift boulders. Graves is also one of the seven major Bordeaux appellations.

Green   Used to describe a wine with excessive fruit acidity, especially if it has a malic (apple-like) aroma.

Gray rot   See **Rot, gray**

Hectoliter   One hundred liters, the equivalent of 22 imperial or 26.5 US gallons. In the EU, wine production is referred to in hectoliters per hectare (hl/ha).

Herbaceous   Aromas and flavors reminiscent of herbs or the leafy and branchy parts of the plant. They are not desirable if they are too strong.

Hybrid A cross between two species of vine. As a result of the phylloxera crisis and the subsequent crossings of American and European species, phylloxera-resistant hybrids have been produced. Such hybrids have not been encouraged because the quality of the wine has tended to be mediocre.

Jammy In red wines, this describes the taste of ripe fruitiness combined with natural berry-like flavors.

Kabinett High-quality German dry white wines (**QmP**) that are never **chaptalized.**

Larousse Gastronomique The wine and food lovers' bible by Prosper Montagné—a gastronomic encyclopedia filled with more than eighty-five hundred recipes and one thousand illustrations, providing not only practical recipes but also a history of cooking, anecdotes, and explanations with sources from Rabelais to Brillat Savarin, August Escoffier, and more. The first French edition was published in 1938; the first English translation in 1961. It is truly a great read and an indispensable tool.

Lees Made up of yeasts in a latent state, tartaric acid, and other residual matter from the harvest, the lees form a dark yellowy deposit at the bottom of the cask. They are removed during **racking.**

Maceration The period during which the red grape skins are in contact with the grape juice, including fermentation.

Madeirized A term meaning "oxidized" or "baked," such as by the heat-treatment method practiced in Madeira and some other countries. It can also refer to a white wine that has oxidized badly and browned in color (usually because of poor storage and/or excessive age). The phenomenon takes its name from the taste of Madeira, and is due to the presence of harmful levels of ethyl aldehyde.

Malic Apple-like aroma of malic acid from incompletely ripened grapes.

Marc The solid parts of the grape, obtained after pressing, forming a cake that is sometimes used for distillation in two different processes: The marc can be sprayed with water and drained off before distillation, or it can be placed in special stills into which steam is forced. The resulting spirit is called eau de vie de marc, or just marc for short.

   In Champagne, the term is the loading unit for the press, corresponding to four thousand kilos of grapes.

Marinate Foods (usually meats) are marinated in marinades to tenderize them and to impart flavor. The marinade is usually of an oil base with an acidic element such as lemon, vinegar, or soy sauce.

Maturation The maturation of a wine is the function of its composition, its origin (***terroir***), and its vintage. No one knows for certain what happens during the aging process. We know that there is an olfactive evolution, or a change from simple aromas to a complex bouquet. During bottle aging, red wines deposit little plaques, grains of coloring agents and other molecules that bond and fall to the bottom of the bottle. The heavier clusters settle faster and quicker than the smaller ones, which need years to settle. As these coloring agents settle in the bottles, the intensity of the wine's color diminishes, becoming more and more reddish brick, and finally yellowish, as the anthocyanins, or coloring agents, in the tannins soften and diminish while the tannins do. Polymerization progresses continually as the wine ages so that tannic wines for long aging become gradually harder and more tannic before reaching a peak where they are more tannic then when they were in the barrel. Then the slope starts a gradual decline. The extra-large molecules lose their ability to combine with other proteins, and their astringency diminishes. At the same time they are combining with other components in the wine, becoming insoluble and precipitating to form the characteristic deposit. At this point the wine is in its mature, mellow phase and is softer, richer, and rounder: This is maturity.

Mercaptan   From the Latin, meaning "capturing mercury," a chemical term referring to the skunk-like smelling compounds formed by yeast reacting with the sulfur in the lees after the primary alcoholic fermentation.

Méthode champenoise   The originality of this way of making sparkling wines lies in the creation of effervescence in the bottle. The wines used have completed their fermentations (alcoholic and sometimes malolactic) and are what the Champenois call clear wines, to which *liqueur de tirage,* made up of sugar solution and yeasts, is added.

This provokes a second alcoholic fermentation in the bottle, which is carefully closed with a metal capsule (or cork). This fermentation produces carbon dioxide, which is trapped in the bottle and mixes into the wine; this is how the effervescence is formed. The bottles are then stored in a cellar *sur lattes* (slats of wood) until they are released to the market (they can be kept for several years in this way without detracting from their freshness).

When the wines are being prepared for shipping, the deposits of dead yeasts that have fallen by force of gravity to the lower side of the bottle are removed. The operation involves raising the bottle progressively on to *pupitres* (racks) and giving it a quarter turn daily (riddling) so that the deposit forms against the cork. Today this traditional way of making Champagne is often replaced by an automatic mechanical operation using *giropallets,* which gives excellent results. The bottles come out neck-down and with the deposit collected against the cork. The neck is immersed in a saline solution that freezes a few centiliters of the wine, forming a plug of ice that includes the deposit. The capsule is then removed in the stage known as *dégorgement* (disgorging). A *liqueur d'expédition* is added; this is a mixture of old wine, pure spirit (or Cognac), citric acid when necessary, anhydride sulfite, and, most important, a sugar solution in quantities that will determine the designation: Brut (0–15 grams), extra dry (12–15 grams), sec (17–35 grams), demi-sec (33–50 grams). The bottle can then be corked, wired, and labeled.

Microclimate   An area where soil combined with other environmental factors produces a distinctive wine. The more American term for the French *climat.*

Mildew   A parasitic mold that attacks the green parts of the vine. It used to be treated with copper sulfate, but today synthetic substances are used.

Moelleux   Describes sweet white wines, the sugar content of which may vary between twelve and forty-five grams per liter, according to a 1984 EU directive.

Musky   A characteristic of wines made with the Muscatel grape as the base, especially during fermentation, when a smell reminiscent of musk is given off.

Must Unfermented grape juice obtained by crushing or pressing.

NV A contraction for "non-vintage," used on port, Champagne, or other wines. Non-vintage wines can also be marketed as VSR (very special reserve).

Native yeast A natural yeast attached to the skins of the grapes, sometimes solely used to start fermentation. If fermentation cannot be started by native, or indigenous, yeasts, then fabricated or synthetic yeasts are used.

Négociant The person who buys wine from the grower or château to sell to wholesalers or foreign importers.

Négociant éleveur The *négociant* who first buys wines from grower, then stores them in order to mature or blend them, or both. See **Elevage.**

Négociant manipulant A term used for traders in Champagne who buy grapes at harvesttime for the preparation of their own Champagne. It is abbreviated to "NM" on the label.

New World The European ex-colonies that began to produce wine in the fifteenth century. Those winemaking countries outside Europe. See **Old World.**

Noble rot See **Rot, noble**

Nouveau Wine of the most recent vintage, which means that, after August 31 of the year following the vintage, wines can no longer claim this designation. Beaujolais Nouveau is the classic example. Today an increasing number of wine-producing regions always declare their vintage on the label—but in the regions of Oporto and Champagne, the vintage is still declared by the trade in the best years only.

Oidium A disease of the vine caused by a microscopic mold that attacks the flowers, leaves, and grapes. The grapes dry out and a whitish dust covers the vine. The only remedy is sulfur treatment.

Old vines A term referring to older vines, usually thirty years or older. This is a good thing. Older vines produce fewer but more concentrated fruits. Quality wine producers in Germany, for example, don't let a vine produce until it is seven years of age, whereas those producers in a bit more of a hurry will make wine from vines as young as three.

Old World The term Old World refers to the countries of Europe and the Mediterranean basin that began to produce wine in the fourth century, as opposed to the term New World, which refers to the European ex-colonies that began producing wine around the fifteenth century. Old World winemakers, in principle, use more traditional winemaking techniques (blending grapes rather than producing single-variety wine, and insisting on smaller yields, for example) rather than modern science. They strive for individual style rather than a homogeneous one and consider *terroir* to be real and important. It might be suggested that the differences between the two are slowly fading, as some Old World winemakers are increasingly producing easy, noncommittal wines for export and to compete in this New World market, while some New World wines countries are embracing more traditional and less commercial styles. That said, the Old World still has time and experience on its side and, in my opinion, hold the ace card as far as possessing the indigenous grape varieties that are so at home in their climates and soils.

Olive oil   Oil extracted from the flesh and stones of the olive. Like wine, the quality of the oil depends greatly on the type of olive, the harvest year, the climate, and the soil. Extra-virgin is the highest quality, as it is unrefined from the first pressing (without aid of heat or chemicals) of the olives. This method is also known as cold-pressed extra-virgin olive oil. The second pressing of the olives produces virgin olive oil, of lesser quality. The oil must be purified and filtered, but it is not refined. The third type, pure olive oil, is a blend of extra-virgin and refined olive oil—the least expensive and most common style.

Organoleptic   Smell, color, and taste make up what are called the organoleptic qualities perceived by the senses.

Overcropping   The practice of allowing vines to produce more fruit than they can ripen.

Oxidation   When oxygen in the air comes into direct contact with the wine, oxidation may cause changes in color and taste.

Oxidized   Sherry-like, madeirized, or nutty flavor caused by the action of oxygen on wine, due mainly to exposure to air, heat, and light.

Palate   The wine-tasting term for "mouth."

Passerillage   The overripening of the grapes at harvest, causing drying out of the grape and higher sugar levels; this is how Vins de Paille, some Muscatels, and the sweet wines of the Jura are prepared. Not to be confused with the sweet wines obtained as a result of **noble rot.**

Pasteurization   To stabilize low-quality wines and get rid of any microorganisms, the wine can sometimes be pasteurized or heat-sterilized.

Perlant   Said of wines that are very slightly sparkling, but less so than semi-sparkling wines.

Pesto   Italian sauce made of basil, Parmesan, garlic, pine nuts, and olive oil.

pH   Measuring unit expressing potential hydrogen, or the concentration of H+ ions. For wines, this means their degree of dryness (between 2.9 and 3.1 for the wines with the best bearing). The lower the pH, the safer the wine is from disease and oxidation, and therefore the greater its aging potential. See also **Acidity, real.**

Phylloxera   This plant louse, imported from the United States, attacks the vine at its roots, and was the cause of the destruction of the European vineyards between 1860 and 1880.

Polymerization   The process by which smaller molecules form and bind together to create larger ones. When wine ages, the phenolic molecules form and become larger tannin polymers, which become so large that they fall out of the wine and form sediment.

Pourriture noble   French for the *Botrytis cinerea* mold, literally "noble rot," *edelfäule* in German, which dehydrates grapes left late on the vine and concentrates their sweet juice.

Press wine   Press wine, or *vin de presse,* is obtained by pressing the more solid elements left over in the vat after the draining off of the free-run wines. Press wines are sometimes blended with the free-run wines at a later stage to obtain the best possible balance for the particular vintage.

Pressing The operation whereby the grape juice is produced.

Primary aromas Those smells in an unaged wine that actually emanate from the grape itself, and are usually straightforward, fresh, fruity smells. These change and become secondary (and tertiary when discussing Burgundies) after the wine has been oak-aged. We then actually call the combination of aromas the wine's **bouquet.** A young wine cannot therefore have a bouquet.

Primeurs These wines, designed to be drunk very young, enjoy this designation provided they are marketed from November 21 until January 31 of the following year. (Not to be confused with *en primeur.*)

QbA Qualitätswein bestimmter Anbaugebeite; German wines that have been **chaptalized.**

QmP Qualitätswein mit Prädikat, a designation is reserved for German wines of quality that have not been **chaptalized.**

Quinta Portuguese equivalent of an estate or property. As with bodegas in Spain, Quinta wines may come from other properties than the one named.

Racking Racking is the operation to separate the wine from the lees; it is called *soutirage* in French. This method aerates and clarifies wine by moving it from one container to another, leaving the lees and sediment behind in the first container.

Récoltant manipulant A category of vine grower in Champagne who makes his own Champagne (manipulates the grapes).

Reduction The opposite, or complement, of oxidation. From Jancis Robinson's *Oxford Companion to Wine,* page 781: "Wines, especially red wines held in the absence of oxygen, may suffer from excess reduction; as a result of the slow polymerisation of tannins and pigments. A wine that is reduced tastes dirty and frequently smells of reduced sulphur compounds such as hydrogen sulphide and mercaptans." Aeration can sometimes cure it.

Refrigeration The physical process used to clarify wines by precipitation of certain solid elements in them.

Remontage For red wine, the operation of pumping the liquid up from the bottom of the vat and spraying the cap. The object is to achieve optimum contact between the liquid and the sediment of skins, pips, and stalks floating on the top.

Reserve For wines and spirits, the term used for special *cuvées* put aside for aging or future use. The term also refers to a minimum aging period for certain spirits such as Calvados, Cognac, and Armagnac.

Residual sugar (RS) The level of sugar that remains in wine after fermentation.

Riddling A spectacular as well as basic operation in the méthode champenoise by which deposits of dead yeasts and mineral salts are collected around the cork so that they can be removed. The French term is *remuage.*

Ripeness   A measurement of acid, pH, and sugar in the grapes; the term is also important in conjunction with the must, in order to extract more color and flavor.

Robe   Literally means "dress" in French and refers to the overall visual appearance of the wine, in both color and general appearance.

Rot, gray   Rot caused by the same mold as the noble rot, *Botrytis cinerea,* which affects grapes damaged by hail or grapeworm. High levels of humidity favor its development. Gray rot affects the quantity of the harvest, alters quality, and can lead to a disease in the wine called oxidasic casse.

Rot, noble   When conditions are favorable—with a dry, sunny end of autumn— grapes develop a beneficial form of decay thanks to the development of *Botrytis cinerea,* the celebrated mold that roasts the Sauternes grapes, producing a concentrated, different type of juice.

Rôti   Meaning "roasted," a characteristic of sweet wines with aromas of dried grapes resulting from noble rot.

Sec, secco, seco   "Dry" in French, Italian, and Portuguese or Spanish.

Selection by mass   Selection of grape varieties coming not from a single clone, but from a group of plants whose genetic structure is different.

Selection de grains nobles **(SGN)**   This expression, meaning « selection of noble grains, » is used particularly in Alsace, but may also be used in other regions such as Sauternes, Barsac, Cadillac, Cérons, Loupiac, Ste-Croix-du-Mont, Monbazillac, Bonnezeaux, Quarts de Chaume, Coteaux du Layon, Coteaux de l'Aubance, Jurançon, and Graves supérieures. It applies to wines made from late-picked grapes affected by noble rot or from *passerillés* grapes with a natural concentration of sugars.

Sorting   In the course of the harvest the sorting, or *triage,* is the stage during which green or rotten grapes are removed. *Sorting* is also the term used for the successive pickings used in the harvest of *passerillés* grapes or grapes affected by **noble rot.** And it can apply to the process of sorting the healthy grapes from the unhealthy, after harvesting, on the sorting tables.

Sour   A fungus (*Mycoderma aceti*) causes wine to change into vinegar when in contact with air. It develops particularly in inadequately filled vats, giving the wine a sour taste and an extremely unpleasant smell.

Spätlese   Late-harvested German wines.

Sparkling   There are several ways of making a sparkling wine: *méthode champenoise;* what is known as the "rural" method (Gaillac, Die) when effervescence is the result of a secondary fermentation; and the Charmat or *cuve close* method. Effervescence may also be produced by adding carbon dioxide.

Stemming   This process of separating the grapes from the stalks. The stalks contain oils and tannins that tend to make the wine bitter and harsh. There is sometimes a need for this process when the grapes are too soft or lacking acidity and structure, for the stems can provide some of the body and firmness that is missing.

Stemmy   An unpleasant aroma and taste of wine fermented with an excess use of grape and stems.

Still wines The opposite of sparkling wines, the term also describes wines that are used as a base in the making of sparkling and semi-sparkling wines.

Sulfur dioxide Winemakers have always used sulfur because of its numerous qualities: It checks premature fermentation in the harvested grapes; destroys undesirable yeasts; eliminates microbes and bacteria; protects oxidation; acts as a dissolving agent; and is a precious ally for sweet white wines inclined to referment in the bottle. Sulfur dioxide is now used either in gaseous form or diluted in water at 5 percent or 18 percent. Too much sulfur dioxide can produce a taste of rotten eggs and induce headaches.

Sur lie Allowing the wine to be aged in contact with the lees, the expired yeast cells from fermentation. Usually considered to give the wine more taste and extracts.

Taille The process of pruning the vines' branches in winter into the shape that will allow them to bear the most fruit, bearing in mind the soil, climate, and grape variety.

In Champagne, it indicates the part of the must that is drawn off by pressing after the **cuvée.** There is a distinction between the first and second *taille.*

Tannin In English we tend to speak of tannin in the singular; this is inaccurate, as there are different types of tannin, all derived from vegetable substances such as nuts, wood, bark, berries, and, of course, grapes. The stalks, skins, and seeds contain tannins that are released during the fermentation process and the pressing, giving the wine its specific character and contributing to its capacity for aging. Storing the wine in new wood allows additional tannin contained in the fibers of the wood to be absorbed by the wine.

Tart A rough and harsh sensation in the mouth caused by excess tannins. These are caused by either a rustic grape variety or excessive fermentation.

Terroir An all-encompassing French term referring to the particular characteristics of a specific piece of vineyard land, including but not limited to the sum total of soil, exposure, drainage, climate, trellising, and grape variety. More poetically, it is the unique and magic trilogy of climate, grape, and soil.

Texture The way a wine feels on the palate; its consistency.

Thermoregulation The process of controlling the temperature of vats during fermentation.

Thinning A few days before the harvest, it is often helpful to remove the leaves covering the grapes to make the grapes riper and more healthy.

Ullage The vacant area in a bottle or cask between the wine and the cork or roof of the cask. Bottle ullage increases with time, as the wine breathes through the cork. Always look out for excessive ullage when buying an older wine.

Varietal A varietal, or *vin de cépage,* is a wine made from a single grape variety. In France the wine must contain 100 percent of the same variety; in some other countries small proportions of other varieties are allowed, and in others there is no relevant regulation.

The term is also used for a wine that has the pronounced aroma and flavor of a grape variety; and it is the general term for wines labeled with names of grape varieties.

Varietal character   The specific characteristics of a grape variety. Good winemaking practices aim to preserve and highlight these and not to dominate them with oak or erase them with high alcohol levels, et cetera.

Vat room   The vat room, or *cuvier,* is where the vats or *cuves* are kept.

Vendanges tardives **(VT)**   This means "late harvesting," which is done to procure overripe grapes for sweet wines.

Viniculture   The science or study of grape production for wine and of the making of wine.

Vins sur lattes   Wines that have been made into Champagne and are stockpiled on their lees prior to **riddling.**

Vintage   Originally meaning "the grape harvest," as there is only one per year, the term has come to refer to the wine made from the harvest of a particular year. Each vintage acquires its specific nature from a combination of climatic factors that will determine the wine's quality and potential for aging.

The differences in quality from one year to another are such that most *négociants* blend wines from different vintages to create a better-balanced product; but the outstanding vintages deserve to stand on their own, so they are kept as single harvest stock to be made available as "vintages." In the past such vintages were very rare, and wines were sold as NV (non-vintage) or VSR (very special reserve).

Viticulture   The cultivation, science, and study of grapes.

Vitis vinifera   The wine-grape species, as opposed to *Vitis labrusca,* the US species producing table wines. All US wines have been produced by *V. vinifera* rootstocks brought over from Europe. The popular conception is that when Europe was devastated by phylloxera, the US wine industry saved them by sending over their healthy rootstocks. But in fact, they were European to begin with . . . so Europe was simply borrowing back their rootstocks.

Well balanced   This is the entire aim of a wine: that all of its components (acid, sugar, tannin, and alcohol) are integrated and none dominates.

Suggested Reading

These are some of my favorite food and wine reference books from my personal library. I am always looking out for good material, so please do not hesitate to contact me with anything you have come across that you find indispensable. For this book, I referred to these, as well as twenty years of my tasting notes, excerpts from my previously published articles in *Vintage Magazine,* my first book *The Wine Collector's Handbook,* my current column in *Taste Italia! Magazine,* my countless international and regional cookbooks, gardening encyclopedias, magazine articles clipped throughout the years, winery brochures, and saved menus from hundreds of wine dinners enjoyed across Europe and other delicious corners of the globe.

Anderson, Burton, *Wines of Italy* (Italian Trade Centre, London, 1992).

Ayrton, Elisabeth, *The Cookery of England* (Purnell Books Services Limited, London, 1975).

Desana, P., and E.Guagnini, *I migliori vini italiani per la buona tavola* (Edizioni Rai Radiotelevisione Italiana, Torino, 1970).

Gribourg, G., and C.Sarfati, *La Dégustation* (Edisud, Université du Vin, Suze-la-Rousse, 1989).

Johnson-Bell, Linda, *The Wine Collector's Handbook* (The Lyons Press, New York, 1997).

Millon, Marc, and Kim Millon, *The Wine and Food of Europe* (Treasure Press, London, 1982).

Montagné, Prosper, *Larousse Gastronomique* (English edition by Paul Hamlyn, London, 1961).

Peynaud, Emile, *Knowing and Making Wine,* translated from the French by Alan Spencer (John Wiley and Sons, Chichester, Sussex, 1981).

Ridgeway, Judy, *The Cheese Companion* (Apple Press, London, 1999).

Robinson, Jancis (ed.), *The Oxford Companion to Wine* (Oxford University Press, 1994).

————, *Guide to Wine Grapes* (Oxford University Press, 1996).

Wilson, James E., *Terroir* (Mitchell Beazley, Reed Books, London, 1998).

Index

Note: Entries in the Food-to-Wine and Wine-to-Food indexes do not appear in the following index. Only text portions of the book have been indexed.